DISTRIBUTED CONTROL SYSTEMS

Their Evaluation and Design

DISTRIBUTED CONTROL SYSTEMS

Their Evaluation and Design

Michael P. Lukas

VNR VAN NOSTRAND REINHOLD COMPANY
New York

Library of Congress Catalog Card Number: 85-22691
ISBN 0-442-26020-2

Manufactured in the United States of America.

Published by Van Nostrand Reinhold Company Inc.
115 Fifth Avenue
New York, New York 10003

Van Nostrand Reinhold Company Limited
Molly Millars Lane
Wokingham, Berkshire RG11 2PY, England

Van Nostrand Reinhold
480 Latrobe Street
Melbourne, Victoria 3000, Australia

Macmillan of Canada
Division of Gage Publishing Limited
164 Commander Boulevard
Agincourt, Ontario MIS 3C7, Canada

15 14 13 12 11 10 9 8 7 6 5 4 3 2 1

Library of Congress Cataloging-in-Publication Data

Lukas, Michael P.
Distributed control systems.

Includes index.
1.Process control—Data processing. 2. Electronic data processing—Distributed processing. I. Title.
TS156.8.L85 1986   629.8′95   85-22691
ISBN 0-422-26020-2

To Marj-
who inspired me
to get this done
and kept things going
while I was doing it.

PREFACE

In less than a decade, microprocessor-based distributed control systems have grown from a technical novelty to a dominant force in the marketplace for industrial automation equipment. The markets involved include the chemical, petroleum, metals processing, pulp and paper, power generation, and similar production industries. Every month, the trade press announces new systems or enhancements to existing systems. These announcements are usually accompanied by glowing claims of technical superiority or cost advantages over competing equipment.

The main purpose of this text is to help the reader navigate through this maze of claims and counterclaims by providing a sound base of technical information for use in evaluating or designing such systems. In one sense, the book is a tutorial on distributed control systems, in that it describes their basic structure and summarizes the functions of each of their elements. However, it goes beyond the level of a tutorial in that it also reviews and compares alternative approaches that have been used to implement each of these functions.

A text of this size cannot provide an exhaustive analysis of each technical area in the distributed control field. My purpose is more modest—to address the needs of several classes of readers:

1. For a potential *user* of a distributed control system, the book provides insight into the major issues to consider when evaluating such systems for purchase and application.
2. For a *designer* of a distributed control system, it reviews typical approaches used in the design of each system element and summarizes issues beyond the designer's immediate area of technical expertise (such as communications or software design).
3. For *managers* and for *students* interested in distributed process control, the book provides an introduction to and survey of industrial practice in the field.

This text is written for people who are not necessarily computer experts but who are familiar with and interested in the field of industrial process control. I have intentionally avoided technical jargon and mathematical derivations, placing emphasis instead on defining and discussing the key concepts of distributed control. Extensive references are provided at the end of each chapter for the reader interested in additional details.

The book is divided into five topical areas:

1. *Chapter 1*—An introduction and background on distributed control systems;
2. *Chapters 2, 3, and 4*—A discussion of the subsystems used to control and gather data from the process;
3. *Chapter 5*—A discussion of the issues dealing with the shared communications facility in a distributed control system;
4. *Chapters 6 and 7*—A description and analysis of the human interfaces in a distributed system;
5. *Chapter 8*—A review of several other key technical issues and a survey of future trends in the distributed control field.

The structure of the discussion in each subject area follows a standard format. First, the subject area is introduced and the distributed control element being discussed is put into the context of the total system. Then, the key requirements on the design of that element are summarized. After reviewing several of the alternative design approaches one can take, the discussion provides some comments on the pros and cons of each alternative. In most cases, I have made no attempt to recommend a best alternative, since that choice usually depends heavily on the intended application of the system. The reader must make that informed decision based on his or her knowledge of the process to be controlled.

This book is based on a working background of fifteen years in the field of distributed control systems. I acquired a good deal of this background at a time when there were no books or papers on the subject. During this period, I learned the basics from several people who were ahead of their time in conceiving distributed control systems: Bud Keyes, John Werme, and Dick Boyd. I also am indebted to several others who, like me, learned the subject on the job from each other: Jim Hoffmaster, Tom Scheib, Chet Slabinski, Tom Bean, and Dave Hankinson; I want to thank these people for their help over the years. There are many others that I would like to thank by name but am unable to do so in a limited amount of space.

Michael P. Lukas
Eastlake, Ohio

CONTENTS

DISTRIBUTED CONTROL SYSTEMS

Their Evaluation and Design

1
EVOLUTION OF DISTRIBUTED CONTROL SYSTEMS

1.1. INTRODUCTION AND HISTORICAL BACKGROUND

The history of man's attempts to control industrial processes through automatic means is a long one (see Refs. 1.1 and 1.5), starting with such early developments as Cornelis Drebbel's furnace thermostat (1620) and James Watt's centrifugal governor for steam engines (1788). However, the major advances in integrated control system architectures, as compared to individual controllers, have taken place over the last fifty years. This section reviews several key developments during these years to provide the rationale for the recent emergence of the distributed control system architecture. The references at the end of the chapter provide additional historical detail.

Control systems have developed from the 1930s to the present day in response to two intertwined influences: user needs and technological advances. One factor that has influenced the control needs of the user is the continual growth in the size and complexity of industrial processes over the past fifty years. Also, the costs of raw materials and energy required to process these materials have increased substantially in this time. Finally, the labor costs involved in plant startup, operation, and maintenance have grown substantially. These influences have motivated the owners and operators of industrial processes to place a greater amount of emphasis on automation and on efforts to optimize their operations. In response to these user needs, the suppliers of industrial controls have been motivated to develop totally integrated plant *management* systems that are more than the combination of individual control, monitoring, and data logging systems.

Fortunately, the explosive advances in technology that have taken place over the past fifty years have provided the capabilities needed for the evolution of such plant management systems. For example, the development of transistors, integrated analog circuits, and solid-state relays resulted in a growth in capability and an increase in reliability of electronic control systems that enabled them to largely replace pneumatic control systems. Similarly, the development of digital technology in the form of improved large-scale integrated logic circuits, microprocessors, semiconductor memories, and cathode-ray tube (CRT) displays has led to even more impressive improvements in digital control system capabilities. These improvements have allowed control systems based on digital technology to replace electronic analog systems in many applications. References 1.2, 1.3, 1.4, and 1.6 trace the history of many of these technological developments.

The lines of technological development can be divided into two separate streams, as illustrated in Figure 1.1. The upper stream with its two branches is the more traditional one, and includes the evolution of analog controllers and other discrete devices such as relay logic and motor controllers. The second stream is a more recent one that includes the use of large-scale digital computers and their mini and micro descendants in industrial process control. These streams have merged into the current mainstream of distributed digital control systems. The dates of several key milestones in this evolutionary process are shown in Table 1.1 to illustrate the pace of these advances.

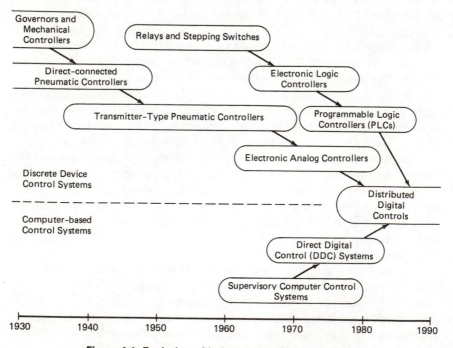

Figure 1.1. Evolution of Industrial Control Technology.

Table 1.1. Key Milestones in Control System Evolution.

1934	Direct-connected pneumatic controls dominate market.
1938	Transmitter-type pneumatic control systems emerge, making centralized control rooms possible.
1958	First computer monitoring in electric utility.
1959	First supervisory computer in refinery.
1960	First solid-state electronic controllers on market.
1963	First direct digital control (DDC) system installed.
1970	First programmable logic controllers (PLCs) on market.
1970	Sales of electronic controllers surpass pneumatic.
1975	First distributed digital control system on market.

1.1.1. Traditional Control System Developments

The concept of distributed control systems is not a new one. In fact, the early discrete device control systems listed in Figure 1.1 were distributed around the plant. Individual control devices such as governors and mechanical controllers were located at the process equipment to be controlled. Local readouts of set points and control outputs were available, and a means for changing the control mode from manual to automatic (or vice versa) usually was provided. It was up to the operator (actually, several operators) to coordinate the control of the many devices that made up the total process. They did this by roaming around the plant and making corrections to the control devices as needed and using the "Hey, Joe!" method of communications to integrate plant operations. This was a feasible approach to the control of early industrial processes because the plants were small geographically and the processes were not too large or complex. The same architecture was copied when direct-connected pneumatic controllers were developed in the late 1920s. These controllers provided more flexibility in selection and adjustment of the control algorithms, but all of the elements of the control loop (sensor, controller, operator interface, and output actuator) were still located in the field. There was no mechanism for communication between controllers other than that provided by each operator to other operators in the plant using visual and vocal means.

This situation changed of necessity in the late 1930s due to the growth in size and complexity of the processes to be controlled. It became more and more difficult to run a plant using the isolated-loop control architecture described above. The emphasis on improving overall plant operations led to a movement towards centralized control and equipment rooms. This was made possible by the development of transmitter-type pneumatic systems. In this architecture, measurements made at the process were converted to pneumatic signals at standard levels, which were then transmitted to the central location. The required control signals were computed at this location, then transmitted back to the actuating devices at the process. The great advantage of this architecture was that all of the process information was available to the operator at the central location. Thus, the operator was able to make better control decisions and operate the plant with a greater degree of safety and economic return.

The centralized control structure described above is still the dominant one in plants operating today. In the late 1950s and early 1960s, the technology used to implement this architecture started to shift from pneumatics to electronics. One of the key objectives of this shift was replacing the long runs of tubing used in pneumatic systems with the wires used in electronic ones. This change reduced the cost of installing the control systems and also eliminated the time lag inherent in pneumatic systems. Both of these advantages became more significant as plant sizes increased. Another consequence of the centralized control architecture was the development of the *split controller* structure. In this type of controller, the operator display section of the controller is panel mounted in the control room and the computing section is located in a separate rack in an adjoining equipment room. The split controller structure is especially appropriate for complex, interactive control systems (e.g., for boiler controls) in which the number of computing elements greatly exceeds the number of operator display elements.

Both pneumatic and electronic versions of the centralized control architecture still exist and are being sold, delivered, and operated today. In fact, it was not until 1970 that the sales of electronic controllers exceeded the sales of pneumatic controllers in the industrial process control marketplace (1.4).

The discussion to this point has focused on *continuous,* or analog, control devices, in which both the inputs and outputs to the controllers vary continuously over a selected range (e.g., 1–5 volts or 3–15 psi). Similar developments have taken place in the realm of sequential logic control devices, in which the inputs and outputs to the controllers take on only one of two discrete states (e.g., On/Off, 0/24 volts). These devices generally are used in controlling certain types of pumps, motors, or valves in a process. They also are used in safety override systems that operate in parallel to and back up the continuous systems described above. The original versions of these logic systems were implemented using simple electronic devices such as relays and stepping switches. Later, the development of solid-state electronic modules allowed logic systems to be implemented using the same level of technology as the corresponding electronic analog controllers.

In the early 1970s, a sophisticated device known as the *programmable logic controller* (PLC) was developed to implement sequential logic systems. This device is significant because it was one of the first special-purpose, computer-based devices that could be used by someone who was not a computer specialist. It was designed to be programmed by a user who was familiar with relay logic diagrams but was not necessarily a computer programmer. This approach to control system configuration was inspired by early efforts of process computer specialists to develop a process-oriented control language. However, it was more successful than most of these efforts in eliminating the user's dependence on a priesthood of computer specialists in running a process control system.

All of the versions of sequential logic systems described above have been implemented in direct-connected distributed architectures as well as in centralized ones. In each case, the logic controller has been associated directly with the corresponding unit of process equipment, with little or no communication between it and other logic controllers. It was not until the late 1970s that PLCs and computers started to be connected together in integrated systems for factory automation. For the purposes of this book, the PLC and networks of PLCs are considered to be special cases of the general distributed control system architecture described later in this chapter.

1.1.2. Computer-based Control System Developments

In addition to the evolution of the traditional types of control systems described above, a more recent (and equally important) evolution of computer-based process control systems has been taking place, as shown in the lower part of Figure 1.1. The first application of computers to industrial processes was in the areas of plant monitoring and supervisory control. In September 1958, the first industrial computer system for plant monitoring was installed at an electric utility power generating station (1.3). This innovation provided an automatic data acquisition capability not available before, and freed the operator from much drudgery by automatically logging plant operating conditions on a periodic basis. Shortly thereafter (in 1959 and 1960), supervisory computer control systems were installed in a refinery and in a chemical plant (1.4). In these applications, analog controllers were still the primary means of control. The computer used the available input data to calculate control set points that corresponded to the most efficient plant operating conditions. These set points then were sent to the analog controllers, which performed the actual closed-loop control. The ability of supervisory control computers to perform economic optimization as well as to acquire, display, and log plant data provided the operator with a powerful tool for significantly improving plant operations.

The next step in the evolution of computer process control was the use of the computer in the primary control loop itself, in a mode usually known as *direct digital control,* or DDC. In this approach, process measurements are read by the computer directly, the computer calculates the proper control outputs, then sends the outputs directly to the actuation devices. The first DDC system was installed in 1963 in a petrochemical plant (1.3). For security, a backup analog control system was provided to ensure that the process could be run automatically in the event of a computer failure. This proved to be a wise precaution, because this early DDC installation (as well as many others) was plagued with computer hardware reliability problems. Despite these problems, it demonstrated many of the advantages digital control has over analog control: tuning parameters and set points do not drift, complex control algorithms can be implemented to improve plant operation, and control loop tuning parameters can be set adaptively to track changing operating conditions.

1.1.3. Resulting System Architectures

As a result of the developments described above, two industrial control system architectures came to dominate the scene by the end of the 1970s. While there are many variations, typical examples of these architectures are shown in Figures 1.2 and 1.3. The first architecture is a hybrid one, making use of a combination of discrete control hardware and computer hardware in a central location to implement the required control functions. In this approach, first level or local control of the plant unit operations is implemented by using discrete analog and sequential logic controllers (or PLCs). Panelboard instrumentation connected to these controllers is used for operator interfacing and is located in the central control room area. A supervisory computer and associated data acquisition system are used to implement the plant management functions, including operating point optimization, alarming, data logging, and historical data storage and retrieval. The computer also is used to drive its own operator interface, usually consisting of one or more video display units (VDUs). A substantial amount of interfacing hardware is required to tie the analog and sequential control equipment to each other as well as to the supervisory computer.

The other dominant architecture, shown in Figure 1.3, is one in which

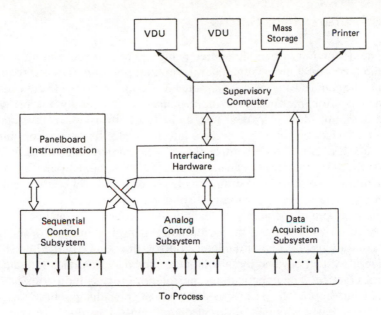

Figure 1.2. Hybrid System Architecture.

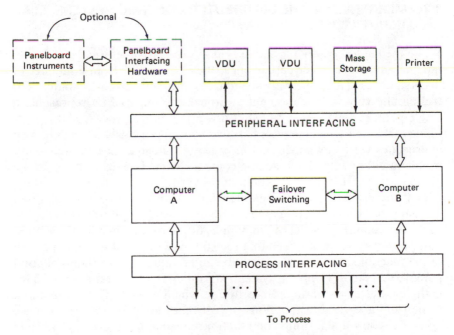

Figure 1.3. Central Computer System Architecture.

7

all system functions are implemented in high-performance computer hardware in a central location. In general, redundant computers are required so that the failure of a single computer does not shut the whole process down. Operator interfacing for plant management functions is provided using computer-driven VDUs, just as in the hybrid control system architecture described above. Operator interfacing for first-level continuous and sequential closed-loop control also may be implemented using VDUs. Optionally, the computers can be interfaced to standard panelboard instrumentation so that the operator in charge of first-level control can use a more familiar set of control and display hardware.

Note that both of the above systems use computers. The main difference between the two systems is the location of the implementation of the first-level continuous and sequential logic control functions. By the late 1970s, the hybrid system became by far the more prevalent approach in industrial control practice. The chemical and petroleum process industries heavily favored this approach, perhaps as a result of their disappointing experiences using early versions of direct digital control systems. In contrast, the use of large centralized computer systems to implement almost all plant control functions was limited primarily to the electric utility industry.

1.2. EMERGENCE OF THE DISTRIBUTED CONTROL SYSTEM ARCHITECTURE

While the central computer and hybrid system architectures provide significant advantages over earlier ones, they also suffer from a number of disadvantages. The biggest disadvantage of the centralized computer control architecture is that the central processing unit (CPU) represents a single point of failure that can shut down the entire process if it is lost. Since early industrial computer hardware was notoriously unreliable, two approaches were developed and have been used to attack the reliability problem: either a complete analog control system is used to back up the computer system, or another computer is used as a "hot standby" to take over if the primary control computer fails. Either approach results in a system significantly more expensive than an analog control system that performs a comparable set of functions. Another problem with these computer-based systems has been that the software required to implement all of the functions is extremely complex, and requires a priesthood of computer experts to develop the system, start it up, and keep it running. This is the natural result of an architecture in which a single CPU is required to perform a variety of functions in real time: input scanning; database updating; control algorithm computation; logging, long-term storage and retrieval of data; and man-machine interfacing (among others). Finally, the centralized system is limited in its capability to accommodate change and expansion. Once the loading on the computer approaches its limit, it becomes very difficult to add on to the system without a significant decrease in performance or increase in cost.

The hybrid system architecture of Figure 1.2 also has its deficiencies. One of the worst is simply that it is composed of many different subsystems, often manufactured by different vendors. Just interfacing the subsystems to one another is a significant challenge, given the variety of different signal levels and conventions that exists in each. Starting them up and making them work as an integrated whole is no less difficult a task. The hybrid approach also is functionally limited compared to the central computer-based system. The benefits of digital control outlined in Section 1.1.2 are lost, since the closed-loop control is done by discrete analog and sequential devices. Also, the speed and accuracy of plant performance computations suffer due to the limitations of the analog input equipment and the problems in accessing the database, which is no longer centralized as in the computer implementation approach.

Because of these problems, it became clear to both users and system designers that a new architectural approach was needed. Control system engineers had been sketching out concepts of distributed systems composed of digital control and communication elements since the middle 1960s. Unfortunately, the technology to implement these concepts in a cost-effective manner was not available at that time. It was not until the microprocessor was introduced in 1971 that the distributed system architecture became practical. Supporting technology also became available during the early 1970s: inexpensive solid-state memories were developed to replace magnetic core memories; integrated circuit chips to implement standard communication protocols were introduced; display system technology flourished with the emergence of light-emitting diode (LED) and color CRT displays; in the software area, structured design techniques, modular software packages, and new on-line diagnostic concepts were developed.

The result of this fortunate confluence of user needs and technological developments was the introduction of a large number of distributed digital control system product lines by vendors in the late 1970s and early 1980s. (See Refs. 1.7–1.12 for tutorial information on distributed control systems and 1.13–1.26 for a review of the development of these systems). While each system has a unique structure and specialized features, the architectures of most of these systems can be described in the context of the generalized one shown in Figure 1.4. The devices in this architecture are grouped into three categories: those that interface directly to the process to be controlled or monitored, those that perform high-level human in-

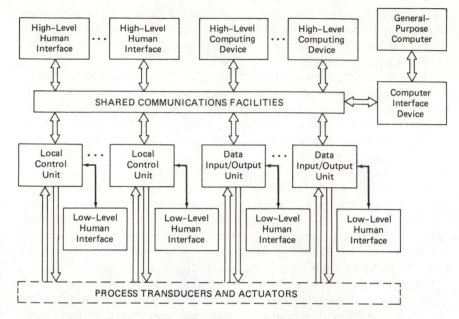

Figure 1.4. Generalized Distributed Control System Architecture.

terfacing and computing functions, and those that provide the means of communication between the other devices. A brief definition of each device is given below, and this terminology is used throughout the book:

1. *Local control unit (LCU)*—The smallest collection of hardware in the system that can do closed-loop control. The LCU interfaces directly to the process.
2. *Low-level human interface (LLHI)*—A device that allows the operator or instrument engineer to interact with the local control unit (e.g., to change set points, control modes, control configurations, or tuning parameters) using a direct connection. LLHIs can also interface directly to the process. Operator-oriented hardware at this level is called a *low-level operator interface*; instrument engineer-oriented hardware is called a *low-level engineering interface*.
3. *Data input/output unit (DI/OU)*—A device that interfaces to the process solely for the purpose of acquiring or outputting data. It performs no control functions.
4. *High-level human interface (HLHI)*—A collection of hardware that performs functions similar to the LLHI but with increased capability

and user friendliness. It interfaces to other devices only over the shared communication facilities. Operator-oriented hardware at this level is called a *high-level operator interface*; instrument engineer-oriented hardware is called a *high-level engineering interface*.

5. *High-level computing device (HLCD)*—A collection of micropro-cessor-based hardware that performs plant management functions traditionally performed by a plant computer. It interfaces to other devices only over the shared communication facilities.

6. *Computer interface device (CID)*—A collection of hardware that al-lows an external general-purpose computer to interact with other devices in the distributed control system using the shared commu-nication facilities.

7. *Shared communication facilities*—One or more levels of commu-nication hardware and associated software that allow the sharing of data among all devices in the distributed system. Shared commu-nication facilities do not include dedicated communication channels between specific devices or between hardware elements within a device.

Not included in the architecture in Figure 1.4 but of vital importance to the design of a distributed control system are the packaging and electrical power systems.

Detailed descriptions of the seven distributed control system elements mentioned above and a discussion of the major issues involved in selecting, using, and designing these elements form the bulk of the remaining chapters in this book, as follows:

1. *Local control unit*—Architectural and hardware issues are discussed in Chapter 2; software and language issues are covered in Chapter 3; and security design issues are discussed in Chapter 4.

2. *Low-level human interface*—The low-level operator interface is dis-cussed in Chapter 6; and the low-level engineering interface is cov-ered in Chapter 7.

3. *Data input/output unit*—Many design issues overlap with local control unit discussions and are found in Chapters 2 and 3; specific process input/output design issues are covered in Chapter 4.

4. *High-level human interface*—The high-level operator interface is discussed in Chapter 6, while Chapter 7 covers engineering interface.

5. *High-level computing device*—Discussed in Chapter 8.

6. *Computer interface device*—Discussed in Chapter 8.

7. *Packaging and power systems*—Discussed in Chapter 8.

A brief discussion of future trends in the development of distributed control systems is provided in the last section of Chapter 8.

1.3. COMPARISON WITH PREVIOUS ARCHITECTURES

One of the main objectives in the development of distributed control systems has been to maintain the best features of the central computer control and hybrid architectures described in the previous section. Most importantly, the new systems have been structured to combine the power and flexibility of digital control with the user-oriented familiarity of the traditional analog and sequential control systems. A summary of some of the key features of distributed control systems compared to previous ones is given in Table 1.2, and additional information on the architectural advantages and disadvantages of distributed systems is provided in references (1.27–1.36). The following discussion of these features expands upon the table:

1. *Scalability and expandability*—Refers to the ease with which a system can be sized for a spectrum of applications, ranging from small to large, and the ease with which elements can be added to the system after initial installation. The hybrid system is quite modular, so it ranks high on both counts; the same holds for the distributed system architecture. On the other hand, the central computer architecture is designed for only a small range of applications. It is not cost-effective for applications much smaller than its design size and it cannot be expanded easily once its memory and performance limits are reached.

2. *Control capability*—Refers to the power and flexibility of the control algorithms that can be implemented by the system. The capability of the hybrid architecture is limited by the functions available in the hardware modules that make up the system. To add a function involves both adding hardware and rewiring the control system. On the other hand, central computer and distributed architectures both provide the full advantages of digital control: driftless set points and tuning parameters, availability of complex control algorithms, ability to change algorithms without changing hardware, remote and adaptive tuning capabilities, and many others.

3. *Operator interfacing capability*—Refers to the capability of the hardware provided to aid the operator in performing plant monitoring and control functions. The operator interface in the hybrid system consists of conventional panelboard instrumentation for normal control and monitoring functions and a separate video display unit

Table 1.2. Comparison of Architectures.

FEATURE	HYBRID ARCHITECTURE	CENTRAL COMPUTER ARCHITECTURE	DISTRIBUTED ARCHITECTURE
1. Scalability and expandability	Good due to modularity	Poor—very limited range of system size	Good due to modularity
2. Control capability	Limited by analog and sequential control hardware	Full digital control capability	Full digital control capability
3. Operator interfacing capability	Limited by panelboard instrumentation	Digital hardware provides significant improvement for large systems	Digital hardware provides improvement for full range of system sizes
4. Integration of system functions	Poor due to variety of products	All functions performed by central computer	Functions integrated in a family of products
5. Significance of single-point failure	Low due to modularity	High	Low due to modularity
6. Installation costs	High due to discrete wiring and large volume of equipment	Medium—saves control room and equipment room space but uses discrete wiring	Low—savings in both wiring costs and equipment space
7. Maintainability	Poor—many module types, few diagnostics	Medium—requires highly trained computer maintenance personnel	Excellent—automatic diagnostics and module replacement

(VDU) for supervisory control. In the central computer and distributed architectures, VDUs generally are used as the primary operator interface for both the normal and supervisory control functions. The VDUs provide significant benefits to the operator: reduction in time needed to access control stations, flexibility of station grouping, graphics displays that mimic the process layout, and others. Since the VDUs in the distributed system are driven by microprocessors rather than by a large computer, they can be applied in a cost-effective way to small systems as well as large ones.

4. *Integration of system functions*—Refers to the degree with which the various functional subsystems are designed to work with one another in an integrated fashion. A high degree of integration minimizes user problems in procuring, interfacing, starting up, and maintaining the system. Since the hybrid system is composed of a variety of individual product lines, it is usually poorly integrated. The central computer architecture is well integrated because all of the functions are performed by the same hardware. The distributed system lies somewhere in between, depending on how well the products that make it up are designed to work together. (There are both good and bad examples of system integration out on the market today.)

5. *Significance of single-point failure*—Refers to the sensitivity of the system's performance to a failure of any of its elements. In the central computer architecture, the failure of a hardware element in the computer can cause the system to stop performing completely unless a backup computer is used. Therefore, this system is very sensitive to single-point failures. On the other hand, both the hybrid and distributed architectures are relatively insensitive to single-point failures due to the modularity of their structure.

6. *Installation costs*—Refers to the cost of system wiring and the cost of control room and equipment room space needed to house the system. The installation costs of the hybrid system are high: much custom wiring is needed for internal system interconnections; long wiring runs are needed from sensors to control cabinets; much control room space is required to house the panelboard instrumentation; and the large volume of control modules needed to implement the system take up a lot of equipment room space. The central computer architecture cuts down on this cost by eliminating the module interconnection wiring and by using VDUs to replace much of the panelboard instrumentation. The distributed system reduces costs further by using a communication system to replace the sensor wiring runs

and by reducing required equipment room space through the use of space-efficient microprocessor-based modules.

7. *Maintainability*—Refers to the ease with which a system can be kept running after installation. Low maintainability implies high maintenance costs, including the cost of spares, costs of process downtime while repairs are being made, and personnel training costs. The hybrid system is particularly poor in this area because of the large number of spare modules required, the lack of failure diagnostics in the system, and the personnel training required to cover the diverse subsystems. The central computer architecture is somewhat better: the range of module types is reduced and a certain number of failure diagnostics are provided. However, relatively sophisticated personnel are required to maintain the complex computer hardware and software. On the other hand, the maintainability of the distributed system architecture is excellent. Since there are only a few general-purpose control modules in the system, spare parts and personnel training requirements are minimal. Automatic on-line diagnostics are available to isolate failures to the module level, and module replacements can be made without disrupting a major portion of the process.

It can be seen from the table that the distributed control system architecture provides the user with many benefits over the hybrid and central computer architectures. The comparison is not all one-sided, however; as with any new venture, moving from a conventional analog control system to a distributed one requires the user to deal with a number of potential difficulties and changes in operation. One of the most obvious changes is that a microprocessor-based control system represents a new technology that plant personnel must learn. A certain amount of retraining of operating, instrument and maintenance people is required to ensure the success of any first installation of a distributed control system in a plant. Operating procedures will change; the operators will be spending a greater percentage of their time monitoring the process from the control room than patrolling the plant. When in the control room, they will be running the process from a video display unit instead of from panelboard instrumentation. During the early introduction of VDUs to the control room, the switch was expected to be traumatic for the operators. However, the transition turned out to be relatively painless; whether this was due to an underestimation of the adaptability of humans or to the pretraining effects of video games and home computers is not clear.

The new distributed systems offer the user a tremendous amount of flexibility in choice of control algorithms and location of equipment in the plant. While this is an advantage in most ways, it also requires that the user plan the installation carefully so that the control system is partitioned properly and that there is appropriate space and protection in the remote locations for the control hardware. These decisions must be well documented so that the installation and startup process proceeds smoothly.

When partitioning the control strategy, the user must be aware of the consequences of the various processing and communication delays that are inherent in a distributed control system. While the rapid advances in digital system hardware are fast making these delays negligible in most situations, the user must be aware of the needs of his or her particular application. If the control system is distributed geographically as well as functionally, the user must make sure that in the remote locations the installed hardware can survive the environment and the proper backup hardware is provided to accommodate any equipment failures.

The above comparisons and design considerations only begin to cover the issues involved in evaluating and designing distributed digital control systems. More detailed comparisons and design discussions on specific technical issues will be provided later in the book. References 1.37–1.44 contain additional information on selecting and evaluating distributed control systems.

REFERENCES

History of Control System Developments

1.1 Mayr, O., *Feedback Mechanisms—In the Historical Collections of the National Museum of History and Technology,* Smithsonian Institution Press, Washington, D.C., 1971.
1.2 Dukelow, S.G., "Boiler Controls—Yesterday, Today, and Tomorrow," 19th ISA Power Instrumentation Symposium, San Francisco, May 9–12, 1976.
1.3 Williams, T.J., "Two Decades of Change—A Review of the 20-year History of Computer Control," *Control Engineering,* vol. 24, no. 9, September 1977, pp. 71–76.
1.4 Kompass, E.J., "The Long-Term Trends in Control Engineering," *Control Engineering,* vol. 26, no. 9, September 1979, pp. 53–55.
1.5 Bennett, S., *A History of Control Engineering, 1800–1930,* Peter Peregrinus Ltd., Stevenage, UK, 1979.
1.6 Williams, T.J., "Computer Control Technology—Past, Present, and Probable Future," *Trans. Inst. Meas. and Control,* vol. 5, no. 1, January–March 1983, pp. 7–19.

Distributed Control Tutorials

1.7 Keyes, M.A., "Distributed Digital Control," *Control Engineering,* vol. 20, no. 9, September 1973, pp. 77–80.
1.8 Kahne, S.J., Lefkowitz, I., and Rose, C.W., "Automatic Control by Distributed Intelligence," *Scientific American,* vol. 240, no. 6, June 1979, pp. 78–90.

1.9 Vandiver, R.L., "What Is Distributed Control?" *Hydrocarbon Processing,* vol. 60, no. 6, June 1981, pp. 91–94.

1.10 Lukas, M.P., and Scheib, T.J., "How Microprocessors Control Process Systems," *Production Engineering,* vol. 28, no. 8, August 1981, pp. 38–42.

1.11 Baur, P.S., "Microprocessors, Data Highways: Building Tomorrow's Control Systems," *Power Magazine,* vol. 126, no. 3, March 1982, pp. 25–32.

1.12 Moore, J.A., and Herb, S.M., *Understanding Distributed Process Control,* Instrument Society of America, Research Triangle Park, 1983.

Distributed Control Surveys and Developments

1.13 Lukas, M.P., "A Distributed System Architecture for Utility and Process Applications," in *Proc. of Third Annual Advanced Control Conference,* ed. by E.J. Kompass, Dun-Donnelly (Control Engineering), Chicago, April 1976, pp. 101–112.

1.14 Keyes, M.A., "Distributed Control—Relevance and Ramification for Utility and Process Applications," *Proceedings of the International Telemetering Conference,* Los Angeles, September 1976; pub. by International Foundation of Telemetering, Woodland Hills, Calif., pp. 692–704, 1976.

1.15 Anon., "The Configurations of Process Control: 1979," *Control Engineering,* vol. 26, no. 3, March 1979, pp. 43–57.

1.16 Martin, J.D., and Lecours, R.E., "Functional Benefits of Distributed Control Systems," *Proceedings of National Research Council Canadian Conference on Automatic Control,* Montreal, Quebec, May 1979; pub. by National Research Council, Ottawa, Ontario, 1979, paper 6.2.

1.17 Kompass, E.J., "The Choices in Distributed Control," *Control Engineering,* vol. 26, no. 6, June 1979, pp. 57–60.

1.18 Schagrin, E.F., "Evolution of a Distributed Control System," *Chemical Engineering Progress,* vol. 76, no. 6, June 1980, pp. 72–75.

1.19 Lukas, M.P., and Willey, M.S.,"A Distributed Control System for Energy Management and Control," IFAC Workshop on Systems Engineering Applications to Industrial Energy Generation and Processes, Houston, Texas, October 1980.

1.20 Denesdi, L., and Zdzieborski, J.H., "Distributed Digital Control and Monitoring for Power Plants," *Power Engineering,* vol. 84, no. 11, November 1980, pp. 76–79.

1.21 Lukas, M.P., "An Advanced System Architecture for Distributed Control," Minutes of 1981 Spring Regional Meetings, International Purdue Workshop on Industrial Computer Systems; Purdue University Engineering Experiment Station Bulletin 143 Series, April 1981, pp. 483–498.

1.22 Bryan, G.C., and Umbers, I.G., *Distributed Systems for Process Monitoring and Control,* Warren Spring Laboratory, Stevenage, Hertfordshire, U.K., 1982.

1.23 Williams, T.J.,"Hierarchical Distributed Control: Progress and Needs," *InTech,* vol. 30, no. 3, March 1983, pp. 45–52.

1.24 Pluhar, K., "Distributed Control Manufacturers Offer Variety of Systems to Worldwide Market," *Control Engineering,* vol. 30, no. 4, April 1983, pp. 80–83.

1.25 Syrbe, M., Saenger, F., and Lang, K.-F., "Centralized and Distributed Control Systems," *Process Automation,* no. 1, 1983, pp. 18–25.

1.26 Krigman, A., "Distributed Control: Pipe Dreams to Reality," *InTech,* vol. 31, no. 4, April 1984, pp. 7–18.

Distributed Control Architecture and Applications Issues

1.27 Borsi, L., and Pavlik, E., "The Concepts and Structures of Distributed Process Automation Systems," *Process Automation,* no. 2, 1980, pp. 63–70.

1.28 Erikson, I.L., and Purvis, J.R. III, "Centralized vs. Distributed Control: A Cost Comparison," *InTech,* vol. 28, no. 6, June 1981, pp. 61–63.

1.29 Natiello, L.F., "Distributed Digital Control: Practical Considerations for Design and Implementation," Third IFAC Workshop on Distributed Control Systems, Beijing, China, August 1981.

1.30 Garrett, L.T., and McHenry, J.M., "Analyzing Costs of Digital and Analog Control Systems," *Hydrocarbon Processing,* vol. 60, no. 12, December 1981, pp. 103–108.

1.31 Leahy, M.J., and Cornell, J.W., "A Discussion of Distributed Microprocessor-based Systems and Applications for Utility Boiler Control," 25th ISA Power Instrumentation Symposium, Phoenix, May 1982.

1.32 Stanton, B.D., "Reduce Problems in New Control System Design," *Hydrocarbon Processing,* vol. 61, no. 8, August 1982, pp. 67–70.

1.33 Damsker, D.J., "Controversial Issues of Distributed Control," *Proceedings of Joint Power Generation Conference,* Indianapolis, September 1983; IEEE, New York, 1984, pp. 522–529.

1.34 Hofmann, W., "Problems in the Application of Digital Automation Systems in the Process Industry," *Process Automation,* no. 2, 1983, pp. 69–76.

1.35 Quietzsch, G., "Comments on the Structures of Digital Automation Systems," *Process Automation,* no. 2, 1983, pp. 77–82.

1.36 Damsker, D.J., chairman, "Application Guide, Distributed Control and Monitoring for Power Generating Stations," *IEEE Power Engineering Society Standard P–1046,* 1986.

Distributed Control System Evaluation and Procurement

1.37 Rapley, D.E., "A Practical Approach for Selection of a CRT-based Distributed Process Control/Data Acquisition System," *ISA Publication* ISBN 87664–432–9, 1979.

1.38 "Selecting Digital Control Systems," *InTech,* vol. 26, no. 5, May 1979, pp. 28–32.

1.39 Lynn, S.R., "Guidelines for Specifying and Procuring Distributed Control Systems," *InTech,* vol. 27, no. 9. September 1980, pp. 87–91.

1.40 Dobrowolski, M., "Guide to Selecting Distributed Digital Control Systems," *InTech,* vol. 28, no. 6, June 1981, pp. 45–52.

1.41 Cocheo, S., "How to Evaluate Distributed Computer Control Systems," *Hydrocarbon Processing,* vol. 60, no. 6, June 1981, pp. 95–106.

1.42 Pollock, W.K., "Evaluating Distributed Control Systems—A Generic Approach," *Proceedings of Third Annual Control Engineering Conference,* Control Engineering, May 1984, pp. 121–124.

1.43 Zimmerman, C.K., "Evaluating Distributed Control Systems: Where Do We Go From Here?" *Control Engineering,* vol. 31, no. 10, October 1984, pp. 109–112.

1.44 Cordova, G.J., Hertanu, H.I., and Doyle, G.T., "Microprocessor-based Distributed Control Systems," *Chemical Engineering,* vol. 92, no. 2, January 21, 1985, pp. 86–95.

2
LOCAL CONTROL UNIT ARCHITECTURE

2.1. INTRODUCTION

As defined in Chapter 1, the local control unit (LCU) is the smallest collection of hardware in the distributed control system that performs closed-loop control. That is, it takes inputs from process-measuring devices and commands from the operator and computes the control outputs needed to make the process follow the commands. It then sends the control outputs to the actuators, drives, valves, and other mechanical devices that regulate the flows, temperatures, pressures, and other variables to be controlled in the plant.

Since an LCU malfunction can cause a condition that is hazardous to both people and equipment, its proper design is critical to the safe and efficient operation of the plant. The issues involved in evaluating or designing LCU architectures are discussed in this chapter. First, the basic elements of a microprocessor-based controller are defined. Then the concept of function blocks is introduced to allow discussion of LCU functionality in the context of a popular control language approach. Next, several LCU architectures prevalent in the distributed control marketplace are compared with respect to cost and performance features. Finally, a number of hardware design issues that affect LCU architecture are discussed. Other issues dealing with LCU languages, security, and input/output capabilities are covered in later chapters.

2.2. BASIC ELEMENTS OF A MICROPROCESSOR-BASED CONTROLLER

To provide a starting point for discussion, the basic elements of a generalized microprocessor-based LCU can be defined as shown in Figure 2.1. The microprocessor along with its associated clock comprise the central processing unit (CPU) of the controller. Read only memory (ROM) is used for permanent storage of controller programs, and random-access semiconductor memory (RAM) is used for temporary storage of infor-

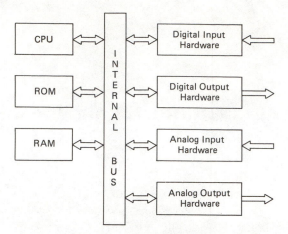

Figure 2.1. Basic Elements of a Local Control Unit.

mation. Depending on the type of microprocessor used, RAM and ROM can be located on the microprocessor chip or on separate memory chips.

The LCU also must have input/output (I/O) circuitry so that it can communicate with the external world by reading in, or receiving, analog and digital data as well as sending similar signals out. Generally, the CPU communicates with the other elements in the LCU over an internal shared bus that transmits addressing, data control, and status information in addition to the data. A detailed description of these microprocessor system elements and how they work is beyond the scope of this book. For more information on the basic operation of digital system components and how they relate to industrial controllers, refer to References 2.1–2.14 at the end of the chapter.

The controller structure shown in Figure 2.1 is the minimum required to perform basic control functions. In a noncritical application in which the control function never changes, this structure might be adequate (e.g., in a home appliance whose failure would not cause a safety problem). The control algorithms could be coded in assembly language and loaded into ROM. After the controller was turned on, it would read inputs, execute the control algorithms, and generate control outputs in a fixed cycle indefinitely. However, because the situation is not this simple in industrial control applications, the controller structure shown in Figure 2.1 must be enhanced to include the following:

1. *Flexibility of changing the control configuration*—In industrial applications the same controller product usually is used to implement a great variety of different control strategies. Even for a particular

strategy, the user usually wants the flexibility of changing the control system tuning parameters without changing the controller hardware. Therefore, the control configuration cannot be burned into ROM but must be stored in a memory medium whose contents can be changed, such as RAM. Unfortunately, RAM is usually implemented using semiconductor technology that is *volatile;* that is, it loses its contents if the power is turned off (whether due to power failure, routine maintenance, or removal of the controller from its cabinet). Therefore, some provision must be made for restoring the control configuration, either from an external source or from a nonvolatile memory within the controller itself.

2. *Ability to use the controller without being a computer expert*—The typical user of an industrial control system is generally familiar with the process to be controlled, knows the basics of control system design, and has worked with electric analog or pneumatic control systems before. However, the user is usually not capable of or interested in programming a microprocessor in assembly language. He or she simply wants to be able to implement the selected control algorithms. Therefore, a mechanism for allowing the user to "configure" the LCU's control algorithms in a relatively simple way must be provided.

3. *Ability to bypass the controller in case it fails so that the process still can be controlled manually*—Shutting down the process is very expensive and undesirable for the control system user. Since all control equipment has the potential of failing no matter how carefully it has been designed, the system architecture must allow an operator to "take over" the control loop and run it by hand until the control hardware is repaired or replaced.

4. *Ability of the LCU to communicate with other LCUs and other elements in the system (as shown in the generalized system architecture in Figure 1.4)*—Controllers in an industrial control system do not operate in isolation but must work in conjunction with other controllers, data I/O devices, and human interface devices. A mechanism for allowing the LCU to perform this interaction must be provided.

The remainder of this chapter, as well as Chapters 3 and 4, will discuss the various ways these needs can be satisfied in designing an industrial-grade LCU.

2.3. FUNCTION BLOCKS—AN INTRODUCTION

As indicated above, the LCU must provide a means for entering the control algorithms to be executed without requiring the user to be a computer programmer. This is usually done by means of a control language supplied with the LCU. Chapter 3 gives a detailed discussion of the issues involved in selecting and evaluating control languages. However, a brief introduction to them is given here to facilitate discussion of LCU architectures.

The control language provided in commercially available industrial controllers usually is one of two types: a control-oriented version of a high-level language such as FORTRAN or BASIC, or a block-oriented language patterned after the control functions traditionally provided as discrete hardware modules in electronic or pneumatic control systems (e.g., summation, square root, or control modules). The discussion of the high-level language approach will be deferred to Chapter 3; this approach is generally used only in computer systems or in the most powerful microprocessor-based LCUs.

By far the more popular approach is to use function blocks to define the control system configuration to be implemented in the LCU. The concept of function blocks can be appreciated most easily through an example, such as that shown in Figure 2.2. In this example, the LCU has two analog inputs and one analog output. Also, the LCU provides the user with a library of function blocks in ROM, which may include proportional-integral-derivative (PID) control, square root, summation, difference, high/low select, and other continuous functions. Logical functions required for sequence control and safety systems also may be provided, such as AND, OR, NOT, time delay, and latching functions. To configure the control

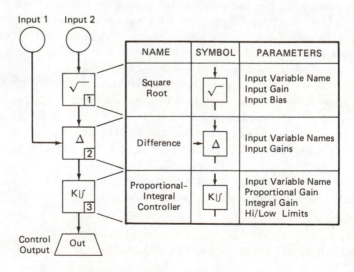

Figure 2.2. Continuous Control Example

logic shown in Figure 2.2, the user would first select the square-root function from the library and give it a block number, say 1 (as shown in the bottom righthand corner). Then, the user would set the various parameters that are associated with the function. In the case of the square-root function, there are three: the source of input to the block (controller hardware input 2), and the gain and bias adjustments to the input signal required to convert it to the proper units in the control structure. Then, the user would select the difference block and identify it as block 2. The parameters associated with this block are the input sources (i.e., hardware input 1 and the output of function block 1) and the gains on the input signals. Next, the user selects the proportional-integral controller function block, labels it, and sets its parameters in a similar manner. The last step is to link the output of function block 3 (control output in the figure) to the physical output of the LCU.

The means by which this function block selection and configuration takes place is not significant here (this subject is covered in Chapter 7). The main point is that the function block concept allows the user not familiar with computer programming to configure and tune the control system. This can be done in a simple procedural fashion using many of the same steps carried out in the past with electronic analog and pneumatic control product lines. In this case, however, the function blocks are implemented in software modules within the LCU instead of as individual hardware modules that must be selected from a catalog and wired up into a control system.

The function block approach has proved to be very successful in relieving the user from the need to learn a programming language in order to use a distributed control system. In this chapter, one of the key parameters in the various control system architectures considered is the size of the control configuration (i.e., the *number* of function blocks) permitted per LCU. Other aspects of evaluating function blocks and selecting control languages will be discussed in Chapter 3.

2.4. A COMPARISON OF ARCHITECTURES

While Figure 2.1 describes the basic elements of all microprocessor-based local control units, the current offerings of controllers in the marketplace exhibit endless variations on this structure. The controllers differ in size, I/O capability, range of functions provided, and other architectural parameters depending on the application and the vendor who designed the equipment. The purpose of this section is to examine the impact of these architectural parameters on the performance, cost, and application flexibility of an LCU.

2.4.1. Architectural Parameters

When evaluating the controllers on the market or when specifying a new one, the control system designer is faced with the problem of choosing a controller architecture that best meets the needs of the range of applications in which the controller is to be used. Some of the major architectural parameters that must be selected include the following:

1. *Size of controller*—This refers to the *number* of function blocks and/ or language statements that can be executed by the controller, as well as the number of process I/O channels provided by the controller.
2. *Functionality of controller*—This refers to the *mix* of function blocks or language statements provided by the controller (e.g., continuous control, logic control, arithmetic functions, or combinations of the above). This also refers to the mix of process input and output types (e.g., analog or digital) provided by the controller.
3. *Performance of controller*—This refers to the rate at which the controller scans inputs, processes function blocks or language statements, and generates outputs; it also includes the accuracy with which the controller performs these operations.
4. *Communication channels out of controller*—In addition to process inputs and output channels, the controller must provide other communication channels to operator interface devices and to other controllers and devices in the system. The number, type, and speed of these channels are key controller design parameters.
5. *Controller output security*—In a real-time process control system, a mechanism must be provided (usually manual backup or redundancy) to ensure that the control output is maintained despite a controller failure so that a process shutdown can be avoided.

Unfortunately, it is not generally possible to select any one of these architectural parameters independently from all of the others, since there is a great degree of interaction among them. Therefore, selecting the best combination for the range of applications to be considered is more a matter of engineering judgment than a science. Each vendor of microprocessor-based systems has a different view of the range of applications intended for the controller, and as a result designs an LCU architecture that quite often differs from that of its competitors.

To illustrate some of the differences in LCU architectures, three representative LCU configurations are shown in Figures 2.3 through 2.5. They are not intended to represent particular commercially available products but rather, different classes of controllers on the market today.

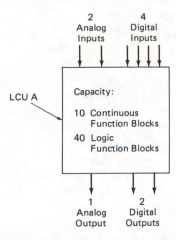

Figure 2.3. LCU Architecture—Configuration A

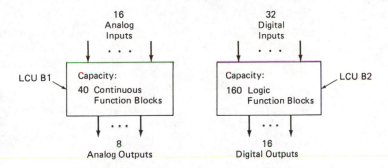

Figure 2.4. LCU Architecture—Configuration B

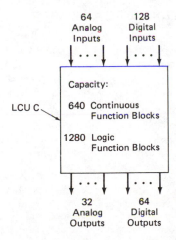

Figure 2.5. LCU Architecture—Configuration C

25

Configuration A (Figure 2.3) represents a class of single-loop LCU that provides both analog and digital inputs and outputs and executes both continuous and logic function blocks. Configuration B (Figure 2.4) represents an architecture in which two different types of LCUs implement the full range of required continuous and logic functions. Configuration C (Figure 2.5) represents a multiloop controller architecture in which both continuous and logic functions are performed. For each example, the architecture is defined in terms of its analog and digital I/O capacity and its continuous and logic function block capacity. In Table 2.1, these architectures are compared on the basis of the parameters defined previously: size, functionality, performance, communications, and output security

Table 2.1. Comparison of Architectures

ARCHITECTURE PARAMETERS	CONFIGURATION A (SINGLE-LOOP)	CONFIGURATION B (2 LCU TYPES)	CONFIGURATION C (MULTI-LOOP)
Controller size	Number of functions needed for single PID loop or motor controller.	Includes functions and I/O needed for eight control loops and a small logic controller.	System size is equivalent to small DDC system.
Controller functionality	Uses both continuous and logic function blocks.	Continuous and logic function blocks split between controllers.	Uses both continuous and logic function blocks; can support high-level languages.
Controller scalability	High degree of scalability from small to large systems	Requires both controller types even in small systems.	Not scalable to very small systems.
Controller performance	Requirements can be met with inexpensive hardware.	Because of functional split, performance requirements are not excessive.	Hardware must be high performance to execute large number of functions.
Communication channels	Need intermodule communications for control; only minimum needed for human interface.	Functional separation requires close interface between controller types.	Large communication requirement to human interface; minimal between controllers.
Controller output security	Controller has single-loop integrity; usually only manual backup is needed.	Lack of single-loop integrity requires redundancy in critical applications.	Size of controller requires redundancy in all applications.

provisions. The following discussion expands on this table for each of the architectures. Additional discussions in the areas of communication requirements and controller output security are given in Sections 4.1 and 4.2 of Chapter 4.

LCU Configuration A. In configuration A, the controller size is the minimum required to perform a single loop of control or a single motor control function or other simple sequencing function. Two digital outputs are provided to allow the controller to drive a pulsed (raise/lower) positioner or actuator. Twice as many inputs as outputs are provided to permit implementation of algorithms such as cascade control, temperature compensation of flows, and interlocking of logic inputs and continuous control loops. A general-purpose controller such as this requires both continuous and sequential (logic) function blocks to be included in its library. In most industrial control applications, the performance of the LCU must be adequate to sample all inputs, compute all of the function blocks, and generate all outputs in the range of 0.1 to 0.5 seconds maximum. Since configuration A has such a small number of inputs, function blocks, and outputs, the performance requirement can be met easily by a simple and inexpensive set of microprocessor-based hardware (e.g., an eight-bit microprocessor and matching memory components).

The communication requirements on configuration A for purposes of human interfacing are minimal because only one loop is controlled and a few input points monitored. However, it is important that a secure inter-controller communication channel be provided so that the single-loop controller can participate in complex control system structures containing other LCUs.

An important architectural feature to be considered when evaluating industrial controllers is the provision for control output security. In commercially available controllers, one or both of the following methods are used to allow continued operation of the process in the event of a controller failure: (1) a backup feature is provided to allow the operator to adjust the control output manually if the automatic controller fails; or (2) a redundant controller is provided to allow continuation of automatic control if the primary controller fails. The choice of method depends on the number of control outputs that would be lost if a controller fails. An operator can handle a small number of loops (usually in the range of one to four) manually, so for small controllers usually only a manual backup is provided. In the case of controller architecture A, the single-loop integrity of the controller configuration allows the simple and inexpensive option of manual backup to be used in most applications. For controllers that implement larger numbers of control loops, some form of control redundancy is usually provided. See Section 4.2 for a more extensive discussion of the issues regarding controller security.

LCU Configuration B. Configuration B differs significantly from configuration A. In the first place, two different types of LCUs (continuous control, or B1 in Figure 2.4, and logic control, or B2) are used to provide the full range of required controller functionality. In general, increasing the number of types of controllers in the system has both positive and negative effects. On the positive side, the specialized design of each controller allows it to match the functional needs of the corresponding application more closely than would a single general-purpose controller. As a result, a particular control application would require a smaller number of controller hardware modules. On the other hand, an increase in the number of controller types from one to two also results in increased interfacing requirements between controllers, additional documentation and training needs, and a decrease in production volume for each controller type (resulting in higher unit costs and longer lead times). In addition, this increase can reduce the scalability of the resulting system, since in the general case *both* of the controller types will be needed in even the smallest system. As usual, the optimum tradeoff is dependent on the range of applications foreseen for the system being designed.

With respect to controller size, configuration B is medium in scale. The continuous control portion has the form of an eight-loop controller, and the logic control portion can be viewed as a small programmable logic controller (PLC) or equivalent. Because of the split in functions and the relatively small size of each controller, the performance requirements on the controller hardware to meet the 0.1–0.5 second cycle time are not excessive. This class of controller usually is implemented using a high-performance eight-bit or an average performance 16-bit microprocessor and matching memory components.

In the area of communication channels required, configuration B calls for a well-designed interface between the two controller types, since in many systems both controllers must operate in close coordination to integrate continuous and logic control functions. The ability to communicate with other controllers in the distributed system must be provided, but the communication performance level need not be as high as in configuration A since a greater percentage of communications takes place within the LCU. Of course, as with Configuration A, a communication channel to human interface devices must be provided, but the channel must have a larger bandwidth because of the larger volume of traffic required per controller.

Finally, regarding output security, the lack of single-loop integrity of configuration B implies that a redundant controller must be used in all critical applications (i.e., those in which a controller failure would cause a significant upset to the process). Of course, if the application requires both continuous and logic control, redundancy must be provided for both of the controller types in the system. It should be noted that full one-on-one redundancy often is not used in commercially available controllers in this class. Instead, one redundant controller may be used to back up several primary controllers. This reduces the cost of redundancy to some extent, but increases the complexity of the hardware used for interfacing the primary and backup controllers.

LCU Configuration C.   LCU configuration C shown in Figure 2.5 is closer in structure to the direct digital control (DDC) systems described in Chapter 1 than are either of the other two configurations. It is designed to be a multiloop controller in which all functions are performed by one CPU in conjunction with its associated memory and I/O boards. This places stringent requirements on the performance of the hardware since all of the control algorithms in the LCU must be executed within 0.5 seconds of less. This LCU configuration is usually implemented with one or more 16-bit microprocessors or a 32-bit microprocessor in conjunction with support hardware such as arithmetic coprocessors to attain the required speed.

Since the objective of this architecture is to implement a large number of functions in one controller, usually both continuous and logic function blocks are provided. Because of the power of the microprocessor supplied in this configuration, it also becomes feasible to include a high-level language (usually BASIC or FORTRAN) in addition to or instead of function blocks.

This architecture has a number of advantages over configurations A and B. For example, requirements for communication among controllers are minimal because of the high density of functions implemented per controller; also, this LCU's high-level language capability allows it to implement complex user-defined control and computational algorithms. However, it is not as scalable to small systems as are the other two architectures, and the communication port or ports to the operator interface hardware must handle a large volume of traffic. In addition, since a failure in this type of LCU could affect a large number of control loops, a redundant CPU (and perhaps redundant I/O hardware as well) must be included in all control applications of any significance. Redundant hardware may not be required if only a few loops are affected by a failure or if the controller is performing only high-level control functions and is not manipulating control outputs directly.

Other LCU features relative to these three architectures will be discussed in more detail throughout the remainder of the book. One particular feature, cost-effectiveness of an architecture in various applications, is covered in the next section.

2.4.2. Impact of Architecture on Cost-Effectiveness

As stated in the previous section, the architecture of the local control unit must be properly matched to the application so that the LCU's performance is acceptable and cost-effective in that application (or expected range of applications). This section will illustrate the effect that selecting certain LCU architectural parameters (e.g., functional capacity, I/O capacity, and number of controller types required) has on the cost of implementing various applications. The applications will be characterized by two parameters: size (in number of loops to be implemented), and complexity (to be defined). The three LCU configurations defined in section 2.4.1 will be compared.

To perform this comparison, a number of assumptions were made. Since the configurations are fictitious, it was impossible to assign an absolute cost to each one. Therefore, a monetary unit no longer in use, the "doubloon," was used in making cost estimates as a reminder that only *relative* costs are being evaluated here, and then only under a particular set of assumptions:

1. *Configuration A*—To serve as a basis of reference, the cost was set at 1,000 doubloons.
2. *Configuration B*—This configuration is composed of two controllers: LCU B1 for continuous functions and LCU B2 for logic functions. Based on the I/O and function block capacity of LCU B1 relative to those of LCU A, it appeared reasonable to assign a cost of 5,000 doubloons to LCU B1. Assuming that LCU B2 is built from similar hardware, its cost also was set at 5,000 doubloons.
3. *Configuration C*—Based on the capacity and hardware complexity of this controller relative to LCU A, assigning a cost of 15,000 doubloons to LCU C appeared to be reasonable.

The following assumptions with respect to the need for redundancy in the various LCU configurations were also made:

1. *Configuration A*—Since LCU A has single-loop integrity, it was assumed that manual backup is adequate in case of controller failure and that no redundancy is required.

2. *Configuration B*—In this case, it was assumed that a redundant controller can back up one to eight primary controllers for both B1 and B2.
3. *Configuration C*—Because of the large number of functions implemented in this controller, it was assumed that each primary controller must be backed up by a corresponding redundant controller.

Two cases will be considered in the following analysis. Case I is a control application that requires only continuous function blocks and analog I/O. Case II is a control application that requires a complete mix of continuous and logic function blocks and both analog and digital I/O.

Case I—Continuous Functions Only.   Using the cost and redundancy assumptions just outlined, it was possible to compute the cost per control loop of each LCU configuration as a function of the total number of control loops that must be implemented. (A control loop was defined to consist of one analog input, one analog output, and five continuous function blocks.) The results are plotted in Figure 2.6. For example, if 12 control loops must be implemented, the following number of controllers are required in each configuration:

1. *Configuration A*—12 controllers are required.
2. *Configuration B*—Three controllers are required (two primary and one backup).
3. *Configuration C*—Two controllers are required (one primary and one backup).

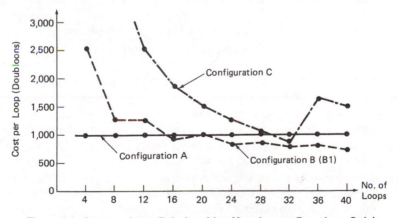

Figure 2.6. Cost-per-Loop Relationships (Continuous Functions Only)

The cost per loop for each configuration was computed by dividing the total cost of the required controllers by the number of loops (12 in the above example).

A number of conclusions can be drawn from the results in Figure 2.6. First, it can be seen that the cost-per-loop relationship for LCU A is a constant at 1,000 doubloons per loop; this is obviously as expected for a single-loop controller. The cost per loop for configuration B (LCU B1) is relatively high for a small number of loops, but decreases quickly as the number of loops increases and the full capacity of the controller is utilized. For 16 loops and beyond, the cost-per-loop of LCU B1 is less than that for LCU A. Since LCU C is designed to be a 32-loop controller, it does not become cost-effective until the application approaches the number of loops in that range. However, if the number of loops required goes above 32, it is again at a significant disadvantage compared to the other controllers, since additional hardware is required beyond that point. A final conclusion can be reached by inspection of Figure 2.6: if the choice of a controller type is based strictly on cost per loop, configuration A would be selected for small systems (under 16 loops) and configuration B would be selected for larger ones.

It should be noted, however, that this conclusion is valid only for the case of simple, single-loop control system configurations. To allow investigation of other configurations, the concept of the *control complexity ratio* (CCR) of a control system structure is defined as follows:

$$CCR = \frac{\text{Number of function blocks in control system}}{\text{Number of control system outputs}}$$

Because case I is concerned with continuous functions only, for this case:

$$CCR = \frac{\text{Number of continuous function blocks}}{\text{Number of analog outputs}}$$

The absolute value of this ratio will vary somewhat depending on the definition of a function block in the particular system considered (some function blocks are more complicated than others). However, for a given definition, this ratio provides a very useful index of control system complexity. For example, the simple control loop defined above has five function blocks per control output, so its CCR is five. If five more function blocks have to be added to this configuration to form a cascade controller, its CCR would then be 10. In more complicated control strategies such as those for a distillation column or an industrial boiler, control complexity ratios may get as high as 30 or 40. It will become clear that the choice of the best or most cost-effective controller architecture depends a great deal on the complexity of the control system to be implemented in the controller.

To determine the effect of control system complexity on the cost-effectiveness of the various LCU configurations, an example control system having 100 control outputs was evaluated. The number of function blocks in the control system was varied to produce a range of CCR values from 1 to 20. For each value of CCR, the number of LCUs required to implement the corresponding control system then was computed for each LCU configuration defined in Figures 2.3 through 2.5. Finally, the cost per function block was determined by dividing the cost of the LCUs by the number of function blocks in the control system. The results of this analysis are plotted in Figure 2.7.

It is evident from the figure that the cost per function is very high for all LCU configurations for low values of complexity. In this range, the number of function blocks implemented is low, while the number of controllers required is fixed by the requirement to provide 100 control outputs. As the complexity of each control configuration increases, the cost per function block decreases until it reaches a minimum level. It is interesting to note that the complexity ratio at which each cost curve reaches its minimum value corresponds closely to the characteristic complexity ratio of the LCU configuration itself. For example, the cost curve for configuration B keeps decreasing until CCR = 5, at which point the curve remains flat. This value of CCR corresponds to the number of continuous

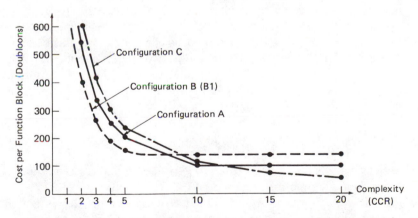

Figure 2.7. Cost-per-Function Relationships (Continuous Functions Only)

function blocks (40) divided by the number of analog outputs (8) provided by LCU configuration B1. Similarly, the curve for configuration A flattens out at CCR = 10 (ten continuous function blocks divided by one analog output), and the curve for configuration C flattens out at CCR = 20 (640 continuous function blocks divided by 32 analog outputs).

Note also that the *value* of the cost per function block at which the curve flattens out is equal to the characteristic cost per function block of the LCU configuration itself, taking into account the effect of redundancy requirements on the configuration. For example, the cost of LCU A is 1,000 doubloons, it implements up to ten continuous function blocks, and no redundancy is required. Therefore, its characteristic cost per function block is (1,000/10) = 100, which is the asymptotic value that the cost curve approaches for high complexities in Figure 2.7. In the case of configuration B, the cost of LCU B1 including the effect of redundancy is 5,000 + (5,000/8) = 5,625 doubloons, because every eight LCUs must be backed up by another LCU. Since LCU B1 implements up to 40 continuous function blocks, its characteristic cost per function block is (5,625/40) = 141. This is the asymptotic value that the cost curve for configuration B approaches for high complexities. A similar computation can be made for LCU C, taking into account the one-on-one redundancy requirement on this configuration.

The cost-per-function curves in Figure 2.7 indicate that LCU B is the most cost-effective configuration for low levels of control system complexity, configuration A is best in the middle range, and configuration C becomes most cost-effective for high levels of complexity.

Case II—Mix of Continuous and Logic Functions.   The conclusions reached for case I change somewhat if the control systems to be implemented require both continuous and logic function blocks. Generally, both types are required in all but the simplest control systems. For this example, it is assumed that a control loop includes two digital inputs, ten logic function blocks, and one digital output in addition to the five continuous function blocks and one analog input and output specified in the previous definition. The same type of analysis as in case I was then performed to determine the cost per loop of each LCU configuration (A, B, and C) as a function of the number of control loops to be implemented. The results of this analysis are plotted in Figure 2.8.

It is clear that the cost curves for configurations A and C have remained the same: the logic functions and digital I/O were included in LCU A and LCU C without incurring any additional cost. However, this is not the case for configuration B. In this configuration, the additional controller, LCU B2, must be added to accomplish the logic functions. This additional hardware causes the corresponding cost curve to move up over the whole

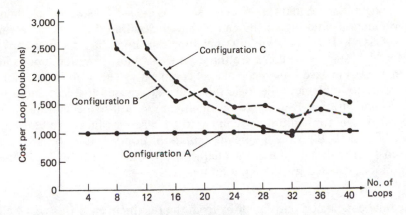

Figure 2.8. Cost-per-Loop Relationships (Mixed Functions)

range of system sizes. As a result, configuration A becomes the most cost-effective one over the entire range except in the vicinity of 32 loops, around which configuration C becomes equally attractive.

A similar evaluation of the cost per function of the various LCU configurations can be made for a range of control system complexities, where now the control systems include both continuous and logic functions. In this case, it is assumed that the control system configuration requires 200 digital outputs in addition to the 100 analog outputs required in case I. Also, it is assumed that there is a ratio of two logic function blocks per continuous function block for all values of system complexity.

The resulting cost-per-function block relationships for each LCU configuration are plotted in Figure 2.9. The general shapes of the cost curves

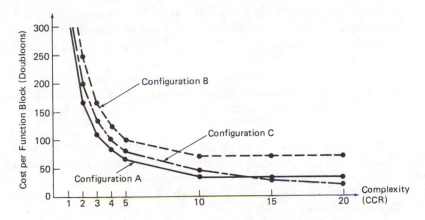

Figure 2.9. Cost-per-Function Relationships (Mixed Functions)

for configurations A and C remain the same as in case I, since the additional logic functions and digital I/O can be handled within the same hardware as in Case I. However, the cost per function block has decreased by a factor of 3, since now there are three times as many function blocks implemented as in case I for each value of complexity. The need for additional hardware to implement the logic functions has caused the cost curve for LCU configuration B to move up significantly with respect to those for the other two configurations (compared to case I). Since now the logic controller LCU B2 is the dominant item in the configuration B hardware, the cost curve flattens out at the characteristic CCR of 10 (160 logic function blocks divided by 16 digital outputs).

The final conclusion one can draw from the results in case II is that LCU B is the least cost-effective configuration for all ranges of complexity due to the additional hardware required to implement the logic control functions. The relationship between configurations A and C remains the same as in case I. LCU A is more cost-effective for small ranges of complexity, and LCU C is better in the higher ranges.

The conclusions reached in the above two architectural evaluations must be tempered by the following cautions:

1. The results obtained are valid *only* for the set of system configuration assumptions and cost assumptions made; different assumptions obviously may lead to different conclusions.
2. The cost assumptions made did not include the cost of the packaging, power, or field terminations for the different configurations; in some cases these costs can be a significant percentage of the total and can change the results of the analysis.
3. The cost assumptions did not include the cost of connections between controllers; if the controllers do not have the capability of communicating over shared buses, the cost of adding separate connections can be significant.
4. The cost-effectiveness of a particular controller configuration is only one criterion for selecting an architecture; many other design and evaluation parameters will be discussed in the rest of the book.

The primary intent of the above discussion has been to alert the reader to the many factors to consider when evaluating a controller architecture for a particular application. The discussion also illustrates some of the quantitative methods that can be used to analyze the cost-effectiveness of various architectures.

2.5. HARDWARE DESIGN ISSUES

The technological developments in microprocessor and memory hardware since 1971 have received a tremendous amount of publicity in the public press as well as in technical publications. This publicity is well deserved, because these developments have made distributed control systems feasible and cost-effective in industrial applications. Often, however, system designers and users alike have a preoccupation with the weekly (if not daily) new product introductions in this field and argue endlessly over which recently announced microprocessor is the best and the fastest. In fact, in most areas of a distributed control system, the selection of one particular chip over another of similar performance usually has little impact on the success of the resulting product. There are many other design areas, such as software structure, communication system architecture, and human interface design, that can make or break the system.

However, there are a few critical hardware design issues that can have a significant impact on the overall system. Issues that primarily affect the design of the local control unit are discussed in this section; those that affect other parts of the system are brought up in the appropriate chapters. In all cases, the discussion will not focus on technology for technology's sake, but rather on how the hardware issues influence system performance or operation from the user's point of view. References 2.15–2.21 at the end of the chapter provide the reader with additional information regarding the impact of semiconductor technology on the capabilities of industrial digital controllers.

2.5.1. Accommodating Technological Change

In selecting or structuring a distributed digital control system for industrial application, the user or designer is faced with a basic contradiction. On the one hand, the pace of development of digital semiconductor technology is breathtaking; on the other, industrial control systems are expected to be installed in the plant and to run satisfactorily for 20, 30, or 40 years with adequate support and maintenance provisions.

It is not possible to slow down the pace of innovation; however, both the user and the designer of these systems can protect themselves from the negative effects of these developments while taking advantage of the benefits. A few of the ways in which this can be done are as follows:

1. Select hardware technology that is state-of-the-art, but has reached a reasonable level of stability. The manufacturers in Silicon Valley are under great pressure to announce products that have barely hit

the drawing board, let alone reached full production. There are countless examples of announced products that never made it to the marketplace or were discontinued shortly thereafter.

2. Make sure that components are available from more than one vendor, and that critical ones have additional sources. A single-sourced (i.e., available from only one vendor) or nonstandard component is a major weak link in a system. Multiple sourcing is another indication that the technology is stable and will not disappear in a month or two.

3. Design or select a distributed system whose architecture can accommodate technological change without the need for scrapping the system or making a major overhaul to it. The communication mechanisms should support a full range of message transmission capabilities between modules in the system. Then, if a module is upgraded to enhance its functionality or performance, the new technology can be accommodated within the basic system structure as long as it is designed to interact with other elements using the same communication mechanisms.

4. The distributed control system vendor must be one that has had prior digital system design experience in the area of interest to the user. It is impossible for the user to write a complete specification for any particular application; only a vendor who has dealt with that application before will have designed the system to include the required features, taking account of (and taking *advantage* of) the technological changes in the hardware likely to occur in the future. In addition, a past history of success in an application area will help guarantee that the vendor will be around in the future to provide support to the system over the long run.

2.5.2. Selecting a Microprocessor

The above discussion on the accommodation of technological change applies especially to the issue of microprocessor selection in a distributed control system. Microprocessor development started with a four-bit chip in 1971 and has gone through stages of eight-bit and 16-bit chip introduction, culminating in the most recent emergence of the 32-bit microprocessor. Each stage has increased the processor's speed, repertoire of instructions, and amount of memory that it can use in a system. The question is, what do all of these advancements mean to the user? From the user's point of view, the precise bit length, speed, and set of machine instructions of a particular processor are unimportant; for example, a fast, state-of-the-art eight-bit microprocessor with supporting arithmetic hardware and optimized software can provide higher effective performance than an older

16-bit microprocessor. What counts is the overall performance, usability and cost of the LCU design that incorporates the microprocessor. The user needs to concentrate on these issues when evaluating a distributed control system.

In addition to the general cautions governing hardware selection given in the previous discussion, the following guidelines should be followed when evaluating the microprocessor used in an LCU:

1. The microprocessor should be a member of a family of processors that share software compatibility. This means that as newer, more powerful processors are added to the family, the vendor will not have to rewrite all of the software for the controller. The user can then take advantage of product upgrades more quickly, and the upgrades are more likely to be compatible with the existing control system.

2. A standard set of off-the-shelf support chips that interface directly with the microprocessor should be available to enhance the microprocessor's performance in such areas as arithmetic computation, communication system interfacing, and direct memory access. This approach will be more cost- and performance-effective than custom designs by the control system vendor.

3. The use of well-established, second-sourced hardware (i.e., available from more than one vendor) is especially important in the area of microprocessor selection. A distributed control system that makes use of an "orphan" processor eventually will suffer from the problems of obsolescence, lack of support, and unavailability of spare parts.

2.5.3. Effects of Developments in Memory

The rapid developments in solid-state memory technology over the last ten years have affected the design of distributed control systems even more than that of microprocessor technology. The progression of memory density (number of bits stored per chip) over the years is graphed as a set of curves in Figure 2.10. Note that the vertical axis uses a logarithmic scale, which means that equal distances correspond to equal *ratios* of numbers instead of equal differences in their value. Next, observe that the various memory technologies maintain their relative density relationships as time progresses. Historically, random-access memory (RAM) has always been denser than ultraviolet-erasable read-only memory (UVROM), which in turn has always been denser than the electrically erasable but nonvolatile memory technologies (electrically alterable read-

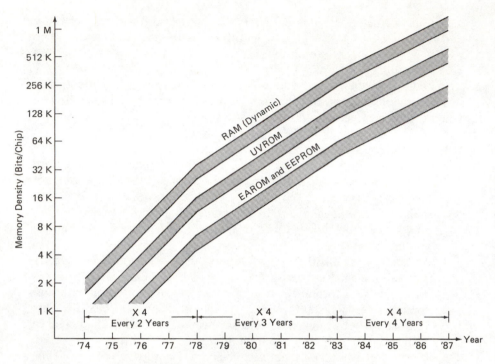

Figure 2.10. Trends in Semiconductor Memory Density.

only memory, or EAROM, and electrically erasable programmable read-only memory, or EEPROM). Note also that the rate of increase in densities has been slowing down somewhat. In the middle 1970s, the memory densities increased by a factor of 4 about every two years; in the early 1980s, this increase took about three years; it is projected that in the late 1980s the quadrupling of density will take about four years to accomplish unless some new breakthrough in chip technology or manufacturing technique is achieved (a likely possibility). At the rates shown, a 1 megabit dynamic RAM will be in full production by about 1987, resulting in a memory density 1,000 times greater than that achieved in 1973.

Accompanying the rapid increase in memory densities shown in Figure 2.10 is a corresponding rapid decrease in the prices of these memories (see References 2.15, 2.17, and 2.18). Bursky (2.18), for example, has observed an order of magnitude (10 to 1) reduction in the price per bit for dynamic RAM in the 14-year period from 1970 to 1984. Others have noted a corresponding order of magnitude reduction in prices in as little as six to ten years, depending on the memory technology and time period studied.

The following discussion summarizes the significance of these trends to the user in each area of memory technology: ROM, RAM, and non-volatile memory.

In microprocessor-based systems, semiconductor ROM is used primarily for program storage. The ROM chips are programmed during the manufacturing process, and their contents are not changed after they are installed in the local control unit. There are two versions of ROM commonly used: mask-programmable ROM (which is what is usually meant by ROM), and ultraviolet-erasable ROM (UVROM). ROM is somewhat less expensive than UVROM, but has the disadvantage that the chip vendor, rather than the control system vendor, must do the programming. This means that the control system vendor must "freeze" the software design at an early date and then allow for the turnaround time for the programming step in the manufacturing process. On the other hand, UVROM can be programmed by the control system vendor at the vendor's facility. If the software design changes, the UVROMs in stock can be erased with ultraviolet light and reprogrammed in a short amount of time. As a result, UVROM has been the preferred read-only memory technology in distributed control systems.

The increasing memory density and decreasing price of UVROM has had a significant impact on LCU design by allowing a dramatic increase in the amount of memory capacity of the LCU without a corresponding increase in physical size or cost. The effect of inexpensive memory on LCU design is that it allows complex programs and sophisticated functions to be implemented in the LCU. For example, high-level and problem-oriented languages can be stored in local memory and executed directly in the LCU. Previously, these programs had to be implemented in a more powerful central computer or "downloaded" from the computer into the LCU. Also, the luxury of inexpensive memory reduces the development time and risk involved in bringing a new LCU design to market, since the software need not be modified or compressed to fit into a limited memory space. From the user's point of view, product price decreases, performance increases, and enhancements are available sooner. Finally, less expensive memory makes it possible to include sophisticated diagnostic and self-checking functions in the system to reduce maintenance costs and increase availability.

The second major area of memory development is in RAM. This type of memory is used primarily for the temporary storage of data. Unlike ROM, information stored in RAM is lost when the electrical power to it is turned off. The availability of inexpensive RAM provides additional impetus to implementing complex control and computational functions at the LCU level. It also permits the storage and manipulation of large data arrays that are used in sophisticated data acquisition and matrix manipulation operations.

The third major area of memory development is in *nonvolatile memory*. This term refers to solid-state memory technologies that have the following characteristics: like RAM, the information stored in the memories can be altered on-line; like ROM, the information is not lost if electrical power to the memories is shut off. Information in a distributed control system that falls into this category includes control logic configurations, control tuning parameters, and control set points and operating modes (e.g., manual or automatic). In analog control systems, this type of information was "stored" mechanically through selection of hardware function modules, hard wiring of control configurations, and setting of switches and potentiometers. One of the significant advantages of digital control systems is that these parameters are stored in memory and therefore can be changed easily on-line; however, the proper precautions must be taken in the system design to ensure that these parameters are not lost if electrical power to the system is lost.

There are several solid-state nonvolatile memory technologies that have been used in distributed control systems. (See References 2.22–2.26 for a survey of these.) A brief description of several representative ones, along with a summary of their advantages and disadvantages, is given below:

1. *Battery-backed RAM*—A small battery is used to provide emergency electrical power to a bank of RAM, usually of the complementary metal-oxide semiconductor (CMOS) type due to its low power consumption. This approach is cost-effective, but the need for battery monitoring and periodic replacement makes it undesirable from a maintenance point of view. Also, in many cases, the batteries are not able to withstand as harsh an environment in terms of temperature and humidity as the rest of the memory system.

2. *EAROM*—This is the original nonvolatile memory used in microprocessor-based systems; it is based on a metal-nitride-oxide-semiconductor (MNOS) process. Memory storage on these chips is not very dense, the time required for the processor to write to the memory is slow, and multiple levels of power supply are required.

3. *EEPROM and nonvolatile RAM (NOVRAM)*—These two technologies have overcome most of the deficiencies of EAROM and have largely supplanted EAROM in distributed control applications. Chip densities are going up rapidly as costs are coming down; if this trend continues, they may provide competition to ROMs and UVROMs for main program storage in micro-based systems.

4. *Bubble memory*—This technology is solid-state (but not semicon-ductor), and relies on the storage of magnetic "bubbles" in a thin sheet of magnetic oxide material. It was once expected that bubble memory would find wide-ranging application as a nonvolatile memory. However, its low speed and complex interfacing requirements have made it most useful as a substitute for rotating memories (e.g., diskettes) in severe operating environments. It is able to withstand extremes of shock, vibration, dust, and temperature better than rotating memories, but at a cost premium. It has not found widespread application in local control unit designs as a board-level nonvolatile memory technology.

In dealing with the preferred nonvolatile memory technologies (EA-ROM, EEPROM, and NOVRAM), the system designer must take certain precautions to ensure reliability of data storage. First, the circuitry used to write the information to the memory must be designed carefully so that the chip specifications on voltage levels and time durations for the write operation are met or exceeded. If this is not done properly, the information stored may not last as long as specified. Second, some of the nonvolatile memory chips are only good for a limited number of write operations; thus, precautions must be taken to ensure that this limit is not exceeded. This is especially important for information such as set points and control modes, which may be changed quite often by the operator. Limits on the allowed number of storage operations per minute must be set and followed so that the write limits are not exceeded over the life of the chip. Third, a mechanism for detecting a memory write error or loss of memory information must be provided. This usually takes the form of a memory *checksum* (arithmetic sum of the contents of memory that is stored in the memory itself and periodically recomputed and checked). Fourth, a means of protecting against a loss of electrical power during a memory write operation must be included in the system. One way of doing this is to have the electrical power system provide a power-fail interrupt signal to the processor when a loss of AC input power is detected. Then, before the memory supply voltage gets too low, the processor can have time to complete any memory operations in progress but not initiate any new ones. Finally, if the nonvolatile memory approach used is battery-backed RAM, proper precautions must be taken to ensure that the batteries are maintained and replaced when needed; automatic alarming of low battery voltage is a desirable feature to ensure that a premature battery failure does not cause a loss of important information.

The architectural and hardware issues discussed in this chapter are the major ones to be considered in designing the computational portion of the

LCU. Other issues concerning I/O capabilities and safety features are discussed in Chapter 4, and communications issues are discussed in Chapter 5.

REFERENCES

Microprocessors in Industrial Controllers

2.1 Kompass, E.J., "A Microprocessor in Every Control Loop," *Control Engineering,* vol. 23, no. 9, September 1976, pp. 123–126.

2.2 Williams, D.L., "Microprocessors Enhance Computer Control of Plants," *Chemical Engineering,* vol. 84, no. 15, pt. 1, July 18, 1977, pp. 95–99.

2.3 Harrison, T.J., "Micros, Minis, and Multiprocessing," *Instrumentation Technology,* vol. 25, no. 2, February 1978, pp. 43–50.

2.4 Harrison, T.J., ed., *Minicomputers in Industrial Control,* Instrument Society of America, Pittsburgh, 1978.

2.5 Shunta, J.P., and Klein, W.F., "Microcomputer Digital Control—What It Ought to Do," *Instrument Society of America Transactions,* vol. 18, no. 1, 1979, pp. 63–69.

2.6 Lukas, M.P., "Using Microprocessors in Industrial Control," *Process Engineering* (Sydney), vol. 9, no. 10, October 1981, pp. 28–33.

2.7 Hampel, J., and Wilkie, D., "A Microprocessor-based Process Controller for Interactive Control Applications," in *Digital Computer Applications to Process Control,* Pergamon Press, Oxford, England, 1980, pp. 457–463.

2.8 Bennett, W.S., and Evert, C.F., *What Every Engineer Should Know About Microcomputers,* Marcel Dekker, New York, 1980.

2.9 Lukas, M.P., Hammon, G.R., and Slabinski, C.J., "A Microprocessor-based Controller for Localized and Distributed Systems," ISA Annual Conference, Houston, October 1980.

2.10 Myron, T.J., "Digital Technology in Process Control," *Computer Design,* vol. 20, no. 13, November 1981, pp. 117–128.

2.11 Chiu, K.C., and Pobanz, N.E., "Distributed Control and Fast Loops: Are All Systems Created Equal?" *InTech,* vol. 31, no. 4, April 1984, pp. 73–74.

2.12 Gupta, A., and Toong, H-M.D., "Microcomputers in Industrial Control Applications," *IEEE Transactions on Industrial Electronics,* vol. IE–31, no. 2, May 1984, pp. 109–119.

2.13 Mizutani, M., and Smith, L.E., "Using Micro-Electronics in Single-Loop Controllers," *Proceedings of Third Annual Control Engineering Conference,* Control Engineering, Barrington, IL, 1984, Control Engineering, pp. 238–243.

2.14 Salim, A., and Eckstein, F.E., "The Function Processor—An Advanced Enhancement for High-Performance Single-Loop Control," *ISA Transactions,* vol. 23, no. 3, 1984, pp. 1–13.

Semiconductor Technology Trends

2.15 Bhandarkar, D.P., "The Impact of Semiconductor Technology on Computer Systems," *Computer,* vol. 12, no. 9, September 1979, pp. 92–98.

2.16 Faerber, G., "Status of Hardware and Software for Microcomputers," in *Digital Computer Applications to Process Control,* Pergamon Press, Oxford, England, 1980.

2.17 Bell, J.R., "Future Directions in Computing," Computer Design, vol. 20, no. 3, March 1981, p. 95–102.

2.18 Bursky, D., "New Processes, Device Structures Point to Million-Transistor IC," *Electronic Design,* vol. 31, no. 12, June 9, 1983, pp. 87–96.

2.19 Bursky, D., "Semicustom ICs," *Electronic Design,* vol. 32, no. 1, January 12, 1984, pp. 208–228.

2.20 Gimson, G.D., "VLSI and Custom/Semi-Custom Applications in Distributed Process Control Systems," *Proceedings of Third Annual Control Engineering Conference,* Rosemont, IL, May 1984, pub. by Control Engineering, Barrington, IL, 1984, pp. 360–366.

2.21 Laduzinsky, A.J., "ICs Deliver More Control Capabilities," Control Engineering, vol. 31, no. 11, November 1984, pp. 81–83.

Nonvolatile Memory Trends

2.22 Hillman, A., "Nonvolatile Memory Selection Mandates Careful Tradeoffs," *EDN,* vol. 28, no. 8, April 14, 1983, pp. 135–139.

2.23 Mortonson, R., and Bassett, S., "Nonvolatile Chip Menu Grows to Suit Various Applications," *Computer Design,* vol. 22, no. 7, June 1983, pp. 153–166.

2.24 Pope, K.W., "No Waiting—EEPROM at Work," *Computer Design,* vol. 22, no. 7, June 1983, pp. 191–196.

2.25 Bursky, D., "Technology Report: Nonvolatile Memories," *Electronic Design,* vol. 32, no. 17, August 23, 1984, pp. 123–144.

2.26 Sommers, R., "Special Edition Report: Nonvolatile Memory," *Electronic Design,* vol. 33, no. 13, June 6, 1985, pp. 78–96.

3
LOCAL CONTROL UNIT LANGUAGES

3.1. INTRODUCTION

Since the local control unit (LCU) is a microprocessor-based device, the only functions of its hardware elements are to bring signals in and out of the device and to provide an environment for the execution of its programs stored in read-only memory. The control and computing functions that the LCU performs are defined by these programs and by the parameters stored in nonvolatile memory, as described in Chapter 2. Of course, the programs and parameters are stored in the LCU memories in the form of *bits* (binary digits - 0s and 1s) and *bytes* (groups of eight bits), as in the case of any computer-based device. Unfortunately, the user of the distributed control system is not likely to be fluent in this machine-level language of bits and bytes. Therefore, a higher-level language must be provided to allow him to interact with the digital hardware in defining the control and computational functions to be implemented in the LCU.

The discussion in this chapter will focus on the control-oriented language issues that are of primary concern to a user of the control system, rather than to the designer. No attempt will be made to discuss the issues involved in the internal design of the real-time software structures in the LCU. This chapter will first summarize the major requirements that a control language must meet. Then several alternative language approaches that have been used in industrial control systems in the past will be described and compared. Examples of the approaches will be provided to illustrate their features and capabilities. The references at the end of the chapter give the interested reader additional information on language issues.

3.2. LANGUAGE REQUIREMENTS

The control-oriented language selected for use in a distributed control system has a critical impact on how well the user accepts the system, since this language is one of the primary mechanisms by which the user interfaces with the system. Therefore, one of the first requirements on the language is that it must allow the user to specify the control and computing functions to be implemented in the LCU in a comfortable manner. The definition of *comfortable* depends to a great extent on the background of the user. A user who has had experience primarily in the area of conventional control devices probably is not interested in becoming a computer programmer simply to use the control system. The user is used to selecting control functions in the form of *dedicated hardware modules* (e.g., summer, integrator, or PID control modules), then interconnecting these modules and tuning them to implement the desired control strategy. Such a user would like to interact with the distributed control system in a similar manner—*configuring* the control strategy instead of *programming* it. On the other hand, a user who comes from a computer control background is used to the power and flexibility of a general-purpose computer language. This kind of user would not be disturbed by the prospect of doing some programming to implement the precise control function in mind for the application. Selecting the control language (or languages) for the LCU must take into account the needs of both these types of user.

Another requirement is that the language must allow the user to implement *at least* the set of control functions that have been provided in the past by conventional analog, sequential, and programmable control systems. Communication functions also are required to allow the LCUs to exchange information with other elements in the distributed control system. A representative list of these control and communication functions includes:

1. Data acquisition and signal conditioning functions, such as input scanning, filtering, linearization, and conversion to engineering units;
2. Limit checking and alarming functions;
3. Modulating control functions, including proportional-integral-derivative (PID) control with all its variations;
4. Sequential control functions for implementing Boolean logic such as AND, OR, and NOT and related functions, such as time delays and latches;
5. Computational functions, such as arithmetic (addition, subtraction, multiplication, and division), trigonometric (e.g., sine and cosine), and dynamic signal processing (integral, derivative, and filter) functions;
6. Signal output functions, both for control and for driving recorders and indicators;
7. Communication functions to allow signal transmissions between the LCU and other controllers and elements in the distributed control system;

8. Communication functions to human interface devices that allow operators and engineers to interact with the LCU.

Another desirable feature is for the language to allow the user to modify these standard functions or to include custom functions within the control language structure.

As the LCUs become more powerful in processing capability, it is becoming feasible and cost-effective to distribute functions previously performed by a central computer into the LCUs. These functions include plant performance monitoring, long-term data storage and retrieval, and computing of optimal set points for plant operation. In the past, these functions have been implemented using a general purpose programming language, such as FORTRAN or BASIC, in the central computer. Therefore, it is essential that the LCUs be able to support these types of high-level languages so that the user can make use of software already in his or her program library or available as standard commercial packages.

As much as possible, the control language selected should be transportable; that is, it should not be dependent on the microprocessor used in the LCU. There are two reasons for this requirement: (1) the user may want to implement the same control logic on systems provided by different vendors, and (2) the same control logic should be usable if the control system vendor decides to upgrade the LCU by going to a new, more powerful microprocessor.

Obviously, the control language must be compatible with the hardware environment in which it will run and with the performance requirements of the control system. The system must provide for sufficient memory capacity to store the control algorithms and data in the LCU. The microprocessor selected must be powerful enough to execute the control algorithms fast enough to meet the needs of the process to be controlled.

3.3. LANGUAGE ALTERNATIVES

While the cost of digital hardware has decreased dramatically over the last several years, the cost of developing and implementing the software portion of digital systems has increased significantly. This is especially true when software costs are evaluated as a percentage of total project costs. According to Boehm (3.1) and others, software development and maintenance now account for over 80% of the total life-cycle costs of a digital computer- or microprocessor-based system.

Because of this trend, the designers of industrial control systems have moved strongly in the direction of *productized software,* that is, software that provides the user with a set of prepackaged functions the user can *configure* (as opposed to *program*) to accomplish the computational or control functions needed for the application. This approach limits the user's flexibility somewhat, but it means the user will be less dependent on software experts (either internal or external to the user's organization) to set up and maintain the control system. If the productized software is well designed for the application, it can offer the user all of the capabilities needed while eliminating a large percentage of the costs that a custom software design would incur.

The major language alternatives currently available to the industrial control user are:

1. Function blocks, preprogrammed functions whose parameters can be set by the user and which can be linked together, much like traditional discrete hardware modules;
2. Problem-oriented languages (POLs) that are customized for a specific type of control application;
3. High-level languages that offer the user some degree of flexibility in designing his or her own control algorithms while maintaining compatibility with function blocks or POLs in the system.

These alternatives are described in more detail in the following sections. References 3.2–3.8 provide additional information on the various types of control languages that are available for use in industrial control systems.

3.4. FUNCTION BLOCKS

In current distributed control systems, the most prevalent prepackaged control language at the LCU level is one of function blocks. (See References 3.9–3.17 for additional information in this area.) In this language approach, the user receives a standard library of control and computational functions that are preprogrammed and stored in ROM. The user then configures the control system by selecting the appropriate blocks from the library, linking them together, and setting the various input and tuning parameters associated with each block. Table 3.1 gives one example of a library of function blocks used in a commercially available controller. It is clear from the example that many of the functions provided are very similar to those available using hardware modules in discrete modulating and sequential control systems. However, the functional capability of the software function blocks goes beyond that of hardware modules in several areas:

1. Functions are provided that would be very difficult or expensive to implement in hardware. Examples include the analog time-delay block (used in the control of processes that have transport delays),

Table 3.1. Example of a Function Block Library

COMPUTATIONAL FUNCTIONS	SIGNAL PROCESSING FUNCTIONS
Sum—2 input/4 input	Integrator
Multiply	Lead/lag
Divide	Moving average
Square root	Analog time delay
y^x, e^x	High/low limit
log x, ln x	Rate limit
Trigonometric	
Generalized polynomial	**SIGNAL STATUS FUNCTIONS**
Function generator	
Two-dimensional interpolation	High/low alarm
Matrix addition	High/low select
Matrix multiplication	Analog transfer
	Digital transfer

CONTROL FUNCTIONS	LOGIC FUNCTIONS
PID control	AND
Pulse positioner	OR
Adapt block	Qualified OR
Smith predictor	NOT
General digital controller	Latch
	Digital timer
INTERMODULE COMMUNICATIONS	Up/down counter
	Remote control latch
Analog input (local/plant level)	Pulse rate counter
Analog input list	
Analog output (local/plant level)	**OPERATOR COMMUNICATIONS**
Digital input (local/plant level)	
Digital input list	Control station
Digital output (local/plant level)	Indicator station
	Cascade station
	Ratio station

the adapt block (which allows tuning parameters in one function block to be adjusted from an externally computed or transmitted signal), and the more complex computational blocks (e.g., exponential functions and matrix operations).

2. Since the function blocks are implemented in software instead of in hardware, one can easily alter the control configuration without changing any controller wiring or purchasing additional hardware (assuming that the controller's function block capacity has not been exceeded).

3. The computational capability of the digital controller allows the conversion of all physical inputs to the system to engineering units (e.g., from milliamps and volts to degrees Celsius or pressure in atmospheres). All of the control and computing operations can then be

carried out using engineering units, thereby eliminating the tedious scaling and conversion operations required in conventional analog control systems.

3.4.1. Example of Continuous Control

To introduce the function block concept, Figure 2.2 gave an example of how function blocks are used in configuring a control strategy. This example can be interpreted as the implementation of a simple flow control loop. Inputs 1 and 2 are the physical inputs to the LCU: input 1 is the flow set point from an external operator input device, and input 2 is a signal input from a differential pressure transducer. To convert input 2 into a flow signal, the user selects the square-root function block from the library and identifies its input as coming from physical input 2. The user then enters appropriate values of the gain and bias parameters to accomplish the desired square-root function and convert the input signal to engineering units (say, flow in gallons per minute). Next, the user selects the difference block in order to generate an error signal between the actual flow and the flow set point. Again, the user identifies the inputs to the difference block and chooses the gain corresponding to input 1 so that the set point also is in units of gallons per minute. Using the output of the difference block as its input, the user then selects a proportional-integral (PI) block to perform the control function. The tuning parameters (proportional gain and integral gain) that are appropriate for the valve and process dynamics then are selected, and the high/low control limits (if any) are set. Once the PI block output is linked to the physical output from the LCU, the control configuration is complete.

This example illustrates the *results* of the control configuration process. Chapter 7 will discuss in detail the devices and techniques by which the user interacts with the LCU to perform these configuration functions.

Once the control configuration has been entered, the LCU can be put on-line so that it can start executing the algorithms in the configuration. In most systems, the function block parameters that do not affect the control configuration can be *tuned* (changed) while the LCU is on-line; however, the LCU generally must be taken off-line if the control configuration itself must be changed. (This is equivalent to rewiring an analog control system.)

3.4.2. Example of Logic Control

The example in the last section was for a continuous control system, one in which the control variables can take on one of many values over a continuous range. Control strategies involving Boolean logic functions also can be configured by means of function blocks. One such example is shown in Figure 3.1. The example illustrates a simplified logic diagram of a motor control circuit. The blocks on the left are manual and process inputs to the logic, and the blocks on the right are outputs of the logic stream. When the operator activates the motor start switch, the latch in the logic diagram is set through the "S" input. This in turn activates the motor current relay through the AND gate, as long as lubricating oil is present in the motor ("lube oil switch on") and the lockout switch has *not* been activated. If the lockout switch has been activated (preventing the start of the motor), this condition is displayed through the lockout indicator light. The operator turns the motor off by activating the motor stop switch, which resets the latch (through the "R" input) and causes the motor current relay to be deenergized. The motor also can be tripped automatically if either the "lube oil pressure low" or "motor vibration high" logic conditions are activated by the corresponding sensors. This control logic is implemented very simply by means of only four function blocks: AND, OR, NOT, and Latch. By means of these and other logic function blocks, one can implement schemes that are much more involved.

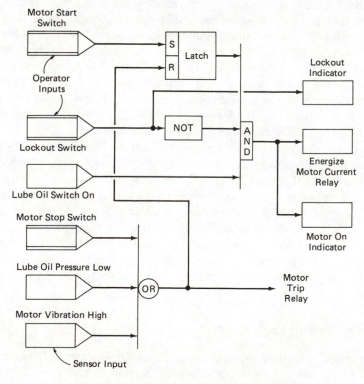

Figure 3.1. Motor Control Function Blocks.

3.4.3. Example of a Batch Reactor

The function block approach also can be used to implement a control strategy that integrates both continuous and logic control functions. For example, to control the simple batch reactor process shown in Figure 3.2, one needs an integrated strategy. The control operations necessary for this process are as follows:

1. When the batch process is started, valve 1 (V1) is opened and the reactor is filled with a liquid called Gonzo-Orthalomido-Organic Polyester (GOOP); then V1 is closed.
2. After the reactor has been filled, the agitator is turned on to mix the GOOP while the temperature controller (TC1) is activated to control the steam valve (V3). This brings the temperature of the GOOP up to 200°F, where it is maintained for ten minutes.
3. After ten minutes, the temperature controller is turned off, the agitator is turned off, and valve 2 (V2) is opened to drain the reactor.
4. After the GOOP has been drained from the reactor, V2 is closed and the process is ready for another batch.

Figure 3.3 shows one possible way to implement this logic in function block form. As in Figure 3.1, the inputs are on the left and the outputs

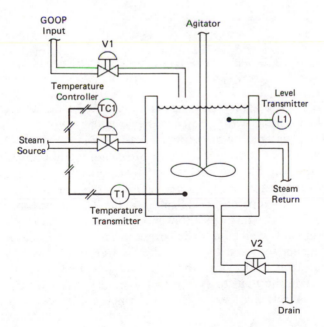

Figure 3.2. Example of a Batch Reactor

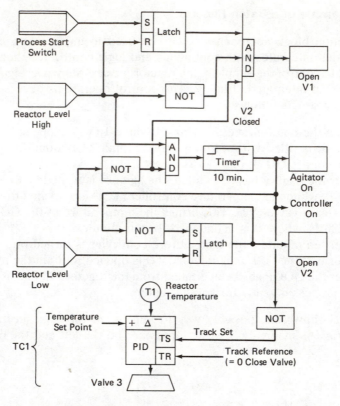

Figure 3.3. Example of Reactor Control Using Function Blocks

are on the right. The sequential logic is implemented using AND and NOT function blocks along with a timer and two latches (both the timer and the latches are triggered by the rising edge of their inputs). The continuous logic consists of only one block, a proportional-integral-derivative (PID) function block. This block includes the PID algorithm itself plus the function of generating an error signal between the temperature set point and the actual reactor temperature (indicated by the "Δ" at the top of the PID function block). It also includes a "switch" feature that causes it to control to the setpoint *only* while the timer output is active (in this case the track set signal equals zero and the controller is free to operate). When the timer output switches to zero, the track set signal switches to one and causes the control output to switch to the track reference value. In this case, the track reference value is zero, which corresponds to a closed valve.

3.4.4. Ladder Diagrams

A special case of logic-oriented function blocks is that of ladder diagrams, as used in programmable logic controllers (PLCs). Ladder diagrams are representations of functions historically provided by such discrete devices as relays, timers, switches, and indicating lights. Figure 3.4 illustrates the

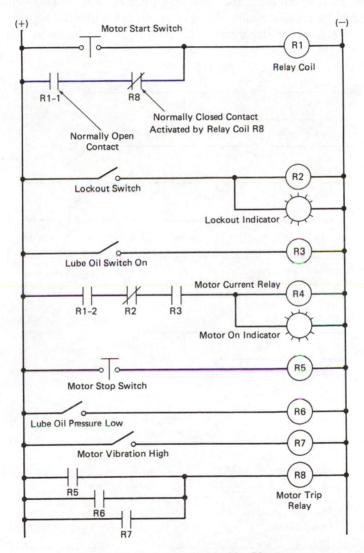

Figure 3.4. Motor Control Ladder Diagram

same logic as in the motor control example in Figure 3.1 but in ladder diagram form. This format of logic description is most popular in applications that are purely sequential in nature, such as motor start/stop control, material handling, and safety alarm and shutdown systems. The more sophisticated programmable controllers also can be used to implement a combination of sequential and continuous control functions, but the ladder diagram representation of the combined logic is more awkward than the function block representation. An example of this combined logic is shown in Figure 3.5, which implements the same logic as shown in Figure 3.3

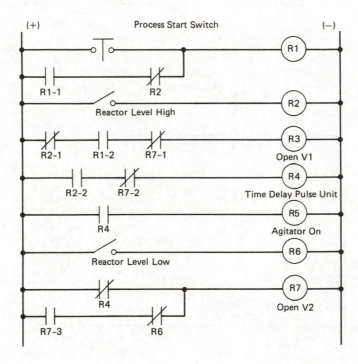

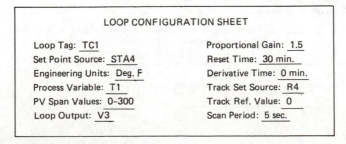

Figure 3.5. Example of Reactor Control Using a Ladder Diagram

for the batch reactor control system. Notice that the relay ladder diagram replaces the logic function blocks in the sequential portion of the control scheme. However, the function block representation of the PID control loop is replaced by a "fill in the blanks" form used to specify the parameters associated with controller TC1. In this representation, there is no direct integration of the continuous and sequential functions, as in the function block diagram in Figure 3.3. The process control engineer must keep this correlation straight mentally or by making notations on the logic drawings. Reference 3.18 gives other examples of sequential control systems implemented in ladder diagram form.

3.4.5. Evaluation of Function Block Libraries

At present, there is little standardization in the libraries of function blocks provided by the various vendors of distributed control systems. Most vendors offer a set of function blocks that emulate the logic diagram symbology defined in one or more standards published by the Instrument Society of America (ISA), the Scientific Apparatus Makers Association (SAMA), or both. (References 3.13–3.16 list the relevant standards.) However, there is rarely (if ever) any direct correspondence between any one vendor's set of function blocks and another's, or between a vendor's set and one listed in a standard. Therefore, it is up to the user to determine whether a particular vendor's offering is adequate to implement the user's control application. Kompass and Morris (3.5) discuss some of the problems involved in making such an evaluation.

Despite this diversity, however, the function block libraries of most vendors tend to fall into one of two general categories:

1. libraries in which the blocks are large; that is, several computational functions are included in a single block (e.g., a PID controller, a square-root function, and output high/low alarms may all be included in one block).
2. libraries in which the blocks are small; that is, each function block performs only a single arithmetic or operational function (e.g., sum, square-root, PID controller, and an alarming operation would all count as separate function blocks).

The first category of function block library generally is patterned after the ISA symbology described in the referenced standards. These macro functions are designed with a specific set of control applications in mind; if they happen to match the user's application, they are probably easier to use than the second category. However, if they do *not* match, the user may find that it is difficult or impossible to implement the specific control algorithm in mind.

The second category of library is more closely patterned after the SAMA symbology described in the referenced standard. With this type of library, the user generally must use a larger number of function blocks to implement a given control strategy. This can take more time, but it allows the user to implement the exact strategy desired. It also can offer the user a great deal of flexibility. If the vendor has provided a good set of application guides to help the user implement the most commonly used control logic configurations, the user can implement a wide variety of applications with little or no penalty in engineering time.

Another variation in the design of function block languages is in the method used to pack the function blocks in an LCU. Some vendors provide only a fixed number of configuration slots in any one LCU, each of which can be filled with only one function block (whether the block is simple or complex). Other vendors assign a numerical weight to each function block that depends on the amount of LCU resources (in memory and computation time) that are required to implement the block. In this approach, function blocks then can be taken from the library and added to the control system configuration until the total weights of the function blocks used match the capacity of the LCU. The weighting method provides more configuration flexibility than the fixed-slot approach but requires a little more bookkeeping (although this is often done automatically by the system) to keep track of the current size of the configuration. Vendors supplying a library consisting of large blocks tend to use the slot-packing approach; vendors using small blocks usually adopt the weighted-packing approach.

When evaluating a particular function block library supplied by a distributed control system vendor, the user needs to keep in mind the range of control applications he or she plans to implement. If the range is limited and the control applications are simple, the large-block approach may be easier to use. If the application range is broad or unknown, the user may wish to select the small-block approach to maintain maximum flexibility. In any case, it would be helpful for the user to define a set of control logics representing the range of applications being considered. The user should then implement this set at the logic diagram level (without necessarily using the actual hardware) using the function block libraries from the various distributed control system candidates. This process will provide valuable data—such as LCU utilization, difficulty of implementation, and flexibility of change—needed to evaluate each distributed control system for particular applications.

Several other points relating to the evaluation of function block libraries are worth mentioning:

1. The libraries of some vendors are incomplete in the sense that auxiliary *hardware* is needed to perform certain control functions. This is clearly undesirable since it increases both the hardware and engineering costs of such a control system and reduces its flexibility.
2. The *number* of function blocks offered is not necessarily a valid measure of the quality of the library. For example, some vendors count ten variations on a PID algorithm as ten different function blocks. What should be of prime importance is the match between the blocks in the library and the needs of the application. For example, if the application requires continuous and logic control blocks, are both included in the same library? Are needed advanced control functions (such as adaptive control or dead-time control blocks) included as a part of the standard offering?
3. The software design approach used in implementing the function blocks must be consistent with the execution capabilities of the processor and the accuracy requirements of the application. For example, early designs of function blocks used fixed-point arithmetic to allow microprocessors with limited capacity to execute the blocks quickly and efficiently. More recent designs use floating-point arithmetic to provide more accuracy in the computations and more flexibility in scaling variables. Even though this approach is more expensive in terms of computational load, the more powerful microprocessors now available allow function blocks to be executed in the same or less time than their predecessors.
4. The user should examine carefully the specific mathematical equations used to implement certain key functions to make sure that the equations are consistent with sound industrial control practice. For example, the PID controller algorithm and the related manual/automatic station algorithm must be designed in such a way that (a) the control output is at the proper value at startup, (b) set-point changes produce a smooth change in the output, and (c) control mode transfers from manual to automatic and back are *bumpless*; that is, the control output does not go through a step change after the transfer. Reference 3.19 discusses some of these algorithm design issues, including protecting against controller *windup* (saturation of the integral term in the PID algorithm when the control output value hits a limit).
5. The user should evaluate each key function block in the library with respect to the number of parameters that the user must set during configuration of the block. (Examples of such parameters are control tuning values, saturation limits, alarms, and option selections.) If this number is large, the block may be quite flexible but very difficult to use. The vendor must provide good documentation on the meaning

of each parameter and its impact on selecting other system configurations. A meaningful default value for each parameter should already be present in the configuration so that the user needs to enter only *changes* from these default values.

3.5. PROBLEM-ORIENTED LANGUAGES

As in the function block approach to defining control system logic, problem-oriented languages (POLs) do not require the user to have a knowledge of computer programming. In general, these are special-purpose languages: each one is tailored to a particular vendor's hardware, specific control application, or both.

There are two popular types of POL: fill-in-the-form and batch languages. In the first type, the user decides what the configuration of the control system will be and then literally fills in forms provided by the vendor. This defines the configuration using the vendor's hardware/software system. A technician then enters the control configuration into the LCU through a terminal or other device, using the form as the source of the input data. This approach was developed during the early years of computer control systems as a first attempt on the part of vendors to provide prepackaged software for nonprogrammers. Figure 3.6 gives an example of the fill-in-the-form approach to defining a single PID loop. Note that this is an expanded version of the PID function in the programmable controller example in Figure 3.5. Since a different form must be filled out for every function, it is clear that a large amount of paperwork is involved in configuring a complex control scheme. On the other hand, once the forms have been filled out, they provide a convenient means of documenting the control system configuration for the user.

While this control language approach does not require user programming as such, it suffers from the following defects:

1. The user cannot easily determine the structure of the control system from the form entries themselves; separate documentation must be maintained to define the overall structure.
2. The definition procedure is tedious and has more of the flavor of programming than any other approach.
3. There is little or no standardization in the forms from one vendor to another.

As a result of these problems, the fill-in-the-form POL has generally been offered only in large computer control systems and has yielded to other language approaches in most distributed microprocessor-based control systems.

DATA FORM—PID CONTROL FUNCTION

LOOP IDENTIFICATION PARAMETERS

LOOP ID NUMBER
LOOP TAG NAME
LOOP DESCRIPTOR

LOOP SCAN PARAMETERS

SCAN PERIOD
SCAN PHASE

SET-POINT PARAMETERS

SET-POINT SOURCE ADDRESS
DEFAULT SET-POINT VALUE

PROCESS VARIABLE PARAMETERS

SOURCE ADDRESS
TAG NAME
LOWER SPAN VALUE
UPPER SPAN VALUE
ENGINEERING UNITS ID

OUTPUT PARAMETERS

OUTPUT ADDRESS
DIRECT (D)/REVERSE (R) ACTION
OUTPUT DEFAULT VALUE
FULL VALUE (F)/INCREMENTAL (I) OUTPUT
OUTPUT CHANGE LIMIT

TUNING PARAMETERS

PROPORTIONAL GAIN
RESET TIME
DERIVATIVE TIME

INITIALIZATION MODE (M=MANUAL, A=AUTO, C=CASCADE)

TRACKING PARAMETERS

TRACK SWITCH SOURCE
EXTERNAL OUTPUT TRACK SOURCE

ALARM PARAMETERS

HIGH ALARM LIMIT
LOW ALARM LIMIT
DEVIATION ALARM LIMIT
ALARM DEADBAND

Figure 3.6. Example of Fill-in-the-Form Language

The second popular type of POL is the batch language, used in control applications of the same name. (See References 3.20–3.24 for more information on batch control languages.) It consists of a set of commands that direct the LCU to perform certain operations, such as opening a valve, ramping a temperature (moving it from one value to another), or filling a tank. Associated with each of the commands is one or more parameters that define the valve to be opened, the beginning and end temperatures in a ramp, the time of the ramp, and so forth. Figure 3.7 lists a set of

Initial Conditions: L1 = 0

V1, V2, V3 are closed.

Agitator is stopped.

Batch Program: START PROCESS

OPEN V1

WAIT UNTIL L1 = 10

CLOSE V1

START AGITATOR

START TIMER

ACTIVATE CONTROLLER C1

WAIT UNTIL TIMER = 10

DEACTIVATE CONTROLLER C1

CLOSE V3

STOP AGITATOR

OPEN V2

WAIT UNTIL L1 = 0

CLOSE V2

STOP PROCESS

CONTROLLER C1 PARAMETERS:

Loop Tag: TC1	Proportional Gain: 1.5
Set Point Source: STA4	Reset Time: 30 min.
Engineering Units: Deg. F	Derivative Time: 0 min.
Process Variable: T1	Track Set Source: R4
PV Span Values: 0–300	Track Ref. Value: 0
Loop Output: V3	Scan Period: 5 sec.

Figure 3.7. Example of Reactor Control Using a Batch Language

batch language statements that implement the same control logic shown in Figures 3.3 and 3.5. Notice that the batch language approach is very concise in its implementation of sequence control logic, compared to the function block and ladder diagram methods. However, like the ladder diagram approach, it requires that the user specify the parameters of continuous control functions separately from the batch language statements. Also, while its format is convenient for the process engineer, a batch language can consume a significant amount of processor and memory resources in the LCU. Therefore, batch languages have not proved to be cost-effective for many general-purpose control applications. As in the case of fill-in-the-form languages, batch control languages have been used mainly in computer control applications. As the computing capabilities of microprocessor-based LCUs continue to increase, however, it is clear that LCUs will be designed to support the use of batch control languages.

There are a variety of other languages that often are called problem-oriented languages, such as PROSPRO, PEARL, AUTRAN, and ATLAS. However, these are generally extensions of what we are calling high-level languages for the purposes of this chapter and are included in the discussion in the next section.

3.6. HIGH-LEVEL LANGUAGES

Until the early 1980s, high-level programming languages (such as FOR-TRAN, BASIC, and PASCAL) were restricted primarily to larger mini-computer systems used in direct digital control, supervisory control, or data acquisition applications. In industrial control, they were not seriously considered for use in dedicated microprocessor-based systems for a number of reasons. First, the performance and memory capabilities of the microcomputer hardware available were not adequate to support these languages. Second, the users of dedicated microprocessor-based control systems generally were not inclined to learn high-level programming languages. They were more comfortable with the other language approaches, including function block and fill-in-the-form languages, discussed earlier.

However, this situation has changed significantly for a number of reasons:

1. The increasingly widespread use of personal computers is creating a class of users who are comfortable with certain high-level languages, such as BASIC.
2. Control system engineers are becoming more sophisticated and are demanding control capabilities that are more specialized than can be provided by means of standard, "canned" functions.
3. The continuing explosion in the performance capability of micro-processor and memory systems is allowing the migration of control functions formerly performed by a computer down into the level of the LCU. Therefore, functions formerly implemented in high-level languages (e.g., supervisory control or plant performance calculations) can now be considered for implementation in the LCU. While many of these functions can be implemented using function blocks or POLs, the remainder require a high-level language implemented at the LCU level.

Because of these trends, a brief discussion of some of the main issues involved in using high-level languages in distributed microprocessor-based control systems is warranted here. No attempt to survey the available languages or to recommend a language has been made. The development of new languages is progressing too quickly and the number of applications is too varied for such an evaluation. Rather, we will limit the discussion to three main areas: (1) a summary of the key high-level language requirements in on-line, distributed systems; (2) a review of the needs for utility software in distributed systems; and (3) a summary of the progress made to date in standardizing high-level languages for process control.

For additional information on the subject of high-level languages in industrial control applications, consult References 3.2–3.4 and 3.32.

3.6.1. High-Level Language Features Required in Distributed Control

High-level languages have been supplanting assembly language for many years in process control computer systems. Many sources have pointed out the advantages of the high-level language approach (see Ref. 3.3, for example): less time required for programming, code that is more readable and understandable, and improved documentation of programs (among others). The use of optimizing compilers and well-written interpreters has made high-level languages nearly as efficient as assembly language in the use of memory and processing time.

However, the designer or evaluator of high-level languages should be aware that a general-purpose language such as FORTRAN and BASIC cannot be used in a real-time process control environment without a significant amount of modification. Most of these general-purpose languages were designed for a batch processing environment, in which the user writes the program, inputs the data, and then runs the program to obtain the desired results. In the process control environment, several programs or tasks may run continuously, occasionally switch into different modes, respond to external events, and keep track of actual time of day and elapsed time. Many of the features required for this environment were missing from the original definitions of the languages, which were oriented to the substantially different environment of the "computer center." To solve this problem, many of these languages have been enhanced with extensions that make them more suitable for real-time process control. However, the success of these extensions has been mixed. More recently, a number of languages have been designed specifically to address the needs of on-line process control (e.g., PEARL, MODULA, and Ada). The user needs to evaluate the various language options carefully to make sure that the selected one meets the needs of the application. The major functional areas to be considered in such an evaluation include:

1. interfacing with the process;
2. coping with the real-time environment;
3. interfacing with other elements in a distributed control system;
4. providing the security features required in a control application;
5. supporting the utilities required to write and maintain the programs.

The first four items are discussed in more detail below; the fifth area will be covered in the next section.

Interfacing with the Process.   The first area involves the interface between the LCU and the sensors and actuators that are the "eyes" and "muscle" of the control system, respectively. Most of the popular high-level languages were designed for a data processing environment in which information is read from or written to data files in memory or to various computer peripherals (e.g., disks, CRTs, magnetic tape units, or printers). However, in a process control environment, information transfer involves continuous devices (such as thermocouples, differential pressure transmitters, or valve positioners) and sequential devices (such as limit switches or motor starting relays). Ideally, the user of the high-level language should be able to write input and output statements that manage this flow of information with minimal human intervention. Thus for analog I/O interfacing, the language should have imbedded in it the functions of input scanning, analog-to-digital and digital-to-analog conversion, linearization, and engineering unit conversion. For digital I/O interfacing, the language should have a bit manipulation capability as well as Boolean operators such as AND, OR, NOT, test bit, set bit, and others. To simplify programming of the control and computational routines, the user ideally should be able to refer to I/O devices symbolically (e.g., by using "tag" names) instead of by hardware addresses.

The makers of distributed digital control systems have attacked this problem in one of two ways: (1) by providing subroutine calls or hardware drivers that accomplish these functions within the language structure or (2) by imbedding the high-level language within a function block structure (see Section 3.4), so that the process interfacing functions are performed by specific function blocks. The latter approach has the advantage of maintaining a relatively simple high-level language structure. The disadvantage is that the LCU then must implement *both* the function block structure and the high-level language.

Coping with the Real-Time Environment.   The second area of functional requirements for high-level languages deals with the fact that the language has to operate in a real-time rather than an off-line or batch-processing environment. An inherent contradiction exists when using a microprocessor (or any other digital computer-based device) in an on-line process control application: On the one hand, any single computer is a sequential device that cannot do more than one thing at a time; further, its basic cycle of operation is governed by an internal clock that times its execution of programs. On the other hand, process control requires the LCU to perform many functions (e.g., read inputs, perform computations, generate outputs, and communicate with other devices) apparently at once. Also, it must be able to respond to events occurring in real time. This contradiction is resolved in designing specific LCUs by taking into account three elements: (1) the speed at which the microprocessor operates (which, if fast enough, makes the LCU *appear* to be performing many functions at once); (2) the hardware in the LCU (which, if properly designed, allows the processor in the LCU to detect the occurrence of outside events); and (3) the structure of the software (including the high-level language), designed so that the LCU can schedule its many operations while being responsive to external events. To be suitable for operation in the real-time environment, the high-level language therefore must have the following features (in conjunction with the hardware and the software operating system):

1. *Interrupt-handling capability to allow programs to respond to external events*. This requires an integrated hardware/software design that can manage several levels of interrupt and allows masking and unmasking of interrupts.
2. *Ability to schedule multiple application programs or tasks executing "simultaneously" (multitasking)*. The scheduling of the tasks must be well-defined under all operating conditions and take into account different priorities of tasks and their triggering by external interrupts, elapsed time, or real time. The tasks must be able to share data with one another and synchronize their operation.
3. *Ability to manage resources (e.g., memory and peripherals) that must be shared by different tasks*.
4. *Software timers and a real-time clock for use by application programs*.

The available high-level languages (with the appropriate extensions) have all these features to a greater or lesser degree, depending on the environment for which they were originally designed—batch processing, interactive, or real-time operation.

Interfacing with Other Elements in a Distributed Control System.   The third functional area to be considered when evaluating or selecting a high-level language is its facility for communicating with devices within the distributed control system other than the sensors and actuators discussed earlier. If a high-level language has been implemented within the LCU, it is likely that the LCU is being used to implement logging, trending, long-term data storage and retrieval, or similar high-level functions. In this case, the high-level language in the LCU must be able to support communication with such peripherals as mass memory (floppy disk, tape drive, or hard disk), CRT, keyboard, and printer. Thus the language must allow for the manipulation of alphanumeric character strings used in driving printers and CRTs. The language also must support interfacing to dedicated operator interface devices such as panelboard indicators or stations, usually over dedicated serial links.

The interfacing capabilities just listed include only those required to communicate within the LCU itself. However, a distributed control system may have a large number of LCUs of different types, each of which performs a dedicated computing or control function. In general, these LCUs must communicate with each other to coordinate their operations. For example, an LCU performing a supervisory control function must communicate with other LCUs that are performing lower-level closed-loop control functions. Or, an LCU may need to acquire inputs from another LCU to perform its own function. In some systems, generating a high-level language program may be done in a separate computing device; the program is then downloaded to the LCU that is to execute it. All of these data transfers are accomplished using the shared communication facilities in the distributed control system (described in detail in Chapter 5). The high-level language in the LCUs must be capable of handling these transactions. Just as with interfacing with the process sensors or actuators, there are two ways to do this: (1) using drivers or subroutines within the language itself or (2) imbedding the language within a function block structure that supports these communications. In either case, the user should be able to link programs or tasks within one LCU with corresponding programs or tasks in other devices without being concerned with the details of the communication operation itself.

Providing Security Safeguards. The fourth requirement for a functional language is that it contain security safeguards to ensure that failures and errors in the LCU do not cause an unsafe condition. Misoperation of a process control system can cause a loss in life, limb, or property; therefore, all reasonable safeguards should be built into the system to detect and/or prevent such a misoperation. Security is not solely a language issue; it concerns the design of the hardware and operating system of the LCU as well. However, the language must support the security features built into the other parts of the system. Some of the security requirements that affect the design of the language and operating system include the following:

1. The language and supporting system software must check for errors during both program entry and compilation (if a compiler is used). Whenever the system detects errors, it must transmit clear and understandable error messages to the user.
2. The language must be able to handle "exceptions," (errors that occur at run time) by detecting them and initiating automatic recovery procedures. Further, the user should be able to specify the recovery procedure the system will use (e.g., restarting using default data, shutting down, or continuing) when an exception is detected. In an on-line system, simply aborting the program in case of an error is unacceptable.
3. In many commercial systems, redundant processors are used in LCUs to increase their reliability. The language and associated system software must support redundancy in such cases, preferably in such a way that the redundant processor or processors are invisible to the user.
4. The software system must support hardware security features. For example, if a *watchdog timer* is used to safeguard against software "crashes," the system must provide a means for resetting the timer. If the LCU includes a nonvolatile memory to maintain parameters during a loss of power, the software must be designed to write the parameters to this memory on a periodic basis. If a *power fail interrupt* is provided to signal the processor that loss of power is imminent, the software must be able to initiate an orderly shutdown sequence in response to the interrupt.
5. In any multiple processor system, the possibility of the memory in one LCU being "scrambled" by the processor in another LCU is always present. To prevent this, the system software must contain orderly procedures for memory access. Error checks should be made on data to be written in a memory, and the software should contain safeguards against two processors attempting to access the same data in memory at the same time.

3.6.2. Utility Software Requirements

A high-level language program does not simply materialize magically in the memory of an LCU. It must be created by a user, who interacts with the LCU through a CRT terminal or other device during the generation of the program. The system software used during this interactive process is usually referred to as *utility* software, since it is an aid to program creation, editing, debugging, and storing but is not a part of the program that is executed on-line. Utility software is required in all applications of high-level languages, not just in those involving distributed control systems. In a large computer installation, these utilities can be quite extensive, and the programming aids provided can be quite sophisticated and powerful as a result. However, the utilities occupy only a small fraction of the resources of the computer system and therefore do not contribute significantly to the system cost.

The situation is somewhat more complicated in the case of industrial distributed control systems. In these systems, the LCU is intended to be a relatively simple and inexpensive device compared to a large process computer. As a result, if the program utilities reside in the LCU, they can occupy a large portion of the LCU's resources. This can lead either to an increase in the cost of the LCU or a reduction in its program capacity. If the utility software must be implemented in a separate programming device, the cost of the LCU remains low, but the system cost rises. The type of high-level language selected strongly affects the best location for the utility software. If the language is an interpretive one such as BASIC, the associated utility software is somewhat simplified and it may well make sense to place it within the LCU. On the other hand, if the selected language requires a compiler (as FORTRAN does, for example) a separate device may be more cost-effective. This dilemma points to the need for minimizing the scope of utility software in a distributed control system while still providing enough capability to meet the needs of the high-level language programmer.

The optimum combination of utility software functions depends to a great extent on the scope of high-level language software that the LCUs will be expected to implement. If the particular distributed control system in question includes a computer that implements the bulk of the high-level language functions, then the utilities required for programming the LCUs can be minimal. On the other hand, if there is a significant amount of high-level language programming to be done and the LCUs are to implement all of the programs, a fairly sophisticated set of utility functions may be indicated. Despite this range of expected requirements, it is likely that the following utility functions will be needed as a minimum:

1. *Text editor*—helps the user create a program file, number and renumber program statements, and make changes to programs;
2. *Debugger*—allows the user to set breakpoints in programs, single-step their execution, read and modify memory, and examine internal registers and I/O registers in an interactive manner;

3. *File manager*—provides a mechanism for storing files on diskette or other storage medium, reloading them into the LCU, and copying, merging and renaming files.

In a distributed control system, there may be a large number of LCUs executing high-level language programs. Keeping track of the various files in the system and their assignment to specific LCUs is likely to require the help of a system-wide file management facility implemented in an LCU or in a separate computer.

3.6.3. Standardization of High-Level Languages

Even a casual reviewer of trade magazines dealing with computer and microcomputer systems cannot fail to notice the variety of high-level languages now in use or proposed for use in these systems. FORTRAN, BASIC, PASCAL, C, and FORTH are among the many. Not only do the languages themselves proliferate, but they also sprout dialects that are designed to be used in specific applications or to take advantage of the capabilities of a particular vendor's hardware. The designer or evaluator of an industrial process control system faces a number of significant questions when attempting to select a high-level language: Is the language a passing fad, or will it be around and supported ten years from now when the system needs updating or modification? If I upgrade my system with the latest hot ZX68800 microprocessor, will I have to rewrite all of my software? Will software modules written for one processor in my distributed control system be usable in the other processors, or will I have to "re-invent the wheel" once again?

In an attempt to attack this problem of software proliferation, various groups have attempted to develop and promote standards for software in real-time process control applications. The benefits of such standardization are obvious: it saves duplicated effort in rewriting programs; it increases the transportability of software from one machine to another; it reduces programmer training time and increases programming efficiency, among others. These efforts have run into the obstacles encountered in any kind of standardization: the snail's pace of standards committee work, the reluctance to accept ideas "not invented here," and the accusation that standardization stifles progress and creativity.

Despite these problems, a few standardization efforts have demonstrated concrete achievements during the last 15 years (see Reference 3.31 for a survey). The most notable example is the International Purdue Workshop on Industrial Computer Systems, started in 1969 by Professor Theodore J. Williams at Purdue University. The Functional Requirements Committee of this workshop was successful in producing a requirements document for industrial computer programming languages in 1971. The Interim Procedural Languages Committee concentrated on defining a standardized process control language that could be applied in the short term. They selected FORTRAN as the base language due to its popularity, and they defined several real-time extensions to the language that gained general acceptance in 1972. In 1978 and 1982, this committee standardized additional FORTRAN extensions. A Purdue-related group, the European Workshop on Industrial Computer Systems (EWICS), has carried on the standardization work in Europe. EWICS generated a unified language document called Industrial Real-Time FORTRAN that is approaching the end of the approval process of the International Standardization Organization (see Reference 3.29). In addition to the FORTRAN-related work, EWICS has formed a Real-Time BASIC Committee that drafted a standard for Industrial Real-Time BASIC in September, 1981 (see Reference 3.30). The committee has been working on obtaining international approval for this document through U.S. and European standards associations.

The other major standardization effort that is worthy of note is the specification and development of the Ada language (see References 3.25 and 3.26, for example). This work has been sponsored by the U.S. Department of Defense, which recognized the need for standardization of software in military systems in the early 1970s. This software is embedded in dedicated processors operating in a real-time environment that is quite similar to that of industrial process control systems. In 1975, the Department of Defense formed a High-Order Language Working Group to address the problem. From its inception through 1978, the group went through an extensive sequence of activities to specify the requirements for a new high-level language for embedded computer systems. In April 1980, after many specification review cycles and a language procurement competition, the group released a draft standard for the resulting language, named Ada. The language is a controversial one (see References 3.27 and 3.28, for example), but the investment the Department of Defense has made in it probably guarantees its acceptance, at least in real-time military and aerospace applications (see Reference 3.34). As the number of programmers familiar with Ada grows, its use may well spread to the commercial and industrial marketplace (see Reference 3.33), but this process is likely to take place gradually over many years.

REFERENCES

Control Language Surveys and Issues

3.1 Boehm, B.W., "Software and Its Impact: A Quantitative Assessment," *Datamation*, vol. 19, no. 5, May 1973, pp. 48–59.

3.2 Gertler, J., and Sedlak, J., "Software for Process Control—A Survey," *Automatica,* vol. 11, 1975, pp. 613–625.

3.3 Diehl, W., "Process Control Software Review," *Instrumentation Technology,* vol. 23, no. 3, March 1976, pp. 49–53.

3.4 Fisher, D.G., "Systems Software for Process Control: Today's State of the Art," *Chemical Process Control 2,* ed. by T.F. Edgar and D.E. Seborg, United Engineering Trustees, New York, 1982, pp. 3–32.

3.5 Kompass, E.J., and Morris, H.M., "Comparing the Relative Complexities of Programming Process Controllers," *Control Engineering,* vol. 28, no. 7, July 1981, pp. 75–78.

3.6 Steusloff, H.U., "Advanced Real-Time Languages for Distributed Industrial Process Control," *Computer,* vol. 17, no. 2, February 1984, pp. 37–46. (Also see other papers in this special issue on software for industrial process control.)

3.7 Bowman, L., "Choosing a Language for Control," *Instruments & Control Systems,* vol. 57, no. 4, April 1984, pp. 57–59.

3.8 Copeland, J.R., and Roland, E.T., "Programming Languages Provide Real-Time Control," *Instruments & Control Systems,* vol. 57, no. 9, September 1984, pp. 65–76.

3.9 Eelderink, G.H.B., Bruijn, P.M., and Verbruggen, H.B., "Microprocessor-based Controllers in a Distributed Network Implemented with a Block-Diagram Language," 3rd Int'l Conf. on Trends in On-Line Computer Control Syst., U. Sheffield, England, March 1979; pub. by IEE, London, 1979, pp. 174–178.

3.10 Pageler, E.L., "An Interactive Process Control Language Designed for the Control Engineer," Instrument Society of America Annual Conference, Chicago, October 1979.

3.11 Tubalkain, K., and Stern, L., "Blockware—A Block-oriented Combustion Control Language," IFAC Workshop on Systems Engineering Applications to Industrial Energy Generation and Processes, October 23–24, 1980.

3.12 King, K.L., Forney, D.E., and Scheib, T.J., "Software Structure for a General Purpose Digital Controller," Instrument Society of America Spring Conference, St. Louis, March 1981.

3.13 Instrument Society of America "Instrumentation Symbols and Identification," Standard ANSI/ISA–S5.1–1975 (R1981), May 29, 1981.

3.14 Scientific Apparatus Makers Association "Functional Diagramming of Instrument and Control Systems," SAMA Standard PMC 22.1–1981, September 1981.

3.15 Instrument Society of America Standard "Binary Logic Diagrams for Process Operations," ANSI/ISA–S5.2–1976 (R1981), October 9, 1981.

3.16 Instrument Society of America "Graphic Symbols for Distributed Control/Shared Display Instrumentation, Logic and Computer Systems," Standard ISA–S5.3–1982, Approved 1982, Second Printing 1983.

3.17 King, K.L., "Using a Building Block Approach to Implement Advanced Control Techniques," Instrument Society of America Spring Conference, Columbus, Ohio, April 1982.

3.18 Cohen, E.M., and Fehervari, W., "Sequential Control," *Chemical Engineering,* vol. 92, no. 9, April 29, 1985, pp. 61–66.

3.19 Gallun, S.E., et al., "Windup Protection and Initialization for Advanced Digital Control," *Hydrocarbon Processing,* vol. 64, no. 6, June 1985, pp. 63–68.

Batch Control Languages

3.20 Willey, M.S., "Higher-Level Languages for Batch and Sequential Control Applications . . . A Textile Example," Tenth Conference on Digital Computers in Process Control, Baton Rouge, La., February 1975; pub. by IEEE, 1975, pp. 16–21.

3.21 DaGraca, J., "Graphic Batch Processing Language Simplified," *Instruments & Control Systems,* vol. 48, no. 12, December 1975, pp. 41–43.

3.22 Mauderli, A., and Rippin, D.W.T., "Scheduling Production in Multi-Purpose Batch Plants: The Batchman Program," *Chemical Engineering Progress,* vol. 76, no. 4, April 1980, pp. 37–45.

3.23 Ward, J.C., and Scalera, M.R., "Developing a Batch Process Computer Control Language," Instrument Society of America Annual Conference, Philadelphia, October 1982.

3.24 Fihn, S.L., and Nyquist, J.A., "Specifying Batch Process Control Strategies: A Structured Approach," *Instrumentation Technology,* vol. 29, no. 10, October 1982, pp. 57–63.

High-Level Languages

3.25 Gordon, M.E., and Robinson, W.B., "Using Preliminary Ada in a Process Control Application," in *AFIPS Conference Proceedings,* vol. 49, AFIPS Press, Arlington, Va., 1980, pp. 597–606.

3.26 Vaughan, W.C.M., "Application of the Ada Language to Process Control," *Chemical Process Control 2,* Proceedings of the Engineering Foundation Conference, Sea Island, GA., January 1981; ed. by T.F. Edgar and D.E. Seborg, United Engineering Trustees, New York, 1982, pp. 71–89.

3.27 Hoare, C.A.R., "1980 ACM Turing Award Lecture: The Emperor's Old Clothes," *Communications of the ACM,* vol. 24, no. 2, February 1981, pp. 75–83.

3.28 Letters and Responses in the ACM Forum, *Communications of the ACM,* vol. 24, no. 7, July 1981, pp. 475–478.

3.29 Netherlands Standards Organization "Draft Standard, Industrial Real-Time FORTRAN," developed by the European Workshop on Industrial Computer Systems and submitted to the International Standards Organization, 1981.

3.30 European Workshop on Industrial Computer Systems, Committee TC2, "Draft Standard, Industrial Real-Time BASIC," September 1981.

3.31 Harrison, T.J., "Process Control Programming Language Standards: Accomplishments and Challenges," *Instrumentation Technology,* vol. 28, no. 11, November 1981, pp. 67–70.

3.32 Gait, J., "A Class of High Level Languages for Process Control," *Computers in Industry* (Elsevier), vol. 4, no. 1, March 1983, pp. 63–67.

3.33 Brandon, C., and Martin, J., "Ada Language Moving Closer to Market," *Control Engineering,* vol. 31, no. 11, November 1984, pp. 89–90.

3.34 Judge, J.F., "Ada Progress Satisfies DOD," *Defense Electronics,* vol. 17, no. 6, June 1985, pp. 77–87.

4
LOCAL CONTROL UNIT—PROCESS
INTERFACING ISSUES

4.1. INTRODUCTION

In Chapters 2 and 3, the local control unit was discussed as if it were a self-contained unit having no interfaces with other elements in the distributed control system. The block diagram in Figure 2.1 illustrates this; only process input and output hardware is shown. In a limited number of dedicated control situations this hardware may be all that is required. However, in the great majority of applications, the LCU must communicate with many other system elements, as shown earlier in the generalized distributed control system structure in Figure 1.4.

Figure 4.1 shows a block diagram illustrating these other interfaces from the point of view of the LCU. This figure expands on the basic LCU elements in Figure 2.1 through the addition of interfaces to external communication facilities and to a low-level human interface device.

The communications interfaces (one or more) permit the LCU to interact with the rest of the distributed system to accomplish several functions:

1. To allow several LCUs to implement control strategies that are larger in scope than possible with a single LCU;
2. To allow transmission of process data to the higher-level system elements (e.g., human interface and computing devices);
3. To allow these higher-level elements to transmit information requests and control commands to the LCUs;
4. To allow two or more LCUs to act together as redundant controllers to perform the same control or computational functions;
5. To augment the I/O capacity of the LCU with that of data input/output units (DI/OUs) in the system.

The low-level human interface device and its associated interface hardware allow several important human interfacing functions to be accomplished through hardware that is connected directly to the LCU rather than over the shared communication facilities. These functions include:

1. Allowing the plant operator to control the process (e.g., select control set points and controller modes);
2. Allowing the operator to override the automatic equipment and control the process manually in case of a controller hardware failure or other system malfunction;
3. Allowing the plant instrumentation engineer to configure the control system logic and later tune the control system parameters.

Later chapters will cover many of the issues involved in implementing these interface functions. Chapter 5 will provide a detailed discussion of the facilities required for generalized communications between LCUs and other system elements. Chapter 6 will cover the issues involved in designing operator-oriented human interface systems, including the low-level human interface device. Chapter 7 will address the same issues with regard to engineer-oriented devices.

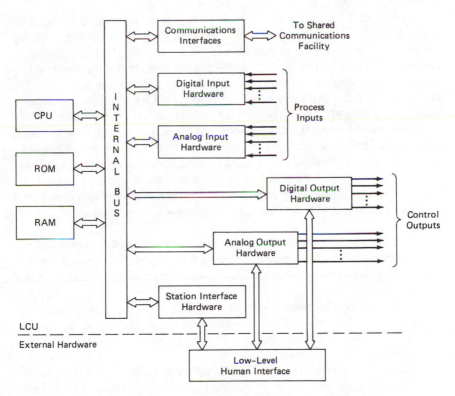

Figure 4.1. LCU Interfaces to Distributed System Elements

This chapter concentrates on process interfacing issues that relate to two specific areas: control system security and the process I/O capabilities of the distributed control system. Section 4.2 will discuss in depth the security issues, including the provision of manual override capability and redundant controllers. Then Section 4.3 will cover the issues involved in meeting a wide range of process interfacing requirements in a distributed system. These include the tradeoffs involved in using DI/OUs to augment the I/O capabilities of the LCU.

4.2. SECURITY DESIGN ISSUES FOR THE LOCAL CONTROL UNIT

4.2.1. Security Requirements

The first priority of the user of any process control system is to keep the process running under safe operating conditions. Downtime that curtails production is extremely expensive; an unsafe condition that leads to human injury or plant damage is even more costly.

Because of this, reliability is one of the major factors considered in evaluating a distributed control system. One way of designing a highly reliable control system is to manufacture it using only the highest-quality components, conduct extensive burn-in testing of the hardware, and implement other quality control measures in the production process. This will increase the mean time between failure (MTBF) of the system, and reduce the probability that it will cause a plant shutdown. However, every plant manager knows that any control system, no matter how reliable, will eventually fail. Therefore, it is important that the control system have adequate security features built into it so that the process can continue safely in spite of the failure of one of the elements of the control system.

One can view the security objectives necessary in designing a distributed control system in the following hierarchy:

1. Maximize the availability of the *automatic* control functions of the system. As much as possible, make sure that the failure of a single control system element does not shut down all automatic control functions.
2. If the failure of a control system element causes the loss of automatic control in a portion of the system, make sure that there is a mechanism that allows the operator to take over manual control of that portion of the process.
3. As much as possible, ensure that the control outputs to the process are safe ones so that, if critical automatic and manual control functions are lost, the operator can shut the process down in an orderly and safe manner.

These security objectives are valid for logic control or sequential control subsystems as well as for continuous control. This hierarchy should be followed most carefully for critical control loops, such as those that control exothermic processes.

This section will discuss in detail a number of security features that can be built into distributed control systems to ensure that the above objectives are met. The manufacturers of these control systems have used a wide variety of approaches to designing security into their systems. Section 4.2.2 will give an overview of these approaches. The first step in triggering any security-related action is to detect that a failure in the control system has occurred; Section 4.2.3 will review the types of diagnostics used to detect such failures. Section 4.2.4 will discuss some of the design techniques used to ensure that the system generates only safe control outputs, even under failure conditions. Section 4.2.5 will cover the design of systems for secure manual backup of automatic control loops. Finally, Section 4.2.6 will summarize several approaches to using redundant hardware that permits automatic control functions to continue under failure conditions.

4.2.2. Overview of Security Design Approaches

Relatively few papers in the literature deal with the design of security features in distributed control systems. Some useful references in this area are given at the end of the chapter (Refs. 4.1-4.12). While each manufacturer of distributed systems takes a somewhat different approach to this design problem, there are three basic categories of security approaches currently in use. These are listed below in approximate order of increasing complexity and cost.

1. *Provide manual backup only (Figure 4.2A)*—In this case, each LCU is designed to implement only one or two control loops, and reliance is placed on the operator to take over manual control in case of a failure of the LCU. Note in the figure that the control output is fed back to the manual backup station and to the computation section of the controller so that the inactive element can synchronize its output with the active element. This ensures that the output to the process will not be bumped when a switchover from the active to the inactive device occurs.
2. *Provide a standby redundant controller (Figure 4.2B)*—In this case, the LCU is backed up by another LCU that takes over if the primary controller fails. In this way, full automatic control is maintained even under failure conditions. As in the first case, the control output is fed back to both controllers to allow bumpless transfers to be accomplished.

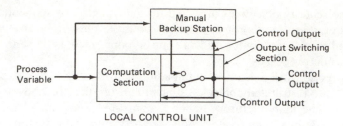

Figure 4.2A. Manual Backup Approach

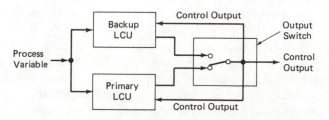

Figure 4.2B. Hot Standby Redundancy Approach

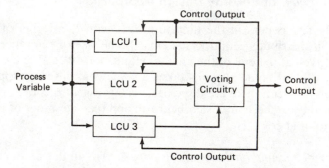

Figure 4.2C. Multiple Active Redundant Controllers

3. *Provide multiple active controllers (Figure 4.2C)*—In this case, several LCUs are active at the same time in reading process inputs, calculating control algorithms, and producing control outputs to the process. Since only one output can be used at a time, *voting* circuitry selects the valid output. The multiple active approach is designed so that a failure of one of the controllers does not affect the automatic control function. The selected control output is fed back so that each controller can compare its own output with the output generated by the voting device.

In each of these three approaches, the intent of the design is (1) to guarantee that multiple control channels (either manual or automatic) are able to generate the control output signal, and (2) to ensure that a safe channel is available or is switched in following the failure of one of the other channels.

The manual backup approach relies on the ability of the operator to control the portion of the process associated with a single LCU. There is some argument on the maximum number of control outputs one operator can manipulate manually; however, handling one to four loops at one time is usually possible, the number depending on the speed of response required to keep each loop under control. This approach has its parallel with the security designs that discrete analog control systems provide, in which each loop is associated with a single physical controller and operator station. If the controller fails, only one loop is affected and the operator takes over manual control until a spare controller can be substituted. The single-loop integrity of this controller structure provides adequate security in the analog case; several manufacturers of distributed systems follow the same approach using microprocessor-based controllers. These controllers provide additional security through the "intelligence" of the microprocessor, which is capable of self-diagnosing potential or actual failures and generating safe control outputs when they occur.

In some situations, however, manual backup control alone does not provide an adequate level of security. This is the case when the LCU has to implement a larger number of control loops (say, five or more). It is unreasonable to expect an operator to handle all of these loops manually while the automatic controller is being repaired. The other situation occurs when the control loop is fast-acting, so that loss of automatic control for even a short time could cause an unsafe plant situation. In both of these cases, some form of redundant controller must be provided to carry on the automatic control functions in the event of a failure of the primary controller. The redundancy approach shown in Figure 4.2B relies on a "hot standby" controller to take over for the primary one. This approach has its roots in the direct digital control (DDC) computer systems described in Chapter 1. Because *all* of the plant control functions are implemented in a single DDC computer, a second computer to provide full backup of the primary computer is essential for control system security. The distributed control architecture uses other versions of backup, which will be described in Section 4.2.6.

The security design approach of using multiple active controllers to perform a control function had its origins in the "fly-by-wire" aircraft controllers developed in the early 1970s for supersonic transport and jumbo jets (see Reference 4.8, for example). These electronic controllers replaced the physical cables the pilot used to manipulate the aircraft control surfaces. In this control application, a simple primary-plus-backup control architecture did not provide an adequate level of automatic control availability. Quadruple redundancy was necessary to provide a secure flight control system. As yet, this approach has not met widespread acceptance in the process control industries because of its high cost and complexity. However, it may become more feasible as hardware costs continue to decrease and specialized components are designed to simplify the system configuration.

4.2.3. On-Line Diagnostics

Every approach to providing control system security through backup elements requires that an on-line failure detection mechanism be included in the design of the LCU. Most distributed control system designs take advantage of the intelligence of the LCU's microprocessor by including a wide range of self-diagnostic routines in the repertoire of LCU functions. Discussed here are on-line routines used for the purpose of detecting impending or actual LCU failures. Section 7.4 will summarize mechanisms that relay this information to the operator.

Depending on the nature of the diagnostic test run and the time required for its execution, each test can be performed at startup of the LCU, during LCU operation, or on a periodic basis. In selecting the set of diagnostics to be used, the designer faces the limitations of memory and time needed to perform the basic LCU functions. The designer can allocate only a relatively small portion of the available resources to diagnostic routines without compromising the cost-effectiveness of the overall design of the LCU.

Table 4.1 lists types of diagnostics for detecting various kinds of failures. For each diagnostic test, the table gives a description, indicates a typical frequency of execution, and identifies the action taken by the LCU if the test is not accomplished successfully. No attempt will be made to describe these diagnostics in great detail since they are relatively standard tests used in systems other than distributed control. Most of them have been used in the past to improve the security of DDC computer applications and have been adapted for use in microprocessor-based systems. However, a few of them may need some further explanation. For example, the primary purpose of the analog-to-digital (A/D) converter check is to ensure that the converter is calibrated correctly (i.e., reads properly at the calibration voltages). Adding the process of detecting excessive calibration corrections makes the function a diagnostic one. The ROM/EAROM sumcheck is a method of verifying that the information stored in the memory at programming time has been retained without error. In the case of ROM, this sum is calculated and stored when the ROM is programmed in the factory. In the case of EAROM, EEPROM, and other alterable nonvolatile memory, the sum must be computed and stored periodically by the LCU processor itself, because the contents of memory change with time. The watchdog timer test provides a mechanism for shutting the LCU down that does not rely on the proper operation of the processor, as do most of the other diagnostics. The timer ensures that unsafe control outputs are not generated if the processor fails and loses track of its location in its program or halts completely.

Once a diagnostic test has detected a failure, the LCU must be able to act on this information in one or more of the following ways:

1. The LCU should be able to alarm or report the failure to both the low-level human interface and to the higher-level human interface and computing elements. If possible, both the *existence* and the *type* of failure should be reported.
2. The LCU should be able to switch a contact ouput to provide an external hardware indication of failure (in case the communication links between the LCU and the other elements are not operational).
3. If the failure affects only a portion of the LCU, the internal application logic of the LCU should be able to drive a failure indicator. The LCU's logic then can trigger the appropriate process trip sequence or cause the control logic to back off to a simpler level of control (e.g., manual instead of automatic, or simple loop instead of cascade.)
4. The LCU should be able to shut itself down in an orderly way, if necessary.

Any of these failure indications can trigger initiation of the manual backup function or transfer of control to a redundant controller.

4.2.4. Secure Control Output Design

This section suggests a number of design practices that can improve the security of the analog and digital control output hardware in an LCU. From a review of the LCU architecture in Figure 4.1, it is clear that the design of this hardware is critical to the security of the LCU. If this hardware is not well designed, incorporating security features into the rest of the system will not be able to compensate for the deficiencies in the output area. This holds for both analog and digital control output channels.

Table 4.1. On-Line LCU Failure Diagnostics

DIAGNOSTIC TYPE	NAME	DESCRIPTION	WHEN PERFORMED	ACTION ON FAILURE
Input diagnostics	A/D converter check	Processor applies known zero and span voltages to converter and uses measurements to correct for input errors.	Periodically during operation	If correction becomes too great, sets alarm and shuts converter down.
	Sensor out of range check	Processor checks that input from sensor is in acceptable range.	Every input scan	Declares sensor input to have bad quality.
	Excessive rate of change check	Processor checks that time rate of change of input from sensor is in acceptable range.	During operation	Declares sensor input to have bad quality.
	Open T/C detection	Processor checks thermocouple for open circuit using standard methods.	During operation	Declares T/C input to have bad quality.
Configuration diagnostics	I/O hardware check	Processor checks that selected I/O hardware options are present.	At startup	Alarms and shuts LCU down.
	Memory check	Processor checks that selected memory options are present.	At startup	Alarms and shuts LCU down.
Memory diagnostics	ROM/EAROM sumcheck	Processor compares the computed sum of the contents of memory with the pre-stored correct value.	Periodically during Operation	Alarms a ROM failure and shuts LCU down.
	RAM test	Processor writes a known pattern into RAM, then reads back and checks the results.	At startup	Alarms a RAM failure and shuts LCU down.

Output diagnostics	D/A converter check	Processor writes a known value to the D/A converter, reads it back through analog channel, and compares results.	Periodically during operation	If error becomes too great, sets alarm and shuts converter down.
	Output register check	Processor writes a known number to the D/A converter and reads digital value back to verify number.	During operation	Sets alarm and shuts converter down.
End-to-end processor/memory diagnostic	Test problem	Processor executes a test control or arithmetic algorithm, then compares results with prestored answer.	At startup	Sets alarm and shuts LCU down.
External hardware check	Watchdog timer	Processor sets an external timer periodically to confirm proper operation.	Periodically during operation	Timer hardware shuts LCU down.
Power system diagnostics	Voltage monitor	Processor uses external hardware to monitor the voltages generated by the LCU power supply.	Continuously during operation	Alarms power supply failure and shuts LCU down.

Some of the techniques the designer should follow to improve the security of the control output circuitry include the following:

1. Keep the number of analog outputs per digital-to-analog (D/A) converter to a minimum (preferably, one output per converter).
2. Design both analog and digital output circuitry so that the control outputs go to a safe state when the LCU fails. The definition of *safe* depends on the application. In the case of digital outputs, the user should be able to select either 0 or 1 as the safe state. In the case of analog outputs, the user should be able to select among the following options: "go to minimum output," "go to maximum output," "hold the last output value," or "go to a preselected output value." Obviously, generating these safe output options should not depend on the proper functioning of the CPU, since the safe state must be generated even if the processor fails.
3. If possible, power the output circuitry from a supply that is independent of the supply used to power the rest of the LCU. The safe output states can then be generated even if the rest of the LCU is not operating, either from loss of power or other failure conditions.
4. Design the output circuitry so that the actual value of the output can be read back by the rest of the LCU. This feature provides two benefits: it permits the LCU to verify that the correct control output has been generated, and it allows the transfer between the LCU and manual backup stations or redundant controllers to be bumpless.
5. For maximum reliability of each output channel, minimize the number of components and electrical connections between the control output driver hardware and the field termination point for the control actuator.

Figures 4.3 through 4.7 illustrate the implementation of these design guidelines. In each case, the LCU structure shown in Figure 4.1 is taken as the base LCU configuration; however, only the elements that deal with output security are shown. Also, the three elements that make up the microprocessor portion of the LCU (CPU, ROM, and RAM) are lumped into one box (labeled "μP").

One common approach used to generate analog control outputs from an LCU is shown in Figure 4.3. In this scheme, a single D/A converter is used to produce several control outputs by including an analog multiplexer (a switching device) in the circuitry. To generate each output, the microprocessor writes the proper value to the output register shown, and the D/A converter generates a corresponding analog voltage. At effectively the same time, the processor instructs the multiplexer (MUX) to switch

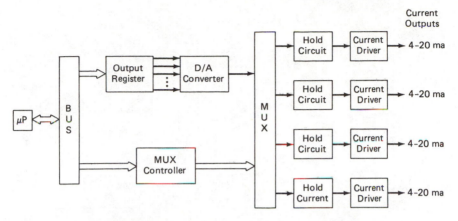

Figure 4.3. Multiplexed Control Output Configuration

the output of the D/A converter to the proper hold circuit. This hold circuit is an analog memory that stores the output value and causes the current driver to generate the appropriate output current, usually in the 4–20 milliampere (ma) range. Then the processor writes the next output value into the register and directs the D/A converter output to the next hold circuit through the MUX as before. This process occurs on a cyclic basis at least several times per second. The effect is to generate multiple control outputs from the LCU using only one D/A converter, which in the past has been one of the most expensive components in a digital system.

While this approach is cost-effective, it suffers from a number of defects from a control security point of view. First, a single failure in any of the common components (output register, D/A converter, MUX, or MUX controller) results in the loss of several control outputs. This type of failure or a loss of power to the output section causes the control outputs to go to zero, which may or may not be a safe state for the process in question. Next, this scheme does not allow the processor to detect an error in the generation of the control outputs. This error could occur through a component failure or through normal drift in component specifications over time or temperature. Finally, the output circuitry is not isolated from the external environment in any way. As a result, a large noise transient at the output terminals could propagate back through the system and wipe out a large number of components and their corresponding control outputs.

Figure 4.4 shows one channel of a much more secure control output configuration. In this case, the D/A converter is dedicated to generating a single control output. Also, provision is made to allow the processor to "read back" the value of the control output. This is done by means of a

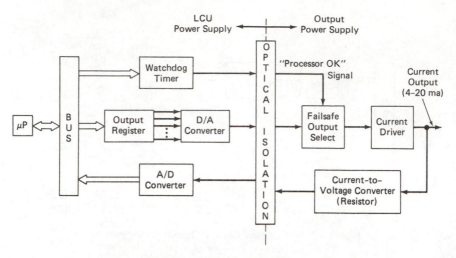

Figure 4.4. Secure Control Output Configuration

current-to-voltage converter (commonly known as a resistor) and an A/D converter. The processor uses this capability to verify that the control output has been generated correctly. In some systems, a known reference voltage is switched into the A/D converter and the processor checks the output value of the converter. The processor can then take into account and correct any errors that occur in the process of reading the A/D converter output and generating the control output values to the D/A converter.

Another feature included in this configuration is the watchdog timer. As described in the previous section, the processor must reset the timer periodically to indicate that the processor is operating properly. If the timer is not reset, the LCU shuts down and the control outputs are put in a safe state. This is accomplished in this configuration through the failsafe output select circuitry, which allows the user to select the safe state appropriate to the process being controlled. These safe states include "hold previous output," "go to zero," "go to maximum value," or "go to a preselected value." The user must select this state before LCU startup by using switches or other hardware in the output section.

Finally, this configuration uses optical isolators to provide electrical separation between the output section and the processing section of the LCU. This has two benefits: it keeps voltage transients from propagating back to the processor from the output terminals, and it allows the output section to be powered by a supply that is independent from the one powering the rest of the LCU. Thus, a failure in the LCU supply will not keep the output section from generating a safe control output value.

It should be mentioned that both the watchdog timer and the A/D converter can be shared among the control output channels in the LCU, since they are not directly involved in the generation of a control output. To some extent, this would reduce the per-channel output cost of the configuration shown in Figure 4.4, which is clearly more expensive than that shown in Figure 4.3. However, the recent dramatic reduction in cost of D/A converters and the significant advantage in security provided by the configuration in Figure 4.4 still makes it the preferred choice.

In Figure 4.5, a somewhat different approach to generating analog control outputs is shown. In this case, the LCU processor is directly involved in the output generation process by generating raise and lower commands to an up/down counter in the output channel. This counter responds to the commands by incrementing or decrementing a digital value in its memory. This value is fed to the D/A converter, which generates a control output through the current driver. The processor keeps track of the output through the current-to-voltage converter and A/D converter circuitry shown and manipulates the raise and lower commands until the output reaches the desired value. The configuration shown in Figure 4.5 is a very basic version which can be enhanced to include the security features described for the configuration in Figure 4.4: watchdog timer, optical isolation, and failsafe output select. This configuration is somewhat more expensive than the previous one due to the addition of the up/down counter, but it has some advantages in simplifying the mechanisms for redundancy and manual backup (which will be discussed in later sections).

This discussion has concentrated on the issue of security in generating analog (continuous control) outputs. Similar considerations must be taken into account in generating digital (logic control) outputs. Figure 4.6 shows a basic and simple digital output configuration. This configuration suffers from many of the same defects as the corresponding analog version in Figure 4.3. The added security features in Figure 4.7 correct these defects.

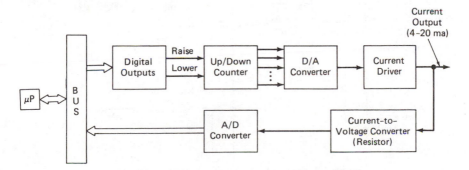

Figure 4.5. Pulsed Control Output Configuration

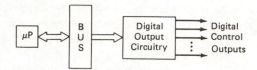

Figure 4.6. Basic Digital Output Configuration

An output readback capability also can be added to this configuration if desired. The failsafe output select section is much simpler in the digital output case than in the analog one. In the digital case, there are only two states (0 or 1), and selecting and generating the safe state is a relatively straightforward process.

4.2.5. Manual Backup Designs

The first line of defense against failures in the control system is to include in the LCU design the output security features discussed in the previous section. The next line of defense is providing a manual backup capability to allow the operator to take direct control over the outputs affected by a control system failure. This is usually accomplished through a low-level operator interface that is directly connected to the LCU. Proper design of the manual backup circuitry is extremely important to control system security, especially in system architectures that rely on manual backup to keep the process running if a controller fails.

It should be pointed out that in analog control systems, manual backup has been the traditional approach used to recover from controller failures.

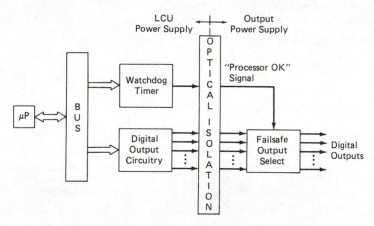

Figure 4.7. Secure Digital Output Configuration

This approach has been adequate, since analog controllers control only a single loop that an operator could handle manually without any difficulty. As a result, the manual backup approach also has been popular in distributed systems using single-loop controllers.

Some of the major principles to follow in designing the manual backup capability for an LCU are as follows:

1. The manual backup signal should enter the LCU as close to the output terminal as possible; that is, there should be a minimal amount of hardware between the low-level operator interface station and the control actuator. This reduces the chance that a hardware failure in the LCU will inhibit the manual backup function.

2. When the manual backup function is activated, the operator should be able to remove and replace the LCU electronics that implement the automatic control function without shutting down the process. Presumably, it is the failure of this portion of the LCU that caused the activation of manual backup in the first place.

3. It should be possible for the operator, through the low-level operator interface, to observe the values of both the manual output signal and the process variable being controlled. These signals must be available even if the automatic control portion of the LCU has failed and is being replaced.

4. The manual output command should be available to the automatic controller so that the transfer from manual backup mode to automatic control mode can be accomplished without bumping the process or requiring manual intervention to balance the output signal.

5. In distributed control applications, the LCU is often located near the process being controlled, while the operator interface hardware is located in a control room some distance away from the LCU. In this case, the low-level operator interface may not be useful as a backup device, since it usually must be located physically near the LCU. In this situation, some mechanism for manual backup from the control room must be provided if there are no other means (such as a redundant controller) for maintaining an output signal on controller failure.

The following paragraphs give several examples of manual backup design approaches used in current distributed control systems.

Figure 4.8 shows the first manual backup configuration. Only the control output section is shown in detail; the other hardware elements in the LCU are grouped together on the left. In this approach, both the LCU processor and the low-level operator interface station communicate with the input/

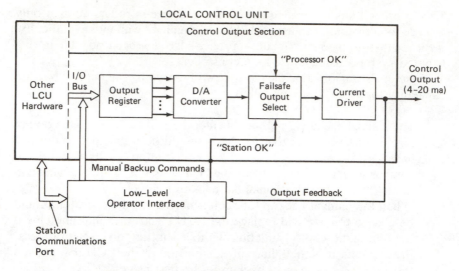

Figure 4.8. Manual Backup—Configuration 1

output cards over a shared bus. Thus, one operator station can back up several output cards. The control output signal is fed back to the interface station and made visible to the operator. A station communications port allows transmission of process variable and control output information between the station and the LCU, thus facilitating bumpless transfer between automatic and manual backup modes. If the LCU processor or another LCU element outside of the control output section fails, the interface station becomes aware of it over the station communications port. The station then takes over the function of generating control outputs over the I/O bus. If both the processor and the station fail, the failsafe output select circuitry takes over to generate a preselected safe output signal, as described in Section 4.2.4.

The manual backup configuration in Figure 4.8 often is used in *multiloop distributed controllers,* in which one or more processors interact with multiple I/O modules over the I/O bus. This approach is cost-effective since one low-level operator interface can be used to back up multiple control output sections in an LCU. However, it is deficient from a security point of view because of the large amount of hardware between the I/O bus and the control output itself. Any failure in this hardware would disable the control output, and any failure in the I/O bus hardware would disable *all* of the control outputs in the LCU. Also, this configuration would not permit the replacement of a failed output section while maintaining the control output through the low-level operator interface. Finally, a manual backup shared among many outputs is less secure than a dedicated backup.

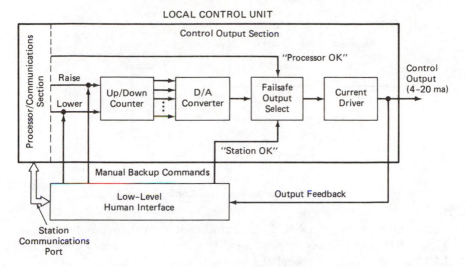

Figure 4.9. Manual Backup—Configuration 2

Configuration 2, shown in Figure 4.9, is similar to the one shown in Figure 4.8 in all respects except for the way in which the manual backup commands are transmitted to the control output section. This type of controller uses an up/down counter to generate the control output signal; therefore, the manual backup commands must use the same input format of raise and lower signals. In this configuration, the low-level operator interface cannot be shared among outputs; it must be dedicated to a single output channel. This increases the cost of backup, but also increases the level of security. However, configuration 2 shares a number of drawbacks with configuration 1 in that the manual backup commands must propagate through a large number of active components before generating a control output signal. Therefore, the same problems in reliability and maintainability apply.

Configuration 3, shown in Figure 4.10, reflects a philosophy that is different from the ones used in designing the previous configurations. Here, the low-level operator interface is completely independent of the LCU and interfaces with it only over the station communications port. This port transfers information needed to keep the LCU and the station aware of each other's status and information base (e.g., control mode, control output, and process variable) so that bumpless transfer between modes can occur. Both the LCU output section and the interface station are capable of generating a current output signal. An external piece of hardware containing only passive components (the diode switching circuitry) selects between the two outputs. The interface station controls this se-

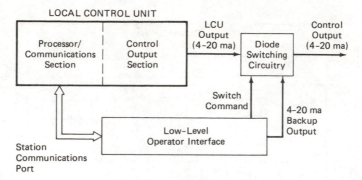

Figure 4.10. Manual Backup—Configuration 3

lection by means of the switch command shown. Although not shown in Figure 4.10, the process variable input to the system is wired to both the LCU and the station in parallel.

Configuration 3 has a number of advantages over the others relative to control output security. First, it is the only configuration that provides a redundant current output capability. The other two rely on a common current driver in the output section of the LCU, a potential single source of failure for both the automatic and manual control functions. Second, the only circuitry between the backup control output and the process is a passive switching circuit, thus minimizing the likelihood of a component failure in the output path. Finally, replacing a failed automatic controller is extremely simple, since the interface station holds the output current while the substitution is being made.

Many high-security logic control applications also require manual backup capability. One approach to providing this capability is shown in Figure 4.11. The front end of this circuitry is similar to the digital output configuration shown in Figure 4.7. However, an output flip-flop or latching circuit is included that will accept a manual output override signal from the low-level operator interface. Feedback of the actual output signal is provided for operator interfacing purposes. The station communications port allows the LCU to be aware of the state of the override circuitry. The security philosophy used in this configuration dictates that the manual backup signal override the failsafe output from the LCU. In situations that may require the automatic failsafe output to override the manual backup signal the "failsafe output select" box would be placed *downstream* of the output flip-flop.

The earlier part of this section listed five principles of manual backup design. The fifth entry in the list deals with the need for a distributed control system configuration to have remote manual backup capability when the LCU is physically remote from the main control center. In such a configuration, the operator controls the plant from a centralized operator's console which usually communicates with the LCU over a shared communication link. If full redundancy is not provided in the LCU, a failure in the LCU could cause the loss of a control output and the potential shutdown of the corresponding portion of the process. A manual bypass capability near the LCU does not provide much help in this case if the physical distance between the control room and the LCU is large and the control loop in question is critical and fast-acting. One solution in this situation is to require full redundancy in the LCU, as will be described in the next section. Figure 4.12 gives another solution—the remote manual backup unit. This unit is designed to interface with the control output circuitry of the LCU using any of the techniques illustrated in Figures 4.8 through 4.11. However, it also includes a port that allows communication with a central operator's station over the shared communication facilities. This port allows the operator to send manual backup commands to the backup unit, which then manipulates the LCU's control output through the "control output override" channel. In this way the control output is maintained *even if* there is a failure in some portion of the LCU itself. This provides a secure method of remote manual backup, because in most cases the communications and operator interface facilities are designed to be redundant. After the instrumentation engineer identifies the failed LCU hardware through manual inspection or through the system diagnostic facilities, the engineer can replace it while the control output is held by the remote manual backup unit.

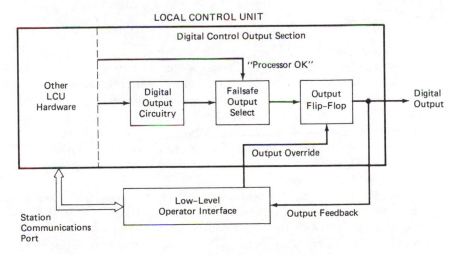

Figure 4.11. Manual Backup for Digital Outputs

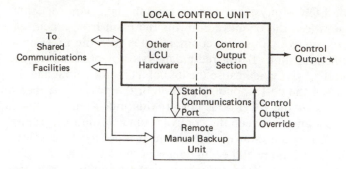

Figure 4.12. Remote Manual Backup Unit

4.2.6. Redundant Controller Designs

As mentioned in Section 4.2.2, the manual backup approach to control system security is viable if the LCU in question handles only a few loops and if the process being controlled is relatively slow. Other situations, however, require some form of controller redundancy to ensure that automatic control of the process is maintained in spite of an LCU failure.

By their very nature, redundant control system structures are more complex than those that rely on manual backup. The addition of redundant elements to the basic control system will always result in an increase in system cost as well as in additional maintenance to service the extra hardware. The redundant structure must be designed carefully to ensure that system reliability actually increases enough to offset these drawbacks. Some of the guidelines to follow in evaluating or designing a redundant control system are as follows:

1. The redundant architecture should be kept as simple as possible. There is a law of diminishing returns in redundancy design. At some point, adding more hardware will *reduce* system reliability.
2. As much as possible, the architecture must minimize potential single points of failure. The redundant hardware elements must be as independent as possible so that the failure of any one does not bring the rest down as well. (In each design, however, there is *always* at least one single point of failure; this element must be designed to be as simple and reliable as possible.)
3. As much as practical, the redundant nature of the controller configuration should be *transparent* to the user; that is, the user should be able to deal with the redundant system in the same way as a nonredundant one. This includes both operational and engineering functions (e.g., control system configuration and tuning.) When one

of the redundant elements fails, the steps to follow in repairing and restarting the system must be clear to the user.
4. The process should not be bumped or disturbed either when one of the redundant elements fails or when the user puts the repaired element back on line.
5. After a control element has failed, the system should not have to rely on it to perform any positive action or to provide any necessary information to the other elements in the system until after repair or replacement.
6. The redundant LCU architecture must have the capability for "hot" spare replacement; that is, allow for the replacement of failed redundant elements without shutting down the total LCU.

The following discussion will describe, in approximate order of increasing complexity, several approaches to designing a redundant LCU architecture:

1. CPU redundancy
2. One-on-one redundancy
3. One-on-many redundancy
4. Multiple active redundancy

In each case, the key advantages and disadvantages of the approach will be listed. No attempt will be made to recommend a best approach; as always, this will depend on the particular control system application.

CPU Redundancy. The first three redundant architectures listed above use the primary/backup approach described in Section 4.2.2. Only one of the redundant elements is active at any one time; the backup element takes over if the primary fails. In the first configuration, shown in Figure 4.13, only the CPU portion (processor and associated memory elements) of the LCU is redundant, while the I/O circuitry is not redundant. This approach is popular in LCU architectures that implement a large number of control loops. In this case, the CPU is redundant because its failure affects *all* of the control outputs. I/O is not redundant because a failure in an output circuit affects only that output. Often, however, a low-level operator interface will back up the control outputs, according to one of the approaches described in Section 4.2.5.

Only one of the CPUs is active in reading inputs, performing control computations, and generating control outputs at any one time. The user designates the primary CPU through the priority arbitrator circuitry shown in Figure 4.13, using a switch setting or other mechanism. After startup,

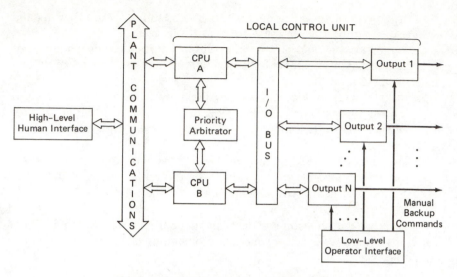

Figure 4.13. CPU Redundancy Configuration

the arbitrator monitors the operation of the primary CPU. If it detects a failure in the primary (through expiration of a watchdog timer or other diagnostic device), the arbitrator transfers priority to the backup. During operation, the backup CPU periodically updates its internal memory by reading the state of the primary CPU through the arbitrator. While both CPUs are connected to the plant communication system, only the primary is active in transmitting and receiving messages over this link. The main operator and engineering interface in this system (other than emergency manual backup) is the high-level human interface shown in the block diagram. This is usually a CRT-based video display unit that interfaces with the LCU over the shared communication facilities. As a result, it can deal with the LCU as if it were nonredundant. Only the primary CPU will accept control commands or configuration and tuning changes transmitted by the VDU. The primary CPU then, in turn, updates the backup CPU with this new information. Following the same philosophy, all monitoring and status information in the LCU is transmitted to the VDU by the primary CPU.

The key advantages of this approach to redundancy are that it is relatively easy to implement and it is cost-effective. The redundant elements interface easily to the plant communication facilities and the I/O bus, which are shared communication channels. The cost of the redundant hardware is not excessive since only the CPU hardware is duplicated. On the other hand, there are problems with this architecture if not designed properly.

For example, the I/O bus and the priority arbitrator represent potential single points of failure in the configuration. They must be designed such that their failure does not render both CPUs in the LCU inoperable. Another potential problem is that the low-level operator interface generally is physically located near the LCU; if the LCU is located at some distance from the central control room, no means of manual backup exists at the central location (where the high-level human interface console is located). This is the same problem as in the manual backup situation described in the previous section and can be solved using the same techniques, either by using full redundancy or by replacing the low-level operator interface station with a remote manual backup unit.

One-on-One Redundancy. The remaining three redundancy approaches provide for redundancy in the control output circuitry as well as in the CPU hardware. As a result, most of these architectures do *not* provide a low-level operator interface for manual backup purposes. The approach shown in Figure 4.14 provides a total backup LCU to the primary LCU. Since the control output circuitry is duplicated in this case, an output switching block must be included to transfer the outputs when the controller fails. As in the first redundant configuration, a priority arbitrator designates the primary and backup LCUs and activates the backup if a failure in the primary is detected. As before, it also serves as the means to update the internal states of the backup LCU with the corresponding information from the primary. In this configuration, the arbitrator has the additional responsibility of sending a command to the output switching

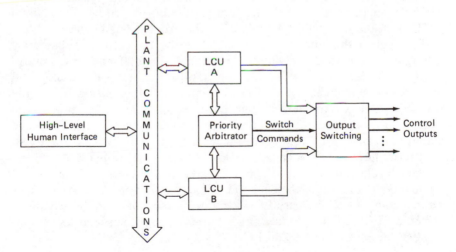

Figure 4.14. One-on-One Backup Redundancy

circuitry if the primary LCU fails, causing the backup LCU to generate the control outputs. Communications with the high-level human interface are handled in the same way as in the CPU-redundant configuration.

The main advantage of the one-on-one configuration, compared to the previous CPU-redundant approach, is that no manual backup is needed, since *all* of the LCU hardware is duplicated. Also, it eliminates any questions that may arise with a partial redundancy approach such as the previous one, particularly regarding the decision on *which* elements are to be redundant. However, it also suffers from a number of disadvantages. First, it is an expensive approach to redundancy, since not only are all of the LCU elements duplicated, but additional elements must be included to manage the redundant ones. Next, it has potential single-point failure problems with the arbitrator and the output switching circuitry. The latter circuitry is particularly vulnerable because it is complex and highly critical to the system.

One-on-Many Redundancy. Figure 4.15 illustrates a more cost-effective approach to redundancy. In this configuration, a single LCU is used as a hot standby to back up any one of several primary LCUs. As in other configurations, an arbitrator is required to monitor the status of the primaries and switch in the backup when a failure occurs. Unfortunately, in this case, there is no way of knowing ahead of time which primary controller the backup would have to replace. As a result, a very general (and complex) switching matrix is necessary to transfer the I/O from the failed controller to the backup. For the same reason, it is not possible to preload the backup controller with the control system configuration of any particular primary LCU. Rather, the configuration is loaded into the backup LCU from the primary LCU only *after* the primary has failed.

The cost of this approach is lower than the other three redundancy configurations because only a small portion of the total amount of control hardware is duplicated. However, this approach violates the second and fifth design guidelines listed at the beginning of this section. First, the switching matrix is an element whose proper operation is essential to the control loops concerned, but it also represents a potential single point of failure. Because of its complexity, it must be designed very carefully so that its failure does not cause the loss of all these loops. Second, the approach relies on the failed controller to provide a copy of the control system configuration to the backup LCU. A better approach would be to store a copy of each primary LCU's control configuration in the arbitrator. When an LCU failure occurs, the arbitrator could then load the proper configuration into the backup LCU.

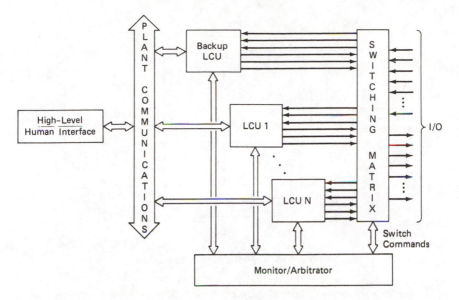

Figure 4.15. One-on-Many Backup Redundancy

Multiple Active Redundancy. In this approach, illustrated in Figure 4.16, three or more redundant LCUs are used to perform the same control functions performed by one in the nonredundant configuration. Unlike the previous architectures, in this one all of the redundant controllers are active at the same time in reading process inputs, computing the control calculations, and generating control outputs to the process. Although not shown in the figure, each LCU has access to all of the process inputs needed to implement the control configuration. Also, a mechanism (usually software internal to the LCUs) is provided to allow the controllers to synchronize their operations in time and to periodically read and check each other's internal states.

An output voting device selects one of the valid control outputs from the controllers and transmits it to the control process. When a controller fails, it is designed to generate an output outside the normal range. The output voting device will then discard this output as an invalid one. In the case of analog control outputs, the output voting device is often designed to select the median signal; in the case of digital control outputs, the voting device is designed to select the signal generated by at least two out of the three controllers. Each controller has access to the output of the voting device to check its own operation and shut itself down if its output disagrees significantly with that of the other controllers.

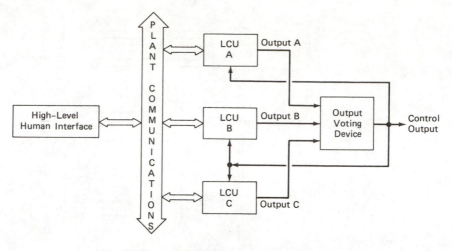

Figure 4.16. Multiple Active Redundancy

The multiple active redundancy configuration is a very sophisticated approach that to date has not been used to any great extent in the industrial process control field. It is very complex and obviously costs more than three times what a nonredundant system costs. However, it is included in the set of approaches listed here because a few control system vendors are beginning to offer it for high-security applications. Indeed, in modified form it has been used in safety systems for nuclear power plants. (If any two out of four devices in a safety channel call for a shutdown, the system initiates a shutdown of the equipment controlled by the channel.) More often, this configuration has been used in high-reliability computer control applications in the aerospace industry (e.g., advanced aircraft, the space shuttle, and unmanned planetary missions). This approach may find its way into selected process control applications as hardware costs continue to decline and configurations become standardized.

The main advantage of this approach is that, as long as the output voting device is designed for high reliability, it significantly increases the reliability of the control system. However, this architecture suffers from a number of problems in addition to cost. One is its questionable ability to manage changes in the control system configuration. In most applications where this configuration has been used so far, the approach has implemented a *fixed* configuration. The process of ensuring that control system configuration and tuning changes have been implemented properly is not trivial. This process needs to be worked out and proven before the industrial control field will accept the multiple active redundancy approach. The other disadvantages are that the added hardware requires increased maintenance and that the system is very complex. Often the KISS principle ("keep it simple, stupid") is still the most effective one to follow in structuring a reliable system.

4.3. PROCESS INPUT/OUTPUT DESIGN ISSUES

The monitoring and control of a large industrial process requires that many inputs of various types be brought into the control system. The control system then computes the proper actions to be taken and transmits the control outputs to the process and the indications to the operator. This section will discuss the issues involved in designing the I/O portion of a distributed control system in a cost-effective manner. First will come a summary of I/O requirements typically placed on a process control system. Then several approaches to the I/O design problem will be discussed, along with their advantages and disadvantages. This section will end with a brief review of the alternatives available in field termination design.

4.3.1. Input/Output Requirements

There are several dimensions to the problem of providing cost-effective I/O hardware for a distributed control system. The first dimension is simply the large *variety* of I/O signals that the control system must handle in order to interface with sensors, analyzers, transmitters, control actuators, and other field-mounted equipment. (See References 4.14, 4.16, and 4.18 for tutorial information in this area.) Table 4.2 lists a typical set of I/O requirements. In addition to the familiar kinds of analog and digital inputs and outputs, the table includes several other types of interfaces that are required for use with "smart" sensors, digital human interface equipment, and pulse-type sensors and actuators. The table does not include other requirements peculiar to retrofit applications. It is not unusual in such applications for a distributed control system to interface with 20- to 30-year-old plant equipment that has another set of electronic and pneumatic signal levels peculiar to its time of manufacture.

The second problem in providing cost-effective I/O hardware is the wide range of input and output *performance specifications* that are imposed to facilitate interfacing with various types of field equipment. These include specifications on:

1. Common and normal mode voltage rejection levels;
2. Voltage isolation requirements between I/O terminals and system electronics;

Table 4.2. Typical Input/Output Requirements

ANALOG INPUT TYPES	DIGITAL INPUT TYPES
Current: 0–20 milliamps (ma) 4–20 ma 10–50 ma Voltage: 1–5 volts (V) 0–10 V −10 to +10 V 0–10 mV 0–100 mV Thermocouple inputs: Types K, T, J, R, S, E Resistance temperature detector (RTD) inputs: 100 ohm platinum bulb	Voltage: 24 V DC 48 V DC 125 V DC 120 V AC, 50/60 Hz 220 V AC, 50/60 Hz Dry contacts (internally or externally powered) Transistor-Transistor-Logic (TTL) voltage inputs: 0/5 V solid-state

ANALOG OUTPUT TYPES	DIGITAL OUTPUT TYPES
Current: 4–20 ma 10–50 ma Voltage: 1–5 V 0–10 V	Open collector transistor outputs: 0/24, 0/48, or 0/125 V Relay outputs TTL voltage outputs: 0/5 V solid-state
	OTHER I/O TYPES
	RS 232/422 serial communications ports Binary coded decimal (BCD) inputs and outputs Pulse count and pulse frequency inputs and outputs Pulse duration outputs

3. Input impedance requirements;
4. Requirements on ability to drive output loads.

These specifications can vary significantly from one industry to another. As a result, both the user and the designer are forced to trade off cost, performance, and flexibility in selecting a particular I/O design.

The third dimension to the I/O design problem is the varying degree of I/O *"hardening"* required in different applications. These include the following levels:

1. *No hardening is required*—Application requires low-cost I/O hardware.
2. *Application is in a hazardous environment (explosive gases or dust)*— I/O hardware must be designed to be explosion-proof or intrinsically safe. (See Reference 4.15 for a discussion of intrinsic safety requirements.)
3. *Field-mounted equipment is subject to lightning strikes or large induced voltage spikes*—I/O hardware must be designed to withstand high-level voltage surges. (See Reference 4.13 for a discussion on surge-withstand requirements.)

4. *Field-mounted equipment is subject to radio frequency interference (RFI) due to presence of walkie-talkies or other RFI-generating equipment such as motor starters or relays.* I/O hardware must be shielded, filtered, or otherwise isolated from the RFI environment to minimize or eliminate errors due to this type of noise. (See Reference 4.17 for a summary of typical RFI requirements.)

The application will determine what combination of these requirements should be imposed.

This range of potential design requirements is not a major problem in centrally located control systems since *all* of the inputs and outputs come into one location in the plant. As a result, a variety of I/O hardware can be provided at that location to handle the full range of requirements. The situation is more complex with a distributed control system. In this situation, the I/O hardware is at least *functionally* distributed and more recently is becoming *geographically* distributed in the plant as well. As a result, the same variety of I/O types and specification levels must be accommodated in equipment that is split up into smaller clusters than in the centralized case. The challenge is to provide I/O hardware that is scalable with respect to cost, performance requirements, and size of application. That is, the I/O hardware design must be able to comply with the full range of performance requirements, perhaps on an optional basis, without making systems that do *not* require the highest level of performance too expensive. Also, the I/O system must be cost-effective for both small and large control and data acquisition systems if it is to be competitive in the full range of potential applications.

4.3.2. Input/Output Design Approaches

In the distributed control systems available on the market in the mid 1980s, the I/O design problem described in the previous section is generally addressed using a combination of two methods:

1. Vendors offer several options on local control unit I/O circuitry to satisfy the range of requirements in the expected applications.
2. Vendors include in their distributed control product line additional products dedicated to signal conversion and I/O handling.

One product that often is used to augment the I/O capability of the LCU is the DI/OU shown in the generalized distributed control system architecture in Figure 1.4. As its name implies, the DI/OU is a microprocessor-based product that is dedicated solely to reading and generating process

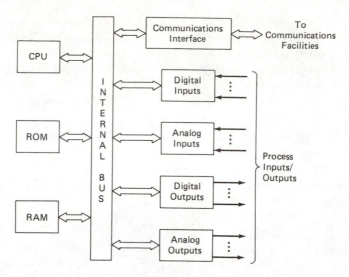

Figure 4.17. DI/OU Architecture

input and output signals. In many distributed systems, this product goes by other names: multiplexer, process interface unit, or data acquisition system. It is essentially a simplified version of an LCU, as the block diagram in Figure 4.17 illustrates. A DI/OU differs from an LCU in the following respects:

1. Its software or firmware is designed strictly for data input/output operations.
2. Its output circuitry does *not* include the security features required for control outputs from an LCU, including interfacing to a low-level operator interface station for control backup purposes. (The station may be used for signal monitoring purposes.)

However, the DI/OU does retain the communications function, which allows it to transmit and receive data to and from other elements in the distributed control system. Therefore, the DI/OU can be used as a "front end" in a computer-based data acquisition system or as an auxiliary I/O device for an LCU.

The advantage of using a DI/OU in the auxiliary mode is that, in general, the cost of an I/O channel in a DI/OU is considerably less than the cost of the corresponding channel in an LCU due to the relative simplicity of a DI/OU. This cost differential is especially significant in applications that call for a large number of input and output points per control function.

The disadvantage of using a DI/OU in a distributed control system is that it adds to the number of product types in the system, thereby increasing spare parts and costs of maintenance. This added overhead is a particular problem in small applications.

The optimum mix of LCUs, DI/OUs, and auxiliary signal conditioning hardware depends to a great extent on the architecture of the LCU used in the distributed control system. In the system illustrated in Figure 4.18, the LCU is a single loop controller. In general, a single-loop controller must be designed to be most cost-effective in applications that call for standard I/O levels without any special I/O hardening, since these represent the majority of applications in the process control field. As a result, it is usually designed to handle only high-level analog inputs and outputs (e.g., 4–20 ma, 1–5 V) and a single digital I/O level (usually 24 V). The other I/O types listed in Table 4.2 must be handled through auxiliary signal conversion equipment or through DI/OUs, as shown in the figure. Signal converters usually are more cost-effective if the number of I/O points is small; otherwise, DI/OUs are a lower-cost option. To minimize the cost of interfacing the signal converters to the LCU, the converters must be designed to fit into the packaging, cabling, and power supply structure of the LCU.

Figure 4.19 illustrates a different situation. In this case, the LCU is a multiloop controller. In the architecture of most multiloop controllers on the market in the mid-1980s the I/O circuitry is located on printed circuit boards that are separate from the rest of the LCU circuitry. As a result, a family of boards handling the full range of I/O requirements in the system can be designed for this type of LCU. Separate signal conversion modules are rarely required in this type of system. DI/OUs are used only if the number of I/O points required by the LCU exceeds its own internal ca-

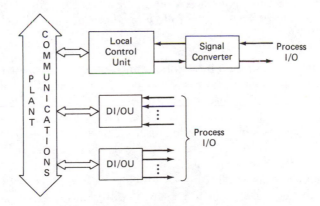

Figure 4.18. I/O Design—Single Loop Controller

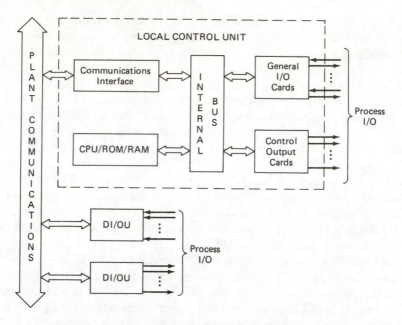

Figure 4.19. I/O Design—Multiloop Controller

pacity or if a large number of data acquisition points (unrelated to control) are included in the application. It should be noted that, in the case of the multiloop LCU architecture, the family of I/O modules used in the LCU can often be the same as those in the DI/OU. This approach reduces the number of different I/O products required in the distributed control system.

If the DI/OU is to provide a cost-effective I/O interfacing capability in a distributed control system, the following guidelines should be followed in its design:

1. The DI/OU should *not* be a stand-alone product that requires special mounting hardware and electrical power. Rather, it should be designed to fit into the packaging, power, and communication structure of the LCUs. This approach minimizes the hardware overhead and interfacing costs involved in using the DI/OU in the distributed system. These added costs are particularly significant in small system configurations.
2. To maximize its application flexibility, each module in the DI/OU should be designed to handle as many different I/O types as possible (voltage levels, thermocouple types, and so forth). Ideally, the user should be able to select each I/O type available on the module on a

point-by-point basis. This approach reduces the number of module types required in the system, and makes more efficient use of module capacity in small systems. A disadvantage is that, if carried to extremes, this flexibility can add an unacceptable cost burden to each I/O point.

3. The user should be able to select the number of I/O points per A/D or D/A converter, perhaps through a master-slave or motherboard-daughterboard arrangement. This would allow the user to trade off I/O cost versus the security of having a small number of points per converter.

4. The DI/OU should be designed to support a number of input conditioning and processing functions, including linearization, bad input detection, engineering units conversion, and alarming. This offloads the other elements in the system and simplifies applications involving the acquisition of a large amount of data.

With regard to the I/O hardening requirements listed in Section 4.3.1, the usual practice in the design of current distributed control systems can be summarized as follows:

1. If the particular hardening requirement in question occurs in most of the applications considered and if the cost of meeting the requirement in the system is relatively low, the necessary I/O hardware is included as a standard feature. Examples of this are (a) optical isolation for surge protection of digital I/O and (b) filtering for RFI protection of analog I/O.

2. If the particular hardening requirement is not a common one and the cost of meeting it is high, the vendor will offer as a base product a low-cost hardware design. Whatever additional hardware is needed to meet the requirement then is offered as an extra-cost option. An example of this approach is the common practice of offering energy-limiting barriers as an option to address intrinsic safety requirements.

As to be expected, the particular needs of the application must be considered carefully when designing or selecting a cost-effective I/O system architecture.

4.3.3. Design of Field Terminations

This section will discuss some of the key issues involved in the design of field terminations for distributed control systems. The discussion is not detailed for two reasons: (1) the design requirements on field terminations vary significantly from one industry to another; and (2) many of the issues involved are not peculiar to distributed systems, but are shared by centralized systems as well.

The basic function of the field termination panels is to provide a point at which the field wiring and shielding can be connected easily to the distributed system cabinets. In most systems, the termination panels also provide a point at which the following additional equipment is connected to the system I/O hardware:

1. Manual backup devices and redundant control devices;
2. Fuses and signal conditioning hardware such as filters;
3. External supplies that provide power to two wire sensors and field contacts;
4. Intrinsic safety barriers and other isolation hardware;
5. Switches and jumpers used to select I/O options.

In some systems, the hardware listed in items 2 and 5 is mounted on the I/O modules themselves. However, this approach can complicate maintenance, since it is usually difficult to gain access to the modules while they are mounted in the system cabinets.

Ideally, the termination panels should be designed to support a high density of terminations per unit area to minimize the cabinet space dedicated to this function. (Because of the steadily increasing number of functions that can be implemented in each active module in the system, the space required for terminations can *exceed* that required for the modules.) Also, the termination panels should be *universal* to the maximum extent possible; that is, any terminal on the panel should be able to handle any I/O type. Finally, to avoid the possibility of damage during installation, no active components should be mounted on the termination panels. Of course, it is often difficult to follow these guidelines due to the special requirements of certain applications (e.g., minimum spacings between terminals on the panels and special signal isolation and conditioning requirements for certain I/O types).

Installation flexibility is maximized if the termination panels are designed to allow mounting either in the same cabinets housing the active electronics modules or in separate termination cabinets. The advantage of separate termination cabinets is that the vendor can ship them to the job site early in the project, thus allowing the field wiring to be connected before the control cabinets are shipped. In some cases, this can expedite the field installation schedule. One of the disadvantages of using separate termination cabinets is that, in general, higher system hardware costs result than if field wiring terminates directly in the control cabinets. Also, using separate termination cabinets means that it is not possible to carry out a complete end-to-end system checkout before it is shipped. Finally, last-minute changes to the I/O configuration can be difficult to manage when the separate cabinets are used, unless the termination panels are designed to be totally universal (any I/O type on any termination block).

If the termination panels are in the cabinets containing the control electronics, good engineering practice suggests that the termination area be separate from the electronic module service area. This avoids conflict between the two categories of plant personnel called on to service the control system: plant electricians (who work in the termination area) and plant instrumentation engineers (who work in the module service area). If the termination panels are located in separate cabinets, the user should be aware of any limitations on the allowed distance between the field terminations and the electronic modules.

REFERENCES

Security Design Issues

4.1 Smith, J.R., "Control Systems Engineering Considerations in the Selection of a Computer-Process Interface System," ISA Publication, *Instrumentation in the Power Industry,* vol. 19, 1976, pp. 65–70.

4.2 Bur, P.W., "Design Considerations for Achieving Reliable Control Within Shared Microprocessor-based Digital Controllers," Instrument Society of America Annual Conference, Houston, Texas, October 1976.

4.3 Depledge, P.G., "Fault-Tolerant Computer Systems," *IEE Proceedings,* Part A, vol. 128, no. 4, May 1981, pp. 257–272.

4.4 Ham, P.A.L., "The Application of Redundancy in Controllers for High Capital Cost or High Integrity Plant," *Proc. 4th Int'l Conf. on Trends in On-Line Computer Systems,* U. of Warwick, UK, April 1982; pub. by IEE, London, 1982, pp. 14–17.

4.5 Goring, C.J., "Cost/Redundancy Trade-Offs in On-Line Control," *Proc. 4th Int'l Conference on Trends in On-Line Computer Systems,* U. of Warwick, UK, April 1982; pub. by IEE, London, 1982, pp. 18–21.

4.6 Sykora, M.R., "The Design and Application of Redundant Programmable Controllers," *Control Engineering,* vol. 29, no. 7, July 1982, pp. 77–79.

4.7 Flood, M.A., and Struger, O.J., "Real-Time Backup Systems for Programmable Controllers," *IEEE Transactions on Industrial Electronics,* vol. IE–29, no. 4, November 1982, pp. 265–272.

4.8 Wensley, J.H., "Industrial Control System Does Things in Threes for Safety," *Electronics,* vol. 56, no. 2, January 27, 1983, pp. 98–102.

4.9 Martinovic, A., "Architectures of Distributed Digital Control Systems," *Chemical Engineering Progress,* vol. 79, no. 2, February 1983, pp. 67–72.

4.10 Griem, P.D., "Security Functions in Distributed Control: Vendor and User Responsibilities," *InTech,* vol. 30, no. 3, March 1983, pp. 57–59.

4.11 Weiss, R., "Fault-Tolerant Computer Systems–Functional Principles and Forms of Realisation," *Process Automation,* no. 2, 1983, pp. 61–69.

4.12 Cocheo, S., "Avoid Vulnerable Distributed Control System Architectures," *Hydrocarbon Processing,* vol. 62, no. 6, June 1983, pp. 59–64.

Input/Output Design Issues

4.13 American National Standard, "IEEE Guide for Surge Withstand Capability (SWC) Tests," *IEEE Standard 472–1974,* July 1974.

4.14 Morrison, R.L., "Getting Transducers to 'Talk' to Digital Computers," *Instruments and Control Systems,* vol. 51, no. 1, January 1978, pp. 27–31.

4.15 Masek, R.C., "Intrinsic Safety," Annual Symposium of the Northern New Jersey Section of the ISA, Cranford, N.J., April 1978.

4.16 Morrison, R.L., "Microcomputers Invade the Linear World," *IEEE Spectrum,* vol. 15, no. 7, July 1978, pp. 38–41.

4.17 Scientific Apparatus Makers Association, "Electromagnetic Susceptibility of Process Control Instrumentation," *SAMA Standard PMC 33.1–1978,* October 1978.

4.18 Zuch, E.L., "Principles of Data Acquisition and Conversion—Parts 1 through 5," *Digital Design,* vol. 9, nos. 7–11, July–November 1979 (five-part series).

5
COMMUNICATIONS FACILITIES

5.1. INTRODUCTION

In conventional nondistributed control systems, the connections that allow communication between the various system elements are configured on a per-job basis. Figure 5.1 shows an example of this for the case of a hybrid system, such as that described in Chapter 1 (see Figure 1.2 and Section 1.1). This system consists of a combination of continuous controllers, sequential controllers, data acquisition hardware, panelboard instrumentation, and a computer system. The controllers communicate with each other by means of point-to-point wiring, usually within the control cabinets. This custom wiring reflects the particular control system configuration selected. The controllers are connected to the corresponding panelboard instrumentation and to the computer system by means of prefabricated cables. The computer obtains information from the data acquisition modules using similar hard wiring or cabling that is specific to the particular module configuration implemented.

This approach to interconnecting system elements has proven to be expensive to design and check out, difficult to change, burdensome to document, and subject to errors (see References 5.1–5.2). It becomes even more cumbersome if the system elements are distributed geographically around the plant. The first step taken to improve this situation was to introduce the concept of *distributed multiplexing* in the early 1970s (see References 5.3–5.4). This concept was first used in the process control industry to implement large-scale data acquisition systems, which at that time had grown to several thousand inputs in size. To reduce the cost of wiring, remote multiplexers located near the sensors in the field were used to convert the inputs to digital form and transmit them back to the data acquisition computer over a shared communication system.

When distributed control systems were introduced in the late 1970s, the use of digital communications was extended to control-oriented systems as well. The communication system began to be viewed as a facility that the various elements and devices in the distributed network share, as the "black box" representation in Figure 5.2 shows. Replacing dedi-

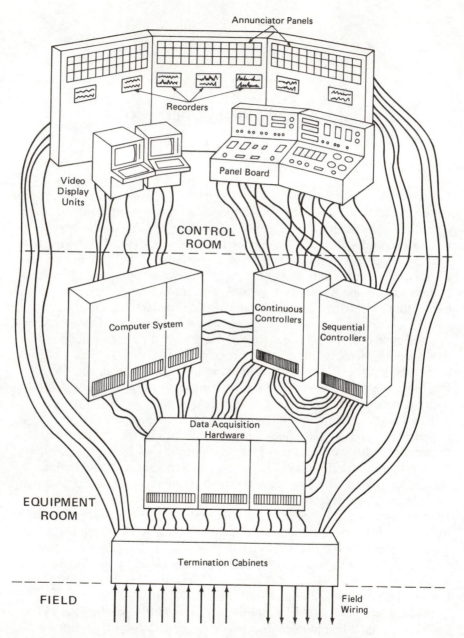

Figure 5.1. Conventional Point-to-Point Wiring

cated point-to-point wiring and cabling with this communications facility provides a considerable number of benefits to the user:

1. The cost of plant wiring is reduced significantly (see References 5.5–5.7 for analyses), since thousands of wires are replaced by the few cables or buses used to implement the shared communication system.
2. The flexibility of making changes increases, since it is the software or firmware configurations in the system elements that define the data interconnection paths and not hard wiring.

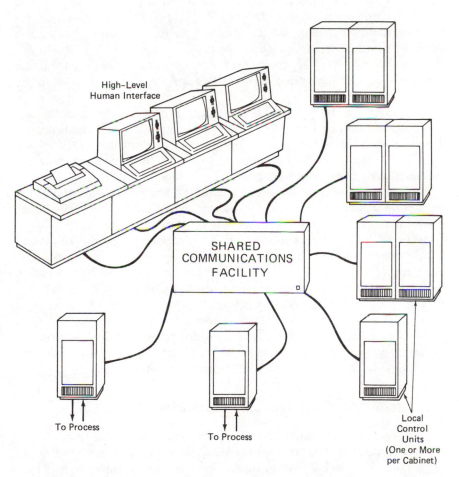

Figure 5.2. Communication Facility as a "Black Box"

3. It takes less time to implement a large system, since the wiring labor is nearly eliminated, configuration errors are reduced, and less time is required to check out the interconnections.
4. The control system is more reliable due to the significant reduction in physical connections in the system (a major source of failures).

However, replacing hard wiring with the shared communications network of a distributed control system also raises a number of questions for the user. In a conventional system, communications between system elements travel at the speed of light, essentially with zero delay. Also, since the hard-wired communication channels between elements are dedicated, there is no danger of overloading a channel. In the case of a shared communication system, the user must be able to judge whether the response time and capacity of the shared system (in addition to many other performance factors) are adequate for the application. This can be a difficult problem for the user, since there are significant differences and few standards among the various communication systems available on the market today.

The purpose of this chapter is to identify the key issues in evaluating and designing a shared communication system used in distributed control. Because of the vast scope of this subject, I have not attempted an exhaustive treatment of these issues. Rather, the discussion concentrates on functional requirements, major design tradeoffs, and critical features to consider. References 5.8–5.11 provide the reader with tutorial information on digital communication systems, while other references at the end of the chapter provide additional details on particular issues.

Section 5.2 lists the various functions implemented by the communication system and discusses the corresponding requirements on the performance of these functions. This section also summarizes the alternative design approaches to consider in evaluating a particular communications system. Section 5.3 covers architectural issues and Section 5.4 deals with protocol issues. Section 5.5 discusses several other issues that are relatively independent of architectural considerations. Finally, Section 5.6 summarizes the status of recent attempts to develop standards for communication networks in distributed control systems.

5.2. COMMUNICATION SYSTEM REQUIREMENTS

As Section 5.1 just implied, the shared communications facility in a distributed control system must at least duplicate the functions previously implemented by the hard-wired connections in a conventional control system. In the context of the distributed control architecture shown in Figure 5.2, these wire-replacement functions include the following:

1. Transmission of control variables between local control units in the system. This is a requirement for all applications in which the control strategy requires multiple interacting controllers. To minimize delays and maximize security of transmission, the LCUs should be able to communicate directly with one another and not through an intermediary.
2. Transmission of process variables, control variables, and alarm status information from the LCUs to the high-level human interfaces and to the low-level human interfaces in the system (i.e., operator and engineer consoles and panelboard instrumentation).
3. Communication of set-point commands, operating modes, and control variables from the high-level computing devices and human interface devices to the LCUs for the purpose of supervisory control.

In addition to these wire-replacement functions, the shared communications facility also may implement functions more closely related to the distributed control architecture:

4. Downloading of control system configurations, tuning parameters, and user programs from the high-level human interfaces to the LCUs.
5. Transmission of information from the data input/output units to the high-level computing devices for purposes of data acquisition or transfer.
6. Transfer of large blocks of data (e.g., console displays, historical trends and logs, or large data bases), programs, or control configurations from one high-level computing device or human interface to another.
7. Synchronization of real time among all of the elements in the distributed control system.

The shared facility can also implement other communication functions, such as transferring voice and video images. However, the current state of technology usually makes it more cost-effective to implement these functions using a separate, dedicated communications medium.

Once the set of functions to be implemented in the shared communications facility is established, the next step is to specify the performance requirements that the system must meet and the features it must include. Often these are highly application-dependent. However, the discussion in the following paragraphs may help the user or designer identify the key parameters to consider.

Maximum Size of the System. This specification includes two parameters: the geographical distances that the communication system must cover, and the maximum number of devices allowed within the system (where a device can be any one of the elements in Figure 5.2). In some communication systems, a third parameter, the maximum distance between devices, is also important. Commercially available systems often extend over several miles of plant area and can handle several hundred devices.

Maximum Delay Time Through the System. As mentioned previously, the delay time across a hard-wired connection is essentially zero on the time scale at which industrial processes operate, since the signals travel at the speed of light. (The actual delay depends on the distance traveled— about 1 nanosecond delay per foot.) In the case of a shared communication system, however, there always are some message delays due to a combination of factors: it takes time to get access to the shared network, to propagate the message, and to process the message at both the sending and receiving ends. The maximum acceptable delay time depends on both the communication function and the particular industrial process. If the shared communication system is used only to monitor temperature signals generated by thermocouples, for example, a delay of several seconds usually would not be significant. On the other hand, if the communication link is part of a fast-acting flow control loop, a delay of a few tenths of a second could introduce instabilities into the loop.

A simple experiment (either actual or hypothetical) for evaluating these communication delays is to introduce a sine wave signal source into an analog input at one end of the distributed system and observe the response at an analog output at the other end, as Figure 5.3 shows. One can hardwire a strip chart recorder to both the input and the output signals to measure the delay and distortion of the input signal as a function of the frequency of the sine wave input. Of course, the results of this experiment are affected by the necessary sampling and digitization of the input and output signals; but the experiment does provide a direct end-to-end check on the effectiveness of the communication-and-control system as a wire replacement medium.

Interactions Between LCU Architecture and the Communications Facility. There is a significant interaction between the architecture of the

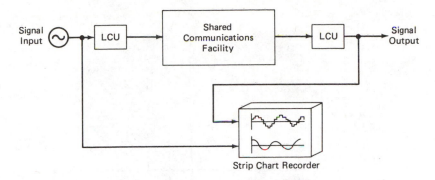

Figure 5.3. Conceptual Time Delay Experiment

LCUs and the shared communications facility in terms of the latter's required performance. One example of this type of interaction is related to the first wire-replacement function listed previously, that of transmitting control variables between LCUs. Figure 5.4 illustrates this interaction. In this figure, each circle represents a single control function, such as a PID controller or a computational block. The lines connecting the circles represent the required transfer of an internal variable from one control function to another. Now, suppose that the LCUs are designed in such a way that each can implement a maximum of nine control functions. In this case, the control logic shown in the figure would have to be partitioned along the solid lines shown, and a total of 12 internal variables would have to be transmitted from one LCU to another across the solid boundaries, using the shared communications facility. On the other hand, if the LCU is designed to implement only four control units, the control logic would be partitioned along the dotted lines shown in the figure. This would result in a total of 24 variables that would have to be transmitted from one LCU to another across the dotted lines, doubling the throughput requirements on the communication facility.

Although this is an artificial example, it illustrates that distributed control systems employing relatively small LCUs usually require a higher rate of communications between elements than those employing large LCUs. In practice, a control system should be partitioned to minimize the need for communications between LCUs, whatever the size of the LCU; however, the trend of interaction from larger to smaller LCUs is clear from the example. Similar relationships between LCU size and required data rates exist with respect to other types of communications, such as transmission of control loop information (e.g., set points and process variables) between LCUs and human interface devices.

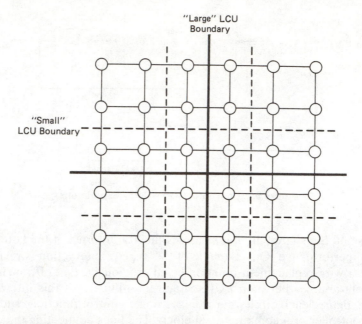

Figure 5.4. Interaction Between LCU Architecture and Communications Facility

Rate of Undetected Errors Occurring in the System.   Every communication link, including a direct hard-wired connection, is subject to errors due to electrical noise in the environment. One advantage of a shared digital communication system is that it can detect these errors at the receiving end and either correct them or request a retransmission of the message. The number of raw errors in a communication system is a function of the noise level and the rate of message transmissions. Most of these errors are detected by the communication system itself; they are not significant in the system's performance except that they increase the number of message delays because garbled information requires retransmission of the data. The significant parameter is the rate of *undetected* errors, since these can cause problems in controlling and monitoring an industrial process. Most industrial communication systems are designed for no more than one undetected error every 100 years. Section 5.5.2 describes some of the design approaches used to achieve this level of security.

Sensitivity to Traffic Loading.   All shared communication systems are designed to operate satisfactorily under *light loading* conditions (i.e., when message traffic on the network is light). The critical test of a shared network is how it behaves under heavy traffic conditions, such as during a major plant upset, when many critical variables are changing rapidly. The message delay time and undetected error rate of the network must not degrade in any significant way during these conditions. One can evaluate the effect of increased loading on a particular network using the same conceptual experiment as shown in Figure 5.3. Adding more input/output signal pairs will increase the traffic loading on the communication network, and one can then evaluate this effect on the delay between any source-destination pair as a function of that loading level. The relationship between loading and the effective communication delays for a particular network involves the network's topology, the physical communication medium, and the message protocols. This chapter will discuss these issues later.

System Scalability. Ideally, the communication facilities should be designed to be cost-effective for a small monitoring or control application but also expandable to larger applications without requiring a major restructuring. This approach provides the user with the most flexibility in configuring the distributed control system. This scalability requirement, together with the requirement on maximum geographical size, often leads to a multilevel architecture of the communications facilities. Section 5.3 will discuss this in more detail.

System Fault Tolerance. It is clear from Figure 5.2 that the shared communications facility is the "spinal cord" of a distributed control system. As such, it must be designed in such a way that the failure of any one of its components will not affect its performance. This requirement for *fault tolerance* leads to the use of failsafe and redundant architectures in the design of its elements.

Interfacing Requirements. In most commercially available distributed control systems supplied by a particular vendor, the communication facility is designed to interface only with elements supplied by the same vendor. However, it is important that the vendor provide a mechanism (sometimes called a *gateway*) that allows connection to other elements using a generally accepted interface standard such as the RS–232C, RS–422, or IEEE 488 standards (described in more detail later in the chapter). This minimizes problems when the user must interface the distributed control system with "smart" instruments, sensors, or computing devices that adhere to these standards.

Ease of Application and Maintenance.   To maximize its ease of application, the communications facility should be designed in such a way that the user can view it as a simple "black box" to which elements of the distributed control system can be connected. As much as possible, any operations for setting up, starting up, or restarting the communications facility should be simple, automatic, or eliminated. There should be application tools that assist the user in configuring the system and automatically checking for potential overloading conditions.

This philosophy also should extend to the area of maintenance. The facility should have self-diagnostic capabilities that detect and announce internal failures. The facility should be modular so that relatively unskilled plant personnel can make repairs quickly. It should be possible to replace modules while the rest of the system is powered and operating; a complete system shutdown should not be necessary.

Of course, all these features are important in designing other elements in the distributed system. However, they are especially important in the case of the communications facility since this is the part of the system with which users are usually least familiar and comfortable.

Environmental Specifications.   Environmental specifications are likely to be much more stringent for the communication facility than for the other elements of the distributed control system, since the former is the least likely to be enclosed in a protective physical environment. The discussion on packaging and power in Chapter 8 lists a typical set of such specifications.

5.3. ARCHITECTURAL ISSUES

Until now, we have viewed the communications facility from the outside in as a black box (Figure 5.2) having certain external characteristics and performance capabilities. This viewpoint is adequate at the first stage of system evaluation and design, during which the main concerns have to do with the communication system's basic scope (How long can the cables extend? How many terminals can the communication system support?) and its overall performance (What is its speed? What kind of delays can be expected?). However, in later stages of evaluation, one has to look at the internals of the communication system to review its architecture and detailed performance characteristics. This is the only way one can understand the system's limitations, strong points, and modes of potential failure. This section will review some of the architectural alternatives available in structuring a communications facility and discuss their advantages and disadvantages.

5.3.1. Channel Structure

The first decision to make in evaluating or designing a communications facility is whether to choose a parallel or serial link as the communication medium. In the *parallel* approach, multiple conductors (wires or fiber optic links) carry a combination of data and handshaking signals (the latter control the flow of data between the nodes in the system). The *serial* approach uses only a single coaxial cable, fiber optic link, or pair of wires. Given the same communication capacity on each link, it is clear that the parallel approach provides a higher message throughput rate than does the serial approach. Also, the existence of separate handshaking lines to control the transfer of data between sender and receiver simplifies the coordination of the communication process. However, the parallel approach requires more circuitry and interconnection hardware at each interface to support the multiple channels, resulting in a higher cost of electronics per node. Also, the timing of the data in the multiple channels can become skewed (i.e., arrive at different times) if the distance between nodes becomes large. As a result, usually only applications requiring high data transfers over relatively short distances (examples are local computer buses and the IEEE 488 instrumentation interface standard) use the parallel approach. Most communication subsystems used in distributed process control use the serial channel approach, especially in the long-distance plantwide communication subsystem (see References 5.12 and 5.13 for examples).

For similar reasons of cost and complexity, frequency multiplexing of multiple communication channels over a single physical link is seldom if ever used in commercial distributed control systems (except in some military applications). Usually, so-called *baseband signaling* is used to transmit a single digital signal over a single physical channel. In this type of signaling, information is transmitted through a change in a voltage or a current level rather than a change in the amplitude, phase, or frequency of a sine wave.

5.3.2. Levels of Subnetworks

The next issue to settle in evaluating or designing a communications facility for distributed control is whether a single network is sufficient for interconnecting all of the elements in the system, or whether multiple subnetworks are necessary; if the latter, then how *many* subnetworks are required? In this context, a *subnetwork* is defined to be a self-contained communication system that:

1. Has its own address structure (that is, a numbering system that uniquely identifies each drop on the subnetwork);
2. Allows communications among elements connected to it using a specific protocol (i.e., data interchange convention);
3. Allows communications between elements directly connected to it and elements in other subnetworks through an interface device that "translates" the message addresses and protocols of the two subnetworks.

Usually, there is a time penalty involved in communicating between subnetworks because the interface device mentioned in (3) adds a message delay greater than the time delay experienced within the subnetwork.

The decision to use subnetworks and if so, how to structure them for a particular application, depends on a number of factors, including:

1. The number and types of system elements to be connected;
2. The geographical distribution of the elements;
3. The communication traffic patterns generated by the elements.

For example, a data acquisition and control application in a small laboratory may involve only a few system elements located in the same geographical area. A single subnetwork may easily handle the amount of message traffic these elements generate. In this case, partitioning the communication system into multiple subnetworks would unnecessarily increase the cost and complexity of the system.

However, in a distributed control system application involving plantwide process control and data acquisition, this is usually not the situation. In this case, there are usually a large number of system elements that must be interconnected over a widespread geographical area. These elements often generate large volumes of message traffic; however, the traffic usually follows certain natural patterns of activity in the plant, such as:

1. Between controllers within a cabinet or in a given plant area;
2. Between high-level devices within the central control room and equipment room area;
3. Between the various plant areas and the central control room area.

In this situation, it often makes sense to partition the communication system into subnetworks that follow the natural patterns of message traffic, while providing a mechanism for the subnetworks to intercommunicate as needed.

Figure 5.5 shows one possible partitioning structure. In this case, several high-level operator interfaces and computing elements located in the central control room area must communicate with each other at moderate levels of message traffic. These elements must also be able to communicate with data acquisition and control elements located near the process units to be controlled. In this example, these latter elements are LCUs (e.g., single-loop controllers) that must communicate with each other at high rates within each process area. The natural communication system partitioning that results from these requirements has three levels:

1. A local bus or subnetwork in each cabinet allows the individual controllers to intercommunicate without interfering with message traffic in other cabinets;

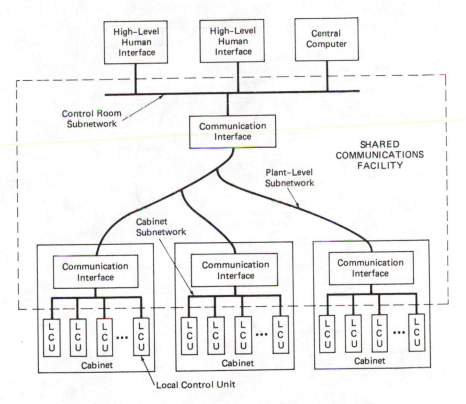

Figure 5.5. Communication System Partitioning—Example 1

2. A local subnetwork in the central control room area allows the high-level devices to intercommunicate;
3. A plantwide communication system interconnects the control room elements with the distributed elements in the process areas.

This partitioning may not be appropriate if the communication requirements and controller structure change, even slightly. For example, suppose that the required communication rates between the high-level elements increase significantly (e.g., to allow for rapid dumps of large databases from one element to another). Also, assume that larger, multiloop controllers are used instead of the single-loop controllers in the previous example. Figure 5.6 illustrates the communication system partitioning that may be appropriate in this case. It consists of the following elements:

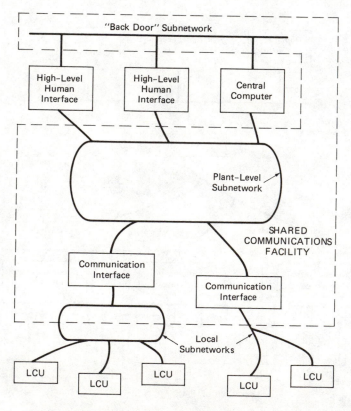

Figure 5.6. Communication System Partitioning—Example 2

1. A local subnetwork that allows the controllers in a given process area to intercommunicate;
2. A plantwide communication system that connects the high-level elements with the local subnetworks;
3. A "back door" subnetwork that allows rapid data transfers between high-level elements to take place without interfering with the process area traffic.

Subnetworks have advantages or disadvantages, depending on the situation. In general, providing multiple levels of subnetworks improves the flexibility of the communication system structure: only the lowest level of subnetwork (presumably the least expensive one) need be used in simple applications, while the higher levels can be added if needed. One can configure very large communication system structures with such a multilevel approach. On the other hand, the multilevel approach suffers from a number of potential disadvantages: (1) message delays through a large number of interfaces between subnetworks can be significant; (2) as more hardware is put in the communication chain between elements, the probability of a failure or error goes up; and (3) the addition of product types increases the complexity and maintenance problems in the system.

5.3.3. Network Topologies

Once the user or designer has established the necessary overall architecture of the communication system (including the use of subnetworks), the next step in the evaluation process is to select the topology of each subnetwork. *Topology* refers to the structure of the physical connections among the elements in a subnetwork.

Rose (5.14) and others (5.15–5.18) have analyzed a number of topologies that have been considered for use in a distributed control system. Figure 5.7 illustrates the most popular ones—star, bus, mesh, and ring configurations. In this figure, the outer six boxes in each diagram represent the system elements to be interconnected; the boxes within the dotted lines represent the devices that make up the communication subnetwork.

The *star topology* has the advantage of being the simplest (and therefore likely to be the least expensive) of the four. In this approach, a single "intelligent" switching device routes the messages from one system element to another. However, a failure of this device would cause the entire subnetwork to stop functioning. Adding a redundant switching device to improve reliability increases the complexity and cost of the star topology considerably. As a result, this approach is rarely used in commercial distributed control systems.

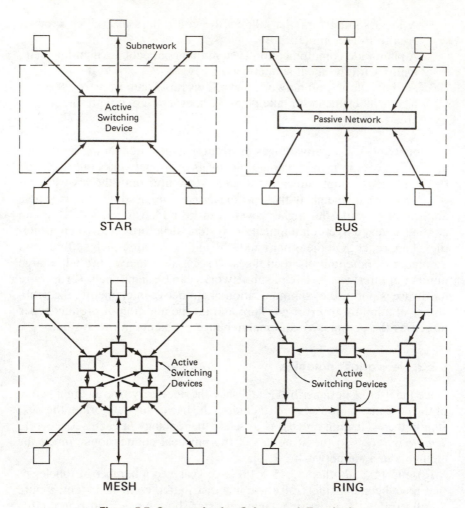

Figure 5.7. Communication Subnetwork Topologies

The *bus topology* is similar to the star topology in that all of the messages in the subnetwork must pass through a common piece of hardware. However, in this case the hardware is a passive network of connections instead of an active switching device. Each element that wishes to communicate over the network obtains control of it in turn (through mechanisms to be discussed later) and transmits its messages directly to the receiving elements. Since the network is passive, introducing redundant connections improves the reliability of this topology without overcomplicating the system. However, in the bus topology the system is vulnerable to a device failure that incapacitates the bus, keeping other devices from gaining control of the bus and communicating on it. For this reason, each device on the bus is designed to be failsafe to the maximum extent possible (i.e., to fail only in a mode that disconnects it from the bus).

The *mesh topology* attempts to overcome some of the disadvantages of the star topology by introducing multiple switching devices that provide redundancy in active hardware as well as alternative message pathways between communicating elements. This results in a very flexible communication structure that has been used successfully in applications requiring that level of security. However, this approach is complex and expensive; it also results in significant delays as each switching device stores and forwards the messages. As a result, industrial distributed control systems generally have not adapted this topology.

The *ring*, or *loop, topology* is a special case of the mesh topology that provides connections only between adjacent switching devices. To simplify the system further, messages usually are permitted to travel in only one direction around the ring from origin to destination. Since no message-routing decisions are necessary in this approach, the switching device can be very simple and inexpensive. For this reason, one can add a redundant ring to increase the reliability of the subnetwork without significantly increasing the cost or complexity of the system. The major potential failure mode in this topology is in a switching device, which would block message traffic around the ring. Therefore, redundant rings with automatic failsafe bypass capabilities usually are used to ensure that a single device failure does not cause a total loop breakdown.

Because of their relative cost-effectiveness and insensitivity to failures, the bus and the ring are the topologies most favored in commercially available distributed control systems. Often the total communication system uses more than one of these types among its various subnetworks.

5.4. PROTOCOL ISSUES

The previous section introduced the architectural concepts of network topologies and subnetworks. These are physical characteristics of communication systems that determine the pathways over which messages can travel. The operations that must take place to accomplish the safe and accurate routing of each message along these pathways from origin to destination also must be defined for a particular communication system. The rules or conventions that govern the transmission of data in the system are usually referred to as *protocols*. Selecting protocols is as critical as (or more critical than) selecting the physical architecture for determining the performance and security of the communication system. This section defines the types of protocols commonly used in distributed control systems and briefly describes several examples of the most popular protocols.

5.4.1. Protocol Reference Model

As implied above in the previous paragraph, many types of communication protocols have been developed over the years (see Refs. 5.19–5.21 for tutorial information on protocols). Some of these have been implemented in software or firmware in the communication processors; others have been standardized to the extent that they have been implemented in hardware (e.g., in special memory or communication processor chips).

To attempt to put some order into the discussion of these protocols, the International Standards Organization (ISO) has developed a reference model for protocols used in communication networks, formally named the Reference Model for Open Systems Interconnection (ISO/OSI). Here, *open* refers to communication systems that have provisions for interfacing to other nonproprietary systems using established interface standards. It will be helpful to refer to this model in the course of discussions in the following paragraphs, so a brief summary of the model follows. (See References 5.22 and 5.23 for more details.)

The ISO model categorizes the various protocols into seven "layers," each of which can be involved in transmitting a message from one system element to another using the communications facility. Suppose, for example, that one LCU in the system (call it LCU A) is executing a control algorithm that requires the current value of a process variable in another LCU (call it LCU B). In this situation, LCU A obtains that information from LCU B over the communication system. All seven layers of protocol may be involved during this process of message transmission and reception. Figure 5.8 illustrates this process. Each layer provides an orderly interface to the next higher layer, thus implementing a logical connection from LCU A down to the communication hardware and then back up to LCU B.

The various layers provide the following services (described in simplified form):

1. *Physical layer*—This layer defines the electrical and mechanical characteristics of the interface between the physical communication medium and the driver and receiver electronics. These characteristics include voltage levels, channel structure (parallel or serial transmission), and the signaling or modulation technique used by the hardware to transmit the data.

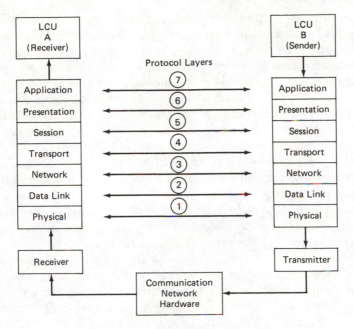

Figure 5.8. ISO Protocol Reference Model

2. *Data link layer*—The communication network hardware is shared among a number of system elements. One function of this layer is to determine which element has control of the hardware at any given time. The other function is to structure the transmission of messages from one element to another at the bit level; that is, this level defines the formatting of the bits and bytes in the message itself so that the arrangement makes sense to both the sender and the receiver. The level also defines the error detection and error correction techniques used and sets up the conventions for defining the start and stop of each message.

3. *Network layer*—Within a network having multiple pathways between elements, this protocol layer handles the routing of messages from one element to another. In a communication system consisting of multiple subnetworks, this layer handles the translation of addresses and routing of information from one subnetwork to another. If the communication system consists of a single subnetwork having only single pathways between elements, this layer is not required in the communication system protocol structure.

4. *Transport layer*—The transport layer is the mechanism in each com-

municating element ensuring that end-to-end message transmission has been accomplished properly. The services provided by the transport protocol layer include acknowledging messages, detecting end-to-end message errors and retransmitting the messages, prioritizing messages, and transferring messages to multiple receivers.

5. *Session layer*—This level of protocol schedules the starting and stopping of communication activity between two elements in the system. It may also specify the "quality" of transport service required if multiple levels of service are available.

6. *Presentation layer*—This layer translates the message formats in the communication system into the information formats required by the next higher layer, the application layer. The presentation layer allows the application layer to properly interpret the data sent over the communication system and, conversely, it puts the information to be transmitted into the proper message format.

7. *Application Layer*—This layer is not strictly part of the communication protocol structure; rather, it is the part of the application software or firmware that calls up the communication services at the lower layers. In a high level language program, it might be a statement such as READ/COM or INPUT/COM that requests information from another system element over the communications facility. In a function block logic structure, it would be an input block that requests a certain process variable to be read from another system element over the communications facility.

These definitions are somewhat abstract and difficult to appreciate fully without referring to concrete examples. The following paragraphs provide some of these examples, and they will illustrate the convenience of the ISO layer structure as a method of organizing a discussion of the functions of a communication system.

5.4.2. Physical Layer Protocols

The purpose of the physical layer is primarily to ensure that the communication system electronics for driver and receiver interface properly with the communication medium itself. Specifications at the physical layer might include:

1. Type of connector and number and functions of connector pins;
2. The method of encoding a digital signal on the communication medium (e.g., the voltage levels and pattern that defines a 1 or a 0 on

the signal wire or coaxial cable—see Reference 5.24 for a summary of the most common encoding schemes);

3. Definitions of hardware functions that deal with the control of access to the communication medium (such as defining handshaking control lines or detecting a busy signal line).

From the examples in this list, it is clear that defining communication system functions at the level of the physical layer is closely tied to selecting the communication medium (e.g., twisted pair wire, coaxial cable, or fiber optics) and the channel structure (e.g., serial or parallel transmission as discussed in the previous section).

A number of standard interface specifications have been developed at the level of the physical layer, including the following:

1. RS–232C—As described in References 5.25 and 5.26, this interface standard defines the electrical characteristics of the interface between a data terminal or computer and a 25-conductor communication cable. The standard covers allowable voltage levels, number of pins, and pin assignments of the connector. It also defines the maximum recommended transmission speed (19,200 bits/second) and distance (50 feet) for the type of voltage-based signaling approach specified. Reference 5.27 describes the speed–distance tradeoffs that can be made to extend the standard while adhering to the RS–232C specifications. The RS–232C standard was written primarily for a communication link having only a single transmitter and a single receiver.

2. RS–449—As described in References 5.28 and 5.29, this interface standard is similar in scope to RS–232C, but specifies a different method of voltage signaling using a "differential" or "balanced" voltage signaling technique. It references two other standards (RS–422A and RS–423) that provide specifics about the voltage driving and receiving approaches allowed. The signaling technique specified in the RS–449 standard is an improvement over RS–232C in several respects. It provides greater immunity to electrical noise, and it permits faster data transmission rates over longer distances (e.g., 250,000 bits/second over 1,000 feet). It also allows multiple receivers to be connected to the same communication link.

3. RS–485—As described in Reference 5.30, this standard goes beyond the RS–232C and RS–449 standards in that it includes the handshaking lines needed to support multiple transmitters and receivers on the same communication link (up to 32 transmitters and/or receiver stations per link). This structure allows multiple devices to intercom-

municate at a low cost and at speeds and distances on the same order of magnitude as the RS–449 standard.

It should be pointed out that *none* of the standards listed above is helpful in defining the formats or meanings of the messages transmitted across the serial communication link; only the higher layers of protocol perform this defining function (described below).

5.4.3. Data Link Layer Protocols

As stated in the definition above, the data link layer of protocol encompasses two functions: (1) controlling access to the shared communication medium and (2) structuring the format of messages in the network. This section describes the two functions and gives examples of their implementation.

Since a communication network (or subnetwork) consists of a single communication medium with many potential users, the data link protocol must provide the rules for arbitrating how the common hardware is used. There is a wide variety of approaches to implementing this function (see Reference 5.12, for example), some of which are used only with certain network topologies. Table 5.1 lists some of the more common network access protocols, along with their key characteristics. They are defined as follows:

1. *Time division multiplex access (TDMA)*—This approach is used in bus-type network topologies. A *bus master* transmits a time clock signal to each of the nodes in the network, each of which has a preassigned time slot during which it is allowed to transmit messages. In some implementations, the assignment of time slots is dynamic instead of static. While this is a simple approach, it does not allow nodes to get rapid access to the network, nor does it handle bursty message traffic (where the messages come in spurts, or bursts) very efficiently. Also, it requires the use of a bus master, which can be a single point of failure unless it is made redundant (which increases cost and complexity).
2. *Polling*—This approach can be used in either bus or ring networks. Like TDMA, it requires that a network "master" be used to implement the protocol. In this approach, the master polls each of the nodes in the network in sequence and asks it whether it has any messages to transmit. If the reply is affirmative, the node is granted access to the network for a fixed length of time. If not, the master moves on to the next node. Since time is not reserved for nodes that

Table 5.1. Network Access Protocols

NETWORK ACCESS PROTOCOL	NETWORK TYPE	ADVANTAGES	DISADVANTAGES
Time division/ multiplex access (TDMA)	Bus	• Simple structure	• Not very efficient for normal (bursty) message traffic • Redundant bus master required to maintain master clock
Polling	Bus or ring	• Simple structure • More efficient than TDMA • Deterministic allocation of access	• Redundant network master required • Slow access to the network
Token passing	Bus or ring	• Deterministic allocation of access • No master required • Can be used in large bus network topologies	• Must have recovery strategies for a dropped token
Carrier sense/ Multiple access with collision detection (CSMA/CD)	Bus	• No master required • Simple implementation • Stable performance at high message traffic levels	• Efficiency decreases in long-distance networks • Access time to network is probabilistic, not deterministic
Ring expansion	Ring	• No master required • Supports multiple simultaneous message transmissions	• Usable only on ring network

do not need to transmit, this protocol is more efficient than TDMA. However, it suffers from the same disadvantages as TDMA: slow access to the network and need for a redundant master for reliability. The polling approach has been used extensively in computer-based digital control systems and in certain proprietary distributed control systems.

3. *Token passing*—This method can be used in either bus or ring networks. In this protocol, a *token* is a special message that circulates from each node in the network to the next in a prescribed sequence. A node transmits a message containing information only when it has the token. An advantage of this approach over the previous protocols

is that it requires no network master. The access allocation method is predictable and deterministic, and it can be used in both large and small distributed networks. The main disadvantage of this approach is the potential danger that a token may get "dropped" (lost) or that two nodes may think they have the token at the same time. Reliable recovery strategies must be implemented to minimize the chance of these errors causing a problem in the network communication function. Token passing is one of the access protocols defined by the IEEE 802 local area network (LAN) standard (described in more detail in Section 5.6).

4. *Carrier sense/Multiple access with collision detection (CSMA/CD)—* This approach is used in bus networks. It is analogous to a party-line telephone network, in which a caller (in this case a node or device in the network) listens on the line until it is no longer busy. Then the device initiates the call (i.e., the message transmission), while listening at all times for any other device trying to use the line. If another device starts to send a message at the same time, both devices detect this and back off a random length of time before trying again. This approach has a number of advantages. It is simple and inexpensive to implement, it does not require a network master, and it provides nodes or devices with fast access to the network. Its efficiency decreases in geographically large networks, since the larger signal propagation times require a longer wait before the device is sure that no other device is trying to use the network. Also, it is not possible to define an absolute maximum time it can take to gain access to the network, since the access process is not as predictable as in other access protocols (the token-passing approach, for example). However, queuing analyses and simulations can provide excellent information on the behavior of a CSMA/CD network, so predicting its performance generally is not a problem (see Reference 5.32, for example). The CSMA/CD protocol is used in the Ethernet proprietary communication system, and is specified in the IEEE 802 local area network standard.

5. *Ring expansion—*This approach is applicable only to ring networks. In this technique, a node wishing to transmit a message monitors the message stream passing through it. When it detects a lull in the message traffic, it inserts its own message, while at the same time buffering (and later retransmitting) any incoming message. In effect, this method "expands" the ring by one message until the original message or an acknowledgment returns back to the original sender. This protocol is very useful in ring networks, since it does not require a network master; it also permits multiple nodes to transmit messages

simultaneously (thereby increasing the effective bandwidth of the communication system). This approach is used in the serial version of the CAMAC (computer-automated measurement and control) system and in certain proprietary communication networks.

Once the control of the communication medium has been established by one of the mechanisms just described, data can be sent from one node to another in the form of a sequence of bits. It is the data link layer of protocol that defines the format in which the bits are arranged to form an intelligible message. It also defines the details of the message transmission and reception operations (including error detection and correction). Most commercial communication systems used in distributed control implement this level using one of a number of protocols that have become standards in the communication industry. Some of the more popular ones are:

1. *BISYNC (binary synchronous communications protocol)*—Character-oriented protocol developed by International Business Machines (IBM).
2. *DDCMP (digital data communications message protocol)*—Character-oriented protocol developed by the Digital Equipment Corporation (DEC).
3. *SDLC (synchronous data link control)*—Bit-oriented protocol developed by IBM.
4. *HDLC (high-level data link control)*—Bit-oriented protocol standard defined by the Consultative Committee for International Telephony and Telegraphy (CCITT).
5. *ADCCP (advanced data communications control procedures)*—Bit-oriented protocol standard defined by the American National Standards Institute (ANSI).

The first two protocols are similar in that they define node-to-node messages on the basis of characters or *bytes* (eight-bit units of data). In contrast, the last three protocols are bit-oriented; that is, the messages are broken up into frames in which the individual message bits have significance. The second group of protocols has largely supplanted the first in current communication systems because of their superior performance and efficient use of the communication medium. The protocols defined in the second group also have been implemented in off-the-shelf chips available from the semiconductor manufacturers, thus simplifying their usage in commercial control systems. References 5.8, 5.9, 5.11, and 5.31 discuss the characteristics and relative merits of these protocols in detail.

5.4.4. Network Layer Protocols

The network layer of protocol handles the details of message routing in communication networks with multiple source-to-destination routes (for example, the ARPANET packet-switching network). The network layer protocol also implements any address translations required in transmitting a message from one subnetwork to another within the same overall communication network. As References 5.9 and 5.29 describe, certain standard protocols (such as CCIT X.25) have emerged to support networking in communication systems. However, due to their cost and complexity, networks allowing alternative routings (such as the mesh topology shown in Figure 5.7) are rare in industrial control systems. Bus and ring topologies with redundant links between nodes are common; however, this type of redundancy generally does not include any options on message routing within the network. It is used only to allow the communication system to continue operating if a cable breaks or a failure disables one of the primary links.

Because of this, most industrial systems need a network layer of protocol primarily to manage the interfaces between subnetworks. The subnetwork interface protocol is usually specific to the particular vendor's proprietary communication system. Industrial systems also need the network layer to implement *gateways,* which are interfaces between the proprietary system and external communication links. The network layer accomplishes this by translating the proprietary message structure into one that conforms to one of the lower-level protocol standards described earlier (e.g., RS–232C or SDLC).

5.4.5. Transport and Session Layer Protocols

In communication systems designed for industrial control, the transport and session layers are often combined for simplicity. These protocols define the method for initiating data transfer, the messages required to accomplish the transfer, and the method for concluding the transfer.

In a distributed control system, each node or element in the system is *intelligent* (i.e., has a microprocessor and acts independently) and performs a particular function in the overall system context. To perform this function, each node requires input information, some of which is generated within the node and the rest obtained from other nodes in the system. One can view the shared communications facility as the mechanism that updates the database in each node with the required information from the other nodes. The updating process is carried out at the level of the session and transport layers of protocol. In industrial control systems, one of the following three methods is used most often to accomplish this updating:

1. *Polling*—The node requiring the information periodically polls the other nodes, usually at a rate consistent with the expected rate of change of the variables in question. The exchange takes place on a request-response basis, with the returned data providing acknowledgment that the polled node received the request and understood it properly.
2. *Broadcasting*—In this approach, the node containing the desired information broadcasts this information to all other nodes in the system, whether the other nodes have requested it or not. In some systems, the receivers acknowledge these broadcast messages; in others, they do not.
3. *Exception reporting*—In this approach, the node containing a particular item of information maintains a "subscriber's list" of the nodes needing that information. When that information *changes* by a specified amount, the subscribers are furnished with the updated value. Usually, the receiving nodes acknowledge this update.

Reference 5.33 describes in detail the characteristics and relative performance of these three implementations of the transport-session layer of protocol. The polling approach is the protocol most commonly used in distributed control systems, particularly those employing computers or network masters to run the communication network. However, this approach is relatively inefficient in its use of communication system bandwidth, since it uses many of the request-response messages to update unchanging information. Also, it responds slowly to changing data. The broadcast method is better in both regards, especially if a pure broadcast approach is used without acknowledgment of updates. However, this latter approach suffers from a potential problem in data security, since the data sender has no assurance that the data user received the update correctly. The exception-reporting technique has proved to be very responsive and efficient in initiating data transfers in distributed control systems (see Reference 5.15). Often a pure exception-reporting approach is augmented with other rules to ensure that:

1. Exception reports on the same point are not generated more often than necessary, which would tend to flood the network with redundant data;
2. At least one exception report on each point is generated within a

selected time interval, even if the point has not changed beyond the exception band. This ensures that the users of that information have available to them a current value of the point.

5.4.6 Higher-Level Protocols

The higher levels of protocols in the ISO model, the presentation and application layers, perform the housekeeping operations required to interface the lower-level protocols with the users of the shared communications facility. Therefore, it is usually not necessary for the user to consider these protocols as separate from the distributed control functions performed through the communication system. (Section 5.2 gave a partial list of these functions.)

One system feature that the higher levels of protocols could implement is to differentiate between *classes* of messages and designate their corresponding priorities in the communication system. For example, a designer may choose to subdivide the types of messages to be transmitted over the shared communications facility into the following priority levels:

1. Messages performing time synchronization functions;
2. Process trip signals and safety permissives;
3. Process variable alarms;
4. Operator set-point and mode change commands;
5. Process variable transmissions;
6. Configuration and tuning commands;
7. Logging and long-term data storage information.

Given this priority scheme, the higher layer of protocols could be used to sort out these messages and to feed the highest priority messages to the lower protocol levels first. While this would appear to be a desirable goal, the complexities and costs involved in implementing such a priority technique in practice are formidable. To date, the suppliers of commercially available distributed control systems have not incorporated a priority message structure in their communication systems. Rather, they have depended on keeping the message traffic in their systems low enough compared to capacity so that messages at all priority levels can get through without undue delays.

5.5. OTHER ISSUES IN EVALUATING COMMUNICATION SYSTEMS

The previous two sections discussed issues dealing with communication system architectures and network protocols. This section reviews a number of other issues to consider in evaluating a communication system. Most are relatively independent of architecture and protocol issues; where there is an interrelationship, it will be identified.

5.5.1. Selecting a Communication Medium

One basic decision to make in evaluating a communication system approach is selecting the physical medium used in conveying information through the system. There are many factors to take into account when choosing the best medium for a particular application, including speed and distance of data transmission, topology of the network, and target costs. While there are many options, the media most often selected for use in industrial control systems are the following:

1. *Twisted pair cable*—A twisted pair of wires usually surrounded by an external shield to minimize noise susceptibility and a rugged jacket for protection against the environment.
2. *Coaxial cable*—An inner metal conductor surrounded by insulation and a rigid or semirigid outer conductor, enclosed in a protective jacket.
3. *Fiber optic cable*—An inner core surrounded by an outer cladding, both layers constructed of glass or plastic material. Fiber optic cables conduct light waves instead of electrical signals. The cable usually includes an internal mechanical member to increase pulling strength, and all elements are encased in a rugged jacket.

Selected industrial applications have employed the technique of transmitting information through free space using infrared light or radio frequencies, but this approach has not been very widespread for a variety of reasons (including problems of cost, security, and noise).

Table 5.2 summarizes the major differences in characteristics of twisted pair cable, coaxial cable, and fiber optic cable, and Figure 5.9 compares typical transmission speed and distance capabilities of the three media.

Cables using a shielded twisted pair of conductors as the communication medium have been used for many years in industrial applications to convey analog signal information and point-to-point digital information. These cables, and their associated connectors and supporting electronics, are low in cost and have multiple sources due to standardization efforts that have taken place over the years. They are easy to install and maintain, and service people can handle and repair them with minimum special training. Twisted pair cable is used most often to implement ring architecture networks, especially the high-speed, long-distance networks characteristic of plant-wide communication systems. These cables are quite suitable for use in rugged environments, particularly if they are built to high-quality

Table 5.2 Characteristics of Communication Media

MEDIUM FEATURE	TWISTED PAIR CABLE	COAXIAL CABLE	FIBER OPTIC CABLE
Relative cost of cable	Low	Higher than twisted pair	Multimode fiber cable comparable with twisted pair
Cost of connectors and supporting electronics	Low due to standardization	Low due to CATV standardization	Relatively high—offset by high performance
Noise immunity	Good if external shield used	Very good	Excellent—not susceptible to and does not generate electromagnetic interference
Standardization of components	High—with multiple sources	Promoted by CATV influences	Very little standardization or second sourcing
Ease of installation	Simple due to two-wire connection	Can be complicated when rigid cable type is used	Simple because of light weight and small size
Field repair	Requires simple solder repair only	Requires special splice fixture	Requires special skills and fixturing
Network types supported	Primarily ring networks	Either bus or ring networks	Almost solely ring networks
Suitability for rugged environments	Good, with reasonable cable construction	Good, but must protect aluminum conductor from water or corrosive environment	Excellent—can survive high temperatures and other extreme environments

standards. As Figure 5.9 shows, point-to-point links using twisted pair cable generally do not operate at transmission speeds over five megabits per second at distances over a few kilometers. Of course, decreasing the distance between nodes in the system allows messages to be sent at higher transmission speeds.

Widespread use of coaxial cable in cable television (CATV) networks has led to a standardization of components and corresponding reduction in costs. As a result, coaxial cable has become quite prevalent in industrial communications systems. If applied properly, this type of medium has a number of advantages over twisted pair cable. First, it can implement a bus network (as well as a ring network) as long as the system uses the appropriate "tee" connectors and bus termination components. Also, it has an advantage in the area of noise immunity, resulting in a potential increase in communication system performance. As Figure 5.9 shows, a communication system using coaxial cable is capable of operating at speeds and distances greater than twisted pair-based systems by a factor of 10 or more. However, more complex and expensive electronics are needed to achieve this higher potential level of performance. As a result, most coaxial-based industrial systems operate at points on the speed-distance graph that are well within the maximum performance limits (i.e., closer to the limits for twisted pair cable). This approach results in communication system costs that are not much higher than those for twisted pair-based systems.

In the area of installation and repair, coaxial cable is somewhat more difficult to handle than twisted pair cable. One type of coaxial cable (broadband cable) has a rigid outer conductor that makes it difficult to install in cable trays or conduit. Coaxial cable requires special connectors, whereas a simple two-wire lug connection is possible with twisted pair cable. Field repair of coaxial cable is more complicated, requiring special fixturing tools and splicing components to perform the operation. Coaxial cable whose outer conductor is made of aluminum requires special care to protect it from water or corrosive elements in underground installations.

The state of the art of fiber optic cable and connector technology has advanced significantly during the 1980s in the areas of performance im-

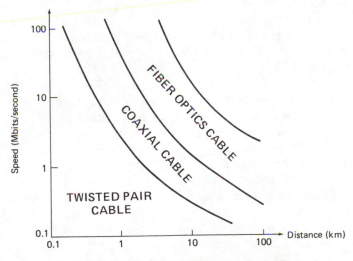

Figure 5.9. Typical Speed-Distance Tradeoffs

provements, standardization of components, and ease of field installation and repair (see References 5.34–5.39). As Figure 5.9 indicates, there is no question that the potential performance of fiber optic communication systems far exceeds that of systems based on coaxial or twisted pair cable. This is primarily due to the fact that fiber optics is not susceptible to the electromagnetic interference and electrical losses that limit the performance of the other two approaches. As in the case of coaxial cable, however, current industrial communication systems employing fiber optics operate well within the possible outside limits of the speed-distance range to keep the costs of the drivers and receivers relatively low and compatible with other elements in the distributed control system. Some systems use fiber optic cable only in selected portions of the total network to take advantage of its high immunity to electrical noise.

Despite recent progress, there still are a number of significant issues to consider when evaluating fiber optic technology for use in industrial applications. First, at its current stage of development, only ring networks can use this medium effectively. (See Reference 5.40.) While short-distance fiber optic bus systems have been implemented and run in specialized situations, cost-effective and reliable industrial-grade bus systems are still being perfected. This is primarily due to the fact that a fiber optic bus system requires the use of special components (light splitters, couplers, and switches) that are still evolving and that require careful selection and installation to be effective. (See References 5.35, 5.38, and 5.42 for additional information in this area.) This development is proceeding rapidly, however, and it is likely that long-distance fiber optic bus systems will emerge eventually.

Another obstacle to the widespread use of this technology is the slow development of standards for fiber optic cables and connectors. At present, the technology is developing much more rapidly than the standardization of its components. The Electronic Industries Association has produced a generic specification for fiber optic connectors (RS–475, see Reference 5.41). While this and related documents on nomenclature and testing are helpful, a standard that would promote second-sourcing and mixed use of cables, connectors, and other components from more than one vendor does not yet exist. As a result, the costs of these components are still relatively high compared to the costs of components used in twisted pair or coaxial systems (although the cost of the fiber optic cable itself is becoming comparable to that of electrical cable in low- or medium-speed applications).

The desirability of fiber optics from the point of view of field installation and repair is still mixed. Because of its light weight and small size, one can easily install fiber optic cable in conduit or cable trays. Since it is immune to electromagnetic interference and cannot conduct electrical energy, it can be run near power wiring and in hazardous plant areas without any special precautions. Fiber optic cable also provides electrical isolation from ground, thus eliminating concerns about ground loops during installation. Recent developments in materials and packaging have made fiber optic cable very suitable for use in high-temperature and other rugged environments. However, although the field repair of fiber optic cable is possible, it requires special fixturing and trained personnel to be accomplished reliably on a routine basis. Also, cost-effective field equipment suitable for locating cable breaks and connector failures is still under development. As in other problem areas, that of field repair is expected to improve dramatically as fiber optic technology matures.

5.5.2. Message Security

As stated in the beginning of the chapter, the communication facility in a distributed control system is shared among many system elements, instead of being dedicated as in the case of an analog control system. As a result, the security of message transmission is a key issue in evaluating alternative communication techniques. There is always a concern that component failures or electrical noise will cut off or degrade the accuracy of information flowing from one system element to another. Section 5.3 noted that one way to avoid a cutoff of information flow is to ensure that the architecture of the communication system does not include any potential single points of failure.

However, additional safeguards are necessary to minimize the chance that message errors due to electrical noise will propagate through the system without detection. Many commercial distributed control systems provide four levels of protection:

1. Handshaking (i.e., acknowledgment of message receipt) between system elements involved in the transfer of information. This ensures that the information has arrived safely. Handshaking is used especially in transmitting critical information such as control system variables.
2. Ability to detect the vast majority of errors in messages caused by external noise.
3. Provision of message retransmission or some other scheme that allows an orderly recovery if a message is lost or contains an error.
4. Inclusion of "reasonableness checks" in the application layer of network protocol to catch any message errors not detected in the lower layers.

This section will discuss these levels in more detail.

The first level of security (handshaking) occurs automatically if the session and transport layers of network protocol use the polling or exception-reporting protocols (Section 5.4). In the polling approach, the node sending a message requesting information is automatically notified that the request arrived safely when it receives the requested information back from the other nodes. If the information is not received, the polling node assumes that an error has occurred and asks for it again. In the exception-reporting approach, the report message usually is followed by an acknowledgment message from the receiving node that informs the sender that it received the information properly. If the broadcast approach is used, a separate mechanism for validating the transfer of information needs to be included to ensure that errors were not introduced in the broadcast messages. For example, this mechanism can consist of a separate set of acknowledgment messages sent by the receiving nodes.

One can best understand the second and third levels of message security by reviewing a typical error handling process, as illustrated in Figure 5.10. In any distributed system, there is a base load of messages that the nodes generate for transmission to other nodes using the shared communications facility. The transmission mechanisms in the nodes handle these messages and send them through the transmission medium. In the process of transmission, the noise environment corrupts some portion of these messages. At the receiving end, an error detection mechanism decides whether each incoming message is *good* (error-free) or *bad* (contains an error). If a message is determined to be bad, the receiving node makes the sending node aware of the error through the acknowledgment process previously described, and the sending node then retransmits the message. As a result, the total message traffic in the communication facility is the sum of the normal message traffic and the retransmitted message traffic. In this scheme, an increase in noise from the environment causes a corresponding increase in total message traffic; however, the error detection mechanism

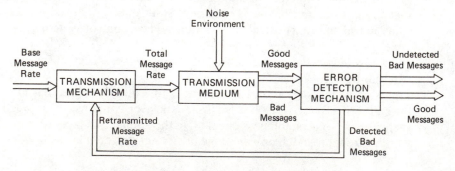

Figure 5.10. Error Handling Process

maintains message security. If this mechanism were perfect, there would be no undetected bad messages received. In practice, however, the mechanism can never be perfect, and a certain number of bad messages get through.

One can see from Figure 5.10 that the error rate of undetected bad messages is a function of the external noise environment, the characteristics of the transmission medium (type of cable, connectors, and driver and receiver electronics), and the effectiveness of the error detection mechanism. Usually, the error detection mechanism is implemented at the data link layer of network protocol by means of *cyclic redundancy check* (CRC) codes built into the message formats (see References 5.9 and 5.43 for detailed descriptions). The CRC code is inserted into the message at the source and checked at the destination for consistency with the transmitted information. In most industrial communication systems, these codes are designed to produce an undetected error rate of less than one bad message per 100 years of operation under an assumed noise environment. (Of course, the error rate in any particular installation is a function of the actual, not the assumed, noise environment that exists.)

To pick up any errors that get through the data link layer of protection, most industrial control systems perform checks on the reasonableness of data acquired over a shared communications facility. For example, if an analog input is outside the expected range or changes faster than is physically possible, then the application logic making use of the input marks the input "bad" and takes appropriate action. In the case of a process variable input to a control loop, this action may consist of putting the loop into manual mode. If the input is used in a calculation, the application logic may substitute a default value or ask the operator to enter a value manually.

5.5.3. Efficiency of Bandwidth Usage

One often-used measure of the performance of a communications facility is the raw bit rate of data transmission between nodes. By this measure, a communication system that uses a 2 Mbit/sec. data rate is assumed to carry twice as much information as one running at 1 Mbit/sec. Unfortunately, the situation is not quite that simple. The efficiency of usage of the information bandwidth provided by 1 Mbit/sec. data links (for example) varies dramatically from one system to another. Some of the factors that can have an impact on this efficiency include the following:

1. *Topology of the communication network*—In ring networks, multiple messages can travel on the ring simultaneously if certain physical

layer network protocols are used. As a result, this type of network can support more message transfers per second than a bus network having the same raw bit transmission rate.

2. *Message formats*—A communication system that supports variable-length message formats can tailor the message size to the type of information to be sent (e.g., an analog input data message would be longer than a message reporting contact status). Therefore, a system with variable-length messages is more efficient than one in which the message length is fixed at the maximum, worst-case size.

3. *Repertoire of message types*—A communication system that supports "packed" messages (e.g., contact status information in groups of eight contacts at a time) is more efficient than a system requiring one message per variable. Similarly, systems that can send a single message to multiple destinations are more efficient than those requiring a separate message for each destination.

4. *Transport and session layer protocol used*—As pointed out previously, the exception-reporting protocol is much more efficient than the polling or broadcast protocols, since the exception protocol initiates messages only when information is changing. One can consider transport layer protocols requiring acknowledgment of messages to be less efficient than those that do not; however, the use of acknowledgments significantly increases message security.

5. *Retransmission rate due to message errors*—If the data rate selected is too high for the noise environment, the transmission medium, or both, there will be a high rate of detected message errors. The resulting load of data retransmission messages can have a significant impact on the true information throughput rate of the system.

It is not possible in this space to discuss all of the factors that can affect the efficiency of bandwidth usage in a shared communications facility. However, the user or designer of such a facility must be aware of these factors and evaluate the alternative communication system approaches with them in mind.

5.6. COMMUNICATION SYSTEM STANDARDS

Since the late 1960s and early 1970s, the industrial controls marketplace has seen a growing flood of products and systems that make use of digital communications, either on a device-to-device basis or as part of a shared network. The introduction and growth of distributed control systems in the late 1970s only augmented that trend. Unfortunately from the user's point of view, very few of the products from different vendors use compatible communication techniques that would allow the products to "talk" to each other without significant modification or special engineering. In many cases, even different product families from the same vendor have trouble "carrying on a conversation." This is a significant problem for the user, who often must either buy from a single vendor, letting the vendor assume the responsibility of interfacing all the system elements, or pay an outside systems house to do the integration. (See Reference 5.44 for a discussion of these problems.)

One solution to this problem would be a universal communication system interface standard, which all devices used in distributed control systems would follow. This would provide significant benefits to the user of such a system. The user would be able to buy a distributed control system adhering to that standard and know that he or she could expand or enhance the system with hardware from the same or even other vendors. The user would not be locked in to buying the enhancements from the original vendor. In addition, a user could assemble multiple vendors' hardware into a total system with a minimum amount of effort and without outside assistance. (See Reference 5.45 for an excellent discussion on the role of standards in improving productivity.)

While the user would find this situation desirable, no such universal communication standard for industrial control systems exists today. One obstacle to establishing a standard is the current rapid pace at which technology in the digital communication system field is developing. To allow true interchangeability of system elements, the standard must specify the communication medium, topology, and protocols to a significant level of detail. If this is done, however, there is a risk that the resulting standard will rapidly become technically obsolete. One example of this is the portion of the CAMAC standard that originally specified an 86-line unidirectional bus structure, which reflected the limitations of digital hardware in the early 1970s. This structure could be simplified significantly and reduced in cost without any loss in function if it took advantage of more recent developments in digital system hardware.

Another obstacle to establishing standards is the fragmentation of the industrial control marketplace, among both vendors and users. Despite widespread impressions to the contrary, most standards are *not* developed by dedicated volunteer committees that produce a standard after months or years of hard work and compromise. Standards develop in one of two ways: (1) when a dominant user demands that the vendors supply products to meet the user's specifications (e.g., General Motors demanding a programmable controller, or the Department of Defense requiring the use of the Ada programming language); or (2) when a dominant vendor puts out a successful product that then becomes a de facto standard in the industry (e.g., the IBM Personal Computer). In the industrial control field, however, there is no dominant user or vendor organization that can force the adoption of such standards. As a result, the standards now in use in industrial control are usually "piggybacked" onto those adopted in other industries.

The communication standards that have achieved the most widespread use are those that are restricted to a single level in the ISO/OSI protocol model. A number of these standards already have been described briefly in Section 5.4 (e.g., the RS–232C and RS–449 interface standards, the Ethernet bus access standard, the SDLC and HDLC data link protocol standards, and the CCIT X.25 network layer standard). The movement towards standardization at the higher levels of protocol is much slower, as References 5.46–5.48 point out.

Over the years, there have been several efforts to define communication system standards that cover an entire distributed system network or at least the communication medium and the first few levels of protocol. The standards of this type that have had the most impact on the field of industrial process control are the following:

1. *CAMAC (computer-automated measurement and control)*—Instrumentation interface standard originally developed by users in the European nuclear physics community.
2. *IEEE 488 Bus*—A bus standard originally developed by Hewlett-Packard for laboratory instrumentation.
3. *PROWAY (PROcess data highWAY)*—A data highway network standard for industrial control systems developed under the auspices of the International Purdue Workshop on Industrial Computer Systems.
4. *IEEE 802 Network*—The dominant local area network (LAN) standard for office and light industrial use.

Another standardization effort that deserves mention is the work being done by the manufacturing automation protocol (MAP) task force at General Motors (GM). The objective of this effort is to establish a unified communication standard that covers all seven levels of the ISO/OSI model. This standard would then be used inside GM for procuring manufacturing automation equipment from multiple vendors. Due to the dominant position of GM in the marketplace, however, this standard may well become influential in the manufacturing automation and industrial controls community outside of GM. To date, the task force has decided on standards at several of the lower layers of the ISO/OSI model, most of which are based on selected portions of the IEEE 802 specifications mentioned in the previous list. Selecting standards for the higher layers and developing and demonstrating hardware conforming to the MAP specification are activities that will continue through the 1980s. (See References 5.49 and 5.50 for additional information on MAP.)

While the MAP standard is still under development, the other four standardization efforts listed previously have been completed and are now influencing the design of industrial control systems. Therefore, the rest of this chapter will concentrate on the key features of the CAMAC, IEEE 488, PROWAY, and IEEE 802 standards. (References 5.51–5.60 provide additional information on each of these standards.)

5.6.1. CAMAC Standard

The CAMAC standard was developed in the late 1960s and early 1970s to solve the problem of interfacing various instruments to computers in high-energy nuclear physics laboratories. The standard originated through the efforts of the ESONE (European Standards Organization for Nuclear Electronics) committee in 1969 and was adopted in 1975 as a set of IEEE standards (583, 595, and 596).

The scope of CAMAC goes beyond defining the communications interfaces between various devices. It includes firm specifications on the size and shape of the electronic modules and the racks that hold them, on the mechanical and electrical interfaces, on the signal and data formats, and on the cabling and connectors. This level of detail in the standard provides a significant benefit to the user: modules from different manufacturers that conform to the CAMAC standard really *can* be used interchangeably in a system.

The IEEE 583 portion of the CAMAC standards covers the configuration of the modules, the specifications on the "crates" or mounting racks, and the rules of operating the 86-pin data bus on the backplane of each crate. The IEEE 595 and 596 documents specify the operation of the serial and parallel communications options available to link the crates to the computer. As Table 5.3 shows, each option has its own limitations on the length of the communication system, speed of data transfer, and maximum number of crates that can be included in the system (or equivalently, the maximum number of drops on the highway). A central computer, a communication driver, or both *must* be included in the system to control the access of devices to the network and all data transfers in the system. In the CAMAC communication structure, all of the layers of the ISO/OSI reference model are specified except for the highest two: the presentation and application layers.

While a few industrial firms have used CAMAC in specific applications (ALCOA being the most active at one time), this standard has not found

Table 5.3. Communication System Standards

FEATURE \ NETWORK	CAMAC		IEEE 488	PROWAY	IEEE 802		
	IEEE 595	IEEE 596			802.3	802.4	802.5
Year started	1971		1974	1975		1980	
Architecture	Serial ring	Parallel bus	Byte-serial bus	Serial bus	Serial bus	Serial bus	Serial bus
Distance constraints	Depends on data rate	300 ft.	20 m.	2000 m.	2500 m. total bus	2500 m. total bus	2500 m. node to node
Maximum rate of data transfer	5 Mbits/sec.	24 Mbits/sec.	250 Kybte/sec. to 1 Mbyte/sec.	1 Mbit/sec.	10 Mbits/sec.	1–20 Mbits/sec.	1.4–40 Mbits/sec.
Access protocol	Centralized polling (computer-controlled)		Centralized polling	Token passing	CSMA/CD	Token passing	Token passing
Transmission medium	Coaxial cable	Multipair cable	Multiconductor cable	Broadband coaxial cable	coaxial cable	coaxial cable	Coaxial cable or fiber optics
Conductors in bus or cable	2	132	16	2	2	2	2
Maximum number of drops	62	7	15	100	1,000	256	256
Original application	Nuclear physics instrumentation		Lab instrumentation	Industrial controls	Local area networks		
Major industrial sponsors	ALCOA		Hewlett-Packard	None	Xerox, DEC, and Intel	CDC and Datapoint	IBM and Modicon

a widespread following in the industrial process control community. No major user group has required it as a condition of purchase, and the major vendors have viewed CAMAC's level of detail as too confining for a technology changing so rapidly. In addition, a number of technical features in the standard make it unsuitable for industrial control applications. For example, it does not support direct communications between crates without going through the communication driver, which makes this driver a potential single point of failure for the network. Also, the methods used to provide redundancy in the communication links are awkward and appear to be an afterthought to the basic system structure.

5.6.2. IEEE 488 Standard

This standard was first developed by Hewlett-Packard to allow easy connection between a computer and laboratory instrumentation (e.g., meters, counters, signal generators) and other peripherals (e.g., printers and plotters). The basic system configuration was first published as an IEEE standard in 1975 and later revised in 1978. It was originally known as the HP-IB (Hewlett-Packard interface bus) and later as the GPIB (general-purpose interface bus).

As shown in Table 5.3, the IEEE 488 standard calls for a *byte-serial bus:* devices transfer information to one another over an eight-bit parallel bus with the help of eight additional lines for bus management and control. In its basic form, there is a distance limitation of 20 meters on the bus and a speed limitation of from 250 Kbyte/sec. to 1 Mbyte/sec., depending on distance. The standard covers the physical and data link layers of the ISO/OSI structure; the network layer is not required. In the basic IEEE 488 configuration, a bus controller (such as a computer) controls device access to the communication medium and implements the transport and session layers of protocol. The higher levels of protocol are dependent on the characteristics of the specific devices connected to the bus.

This network is intended for use in low-noise environments and has little in the way of error detection or other security features in its basic structure. Because of this, the limited length of the bus, and the small number of devices supported, the IEEE 488 bus has not been used to any great extent in industrial process control applications. However, a number of distributed control systems have been designed to interface with the IEEE 488 bus to allow use of laboratory instrumentation data in the rest of the distributed control system. Interfacing to the bus is not a difficult task, since integrated circuit chips that implement the bus protocol have been available for a long time. A number of vendors have provided extensions to the basic bus capabilities, including: (1) repeater hardware that increases the allowed length of the bus; (2) a token-passing mechanism to allow true networking of multiple devices on the bus; and (3) interfaces to standard computer buses to simplify networking of computers on the bus.

5.6.3. PROWAY Standard

This standard had its origins in the early 1970s at meetings of the International Purdue Workshop on Industrial Computer Systems. Work on the standard began officially in 1975 in a subcommittee of the International Electrotechnical Commission. Of the four communication network standards discussed in Section 5.6, only PROWAY was conceived from the beginning with the specific needs of the industrial control application in mind. The main characteristic that differentiates this standard from others is its concentration on high data integrity and high availability of the communication system. The targeted undetected error rate for PROWAY is less than one undetected error in every 1,000 years, as compared to a target in the IEEE 802 system of one undetected error per year.

The architecture selected for PROWAY is a serial bus structure having a maximum distance of 2,000 meters, a speed of 1 Mbit/sec., and a token-passing media access form of protocol. Because of the similarities between the PROWAY bus and the IEEE 802 token bus, the PROWAY standardization committee coordinated closely their efforts with those of the IEEE 802 committee. In fact, the PROWAY committee contributed Appendix B to the 802.4 section of the IEEE standard to define the areas in which the 802.4 standard should be enhanced to meet the security needs of industrial control applications. The result of this cooperative effort is that the industrial control community can take advantage of the 802-oriented integrated circuit chips that are being produced to meet the needs of the larger local area network marketplace.

5.6.4. IEEE 802 Standard

The growth of intelligent devices such as word processors, desktop computers, and associated peripherals (e.g., printers, plotters, and mass storage media) in offices and other light industrial environments has generated a need for associated communication systems that allow the devices to share data. These systems have become known as *local area networks* (LANs), which are characterized by medium to high communication speeds, limited geographical distribution, and low error rate operation in a relatively benign noise environment. (See References 5.16 or 5.60 for a complete definition of LANs.) In 1980, the IEEE Local Network Standards Committee was formed to develop hardware and protocol standards that would guide the future designs of LANs. To maximize the impact of its work by achieving results in a short time, the committee limited the scope of its efforts to the lowest two layers of the ISO/OSI protocol reference model: the physical and the data link layers. The major results of the committee's work are as follows:

1. At the physical layer, the committee defined the specifications on a "media access unit," which is the device used to generate the signal transmitted on the communications medium. This definition permits the use of several types of physical communication media: coaxial cable, twisted pair wire, fiber optics, and others. This concept allowed the choice of media to become independent of the choice of higher level protocols.
2. Recognizing that different applications might require variations in network topologies and media access protocols, the committee incorporated three network configurations into the standard.
3. The committee selected the HDLC (high-level data link control) format, with some modifications, to be the standard data link protocol for all 802 networks.

Table 5.3 summarizes the characteristics of the three selected network configurations. The configurations are labeled 802.3, 802.4, and 802.5 in accordance with the number of the corresponding section of the 802 standard. The 802.3 configuration is a CSMA/CD bus network that was derived from the Ethernet system developed and sponsored by Xerox, Intel, and Digital Equipment Corporation. The 802.4 configuration is a token-passing bus network, while the 802.5 standard describes a token-passing ring network. The protocols for all three of these configurations have been incorporated into integrated circuit chips, so the standards can be implemented in a very cost-effective manner. The implementation in silicon ensures that the 802 standard will be adopted widely.

It should be pointed out that the 802 standard was not originally intended for use in high-noise, high-security industrial control applications. However, as mentioned in the previous section, the PROWAY committee adopted the 802.4 version of the standard as being most suitable for the industrial control application. This committee identified several modifications to the 802.4 standard that would increase the security and noise immunity of the token-passing bus system and make it acceptable for industrial use. An appendix to the 802 standard describes these modifications.

The development of the IEEE 802 standard represents a significant step in controlling the proliferation of local area network types. However, the user should be cautioned that the variety of options in topologies, access methods, bit rates, and encoding techniques permitted within the 802 structure makes the standard less than perfect. A communication device that carries the label "conforms to IEEE 802" does not necessarily interface directly with another device carrying the same label.

This concludes the discussion on the communications facilities that support the transfer of information from one element to another within the distributed control system. The next two chapters focus on communications of a different type—those that support the transfer of information between man (i.e., operators and plant engineers) and machine (i.e., the distributed control system).

REFERENCES

Background and Tutorials

5.1 Erickson, I.L., "Centralized vs. Distributed Process Control," Instrument Society of America International Conference, Houston, Texas, October 1980.

5.2 Damsker, D.J., "Control and Communication Systems for Power Plants," *Power Engineering,* vol. 82, no. 1, January 1978, pp. 58–61.

5.3 Linn, E.Y., Schoeffler, J.D., and Rose, C.W., "Distributed Microcomputer Data Acquisition," *Instrumentation Technology,* vol. 22, no. 1, January 1975, pp. 55–61.

5.4 Kinginger, J.H., et al., "Study of Remote Multiplexing for Power Plant Applications," *ISA Transactions,* vol. 18, no. 2, 1979, pp. 3–20.

5.5 Keyes, M.A., "Distributed Control—Relevance and Ramification for Utility and Process Applications," *International Telemetering Conference Proceedings,* Los Angeles, September 1976; pub. by International Foundation of Telemetering, Woodland Hills, Calif., 1976, pp. 692–704.

5.6 Zahr, K.M. and Summers, W.A., "Microprocessor-based Multiplexing . . . an Engineering and Cost Analysis," *Instrumentation Technology,* vol. 25, no. 4, April 1978, pp. 47–51.

5.7 Laduzinsky, A.J., "Microprocessor-based Terminals Provide Masterless Distributed Control," *Control Engineering,* vol. 29, no. 4, April 1982, pp. 102–104.

5.8 Sherman, K., *Data Communications: A Users Guide,* Reston Publishing Company, Reston, Va., 1981.

5.9 Davies, D.W., et al., *Computer Networks and Their Protocols,* John Wiley & Sons, Chichester, UK, 1979.

5.10 Gooze, M., and Nelson, G., "What Do You Have to Know About Serial Data Communication," *InTech,* vol. 28, no. 6, June 1981, pp. 65–68.

5.11 Goldberger, A., "A Designer's Review of Data Communications," *Computer Design,* vol. 20, no. 5, May 1981, pp. 103–112.

Architectural Issues

5.12 Schoeffler, J.D., "Data Highway Structures and Their Effect on Applications," Instrument Society of America Annual Conference, Niagara Falls, New York, October 1977.

5.13 Cox, H., "The Advantages of Pure Bit Serial Interfaces for Microcomputers and Other Controllers," in *IEE Conference Publications no. 172*, 3rd Int'l Conf. on Trends in On-Line Computer Control Systems, U. Sheffield, England, March 1979; pub. by IEE, London, England, 1979, pp. 26–28.

5.14 Rose, C.W., "The Structuring of Distributed Intelligence Computer Control Systems," in *Chemical Process Control 2*, United Engineering Trustees, New York, New York, 1982, pp. 565–579.

5.15 Schoeffler, J.D., "Distributed Computer Systems for Industrial Process Control," *Computer*, vol. 17, no. 2, February, 1984, pp. 11–18.

5.16 Rosenthal, R., ed., "The Selection of Local Area Computer Networks," *Special Publication 500–96*, National Bureau of Standards, November 1982.

5.17 Saltzer, J.H., Clark, D.D., and Pogran, K.T., "Why a Ring?" IEEE Seventh Data Communications Symposium, Mexico City, October 1981.

5.18 Salwen, H.C., "In Praise of Ring Architecture for Local Area Networks," *Computer Design*, vol. 22, no. 3, March 1983, pp. 183–192.

Protocol Issues

5.19 Pouzin, L., and Zimmerman, H., "A Tutorial on Protocols," *Proceedings of the IEEE*, vol. 66, no. 11, November 1978, pp. 1346–1370.

5.20 Goldberger, A., and Lau, S.Y., "Understand Datacomm Protocols by Examining Their Structures," *EDN*, vol. 28, no. 7, March 3, 1983, pp. 109–118.

5.21 *Computer*, vol. 12, no. 9, September 1979. Special issue on computer network protocols.

5.22 International Organization for Standardization, "Data Processing–Open Systems Interconnection—Basic Reference Model," Draft proposed for Standard 7498, February 1982.

5.23 "Networking for Control" *I&CS*, vol. 58, nos. 4–6, April–June 1985. Installments 3, 4, and 5 of the series.

5.24 Sanders, L.S., "Pulse Codes in Serial Data Communications," *Computer Design*, vol. 21, no. 1, January 1982, pp. 203–210.

5.25 Electronic Industries Association, "Interface Between Data Terminal Equipment and Data Communication Equipment Employing Serial Binary Data Interchange," Standard RS–232–C, August 1969.

5.26 Leibson, S., "What Are RS–232C and IEEE 488?" *Instruments and Control Systems*, vol. 53, no. 1, January 1980, pp. 47–53.

5.27 Pearson, L.T., "Extending the Limits of an RS–232 Interface," *Computer Design*, vol. 20, no. 10, September 1981, pp. 163–166.

5.28 Electronic Industries Association, "Electrical Characteristics of Balanced Voltage Digital Interface Circuits," Standard RS–422, April 1975.

5.29 Eckard, M., "Tackling the Interconnect Dilemma," *Instruments and Control Systems*, vol. 55, no. 5, May 1982, pp. 36–43.

5.30 Baker, S., "RS–485 Interface Standard Gains Acceptance," *Electronic Engineering Times*, pp. 47 and 50, February 27, 1984.

5.31 Berglund, R.G., "Understanding SDLC," *Modern Data*, vol. 8, nos. 2–9, February–September 1975. Series of articles.

5.32 Shepherd, W.D., Blair, G.S., and Hutchison, D., "Comparison of an Ethernet-like Communication System with the Cambridge Ring," *IEE Proceedings*, vol. 129, pt. E., no. 4, July 1982, pp. 147–155.

5.33 Lukas, M.P., Dziubakowski, D.J., and Schoeffler, J.D., "The Use of Exception Transmission in a High–Performance Distributed Control System," *ISA Transactions*, vol. 23, no. 3, 1984, pp. 73–82.

Other Issues

5.34 Pingry, J., "Problem Solving with Fiber Optics," *Digital Design,* vol. 13, no. 7, July 1983, pp. 76–87.

5.35 Gruchalla, M.E., "Practical Problems of Fiber Optics in Field Applications," *ISA Transactions,* vol. 23, no. 1, 1984, pp. 29–39.

5.36 Winard, H., "Focus on Fiber Optic Cables: Steadily Forging the Link," *Electronic Design,* vol. 32, no. 7, March 8, 1984, pp. 177–187.

5.37 Stier, R., and Ohlhaber, R., "Fiber Optics or Electronic Cable?" *Instrumentation & Control Systems,* vol. 57, no. 7, July 1984, pp. 39–42.

5.38 Storozum, S.L., and Uhlhorn, R.W., "Fault-Tolerant Fiber Optic LANs," *Photonics Spectra,* vol. 18, no. 9, September 1984, pp. 61–68.

5.39 Kapron, F.P., "Fiber-Optic System Tradeoffs," *IEEE Spectrum,* vol. 22, no. 3, March 1985, pp. 68–75.

5.40 Damsker, D.J., "Fiber Optic Links for Power Plant Control and Data Communications Systems," *Power Engineering,* vol. 86, no. 2, February 1982, pp. 54–57.

5.41 Electronic Industries Association, "Generic Specification for Fiber Optic Connectors," *Standard RS–475,* November 1981.

5.42 Ormond, T., "Multiple-Access Fiber-Optic Couplers Enhance Data Link Performance," *EDN,* vol. 30, no. 13, June 13, 1985, pp. 75–78.

5.43 Swanson, R., "Understanding Cyclic Redundancy Codes," *Computer Design,* vol. 14, no. 13, November 1975, pp. 93–99.

5.44 Reason, J., "Update Powerplant Controls—and Update and Update and Update," *Power,* vol. 129, no. 6, June 1985, pp. 48–51.

5.45 Bell, C.J., "Standards Can Help Us," *Computer,* vol. 17, no. 6, June 1984, pp. 71–79.

Communication System Standards

5.46 Rauch-Hindin, W.B., "Upper-Level Network Protocols," *Electronic Design,* vol. 31, no. 7, March 3, 1983, pp. 181–194.

5.47 Berry, D., "Standardizing Upper-Level Network Protocols," *Computer Design,* vol. 23, no. 2, February 1984, pp. 175–185.

5.48 Hindin, H.J., "Formal Protocol Specification Ready to Make Its Mark," *Computer Design,* vol. 23, no. 7, June 1984, pp. 57–64.

5.49 Special Issue on Manufacturing Automation Protocol, *Control Engineering,* vol. 32, no. 11, October 1985 2nd Edition.

5.50 Cleaveland, P., "Local Area Networks for Industrial Control," *Instruments & Control Systems,* vol. 57, no. 8, August 1984, pp. 31–37.

5.51 Horelick, D., and Larsen, R.S., "CAMAC: A Modular Standard," *IEEE Spectrum,* vol. 13, no. 4, April 1976, pp. 50–55.

5.52 Merritt, R., "Universal Process Interfaces—CAMAC vs. HP–IB," *Instrumentation Technology,* vol. 23, no. 8, August 1976, pp. 29–36.

5.53 Wilson, D., "Designer's Guide to the IEEE 488 Bus," *Digital Design,* vol. 14, no. 1, January 1984, pp. 54–61.

5.54 McGowan, M.J., "The Proway Project: Is a Standard Process Control Bus in Sight?" *Control Engineering,* vol. 26, no. 8, August 1979, pp. 29–34.

5.55 Capel, A.C., and Lynch, G.F., "Proway: The Evolving Standard for Process Control Data Highways," *InTech,* vol. 30, no. 9, September 1983, pp. 91–94.

5.56 Instrument Society of America, "PROWAY-LAN (Local Network), An Industrial Data Highway," Draft Standard ISA–dS72.01, revision D, version June 1984.

5.57 Graube, M., "Local Area Nets: A Pair of Standards," *IEEE Spectrum,* vol. 19, no. 6, June 1982, pp. 60–64.

5.58 Laduzinsky, A.J., "Local Area Networks Expand the Horizons of Control and Information Flow," *Control Engineering,* vol. 30, no. 7, July 1983, pp. 53–56.

5.59 Bolton, A., "Update on Local Area Network Standards," *Instruments and Control Systems,* vol. 56, no. 11, November 1983, pp. 27–31.

5.60 Graube, M., and Mulder, M.C., "Local Area Networks," *Computer,* vol. 17, no. 10, October 1984, pp. 242–247.

6
OPERATOR INTERFACES

6.1. INTRODUCTION

The control and communication equipment described in the previous chapters performs the bulk of the automated functions that are required for operating an industrial process. For this automated equipment to be used in a safe and effective manner, however, it is absolutely necessary to have a well-engineered human interface system to permit error-free interactions between the humans and the automated system. Two distinct groups of plant personnel interact with the control system on a regular basis:

1. *Instrumentation and control system engineers*—These people are responsible for setting up the control system initially and adjusting and maintaining it from time to time afterwards;
2. *Plant operators*—These people are responsible for monitoring, supervising, and running the process through the control system during startup, operation, and shutdown conditions.

As the generalized distributed control system architecture in Figure 1.4 shows, a human interface capability can be provided at one or both of two levels:

1. Through a low-level human interface (LLHI) connected directly to the local control unit or data input/output unit (DI/OU) via dedicated cabling;
2. Through a high-level human interface (HLHI) connected to an LCU or DI/OU only through the shared communications facility.

The low-level human interface equipment used in distributed control systems usually resembles the panelboard instrumentation (stations, indicators, and recorders) and tuning devices used in conventional electric analog control systems. The HLHI equipment makes maximum use of the latest display technology (e.g., CRTs or flat-panel displays) and peripheral devices (e.g., printers and magnetic storage) that are available on the market; it is configured in a console arrangement that allows operator and engineer to be seated during use.

When it is included in the system configuration, the LLHI generally is located geographically close to (within 100–200 feet of) the LCU or DI/OU to which it is connected. On the other hand, the HLHI can be located anywhere in the plant, including the central control room. The needs of the application will determine whether the particular installation has one or both levels of interface. Figures 6.1, 6.2, and 6.3 show some examples of typical installations and their corresponding equipment configurations.

Figure 6.1 illustrates a relatively small and simple installation. A single LCU located in the plant equipment room (sometimes called the *relay room*) performs all of the required control functions. Low-level human interface units located in the equipment room and the plant control room provide the complete operator and instrument engineer interface for the control system. This type of equipment configuration is typical of a stand-alone control system for a small process or of a small digital control system installed in a plant controlled primarily with conventional electrical analog or pneumatic equipment.

Figure 6.2 shows a typical structure of a complete plantwide control system. Several LCUs are used to implement the functions required in controlling the process; therefore, the control is *functionally distributed*. However, the LCUs are all located in a central equipment room area, and so it is not a *geographically distributed* control system. Both high-level and low-level human interface devices are located in the control room area for operational purposes. Most of the operator control functions are performed using the high-level interface; the low-level interface is included in the configuration primarily to serve as a backup in case the high-level

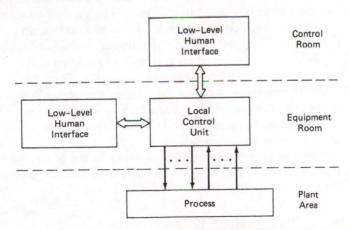

Figure 6.1. Stand-Alone Control Configuration

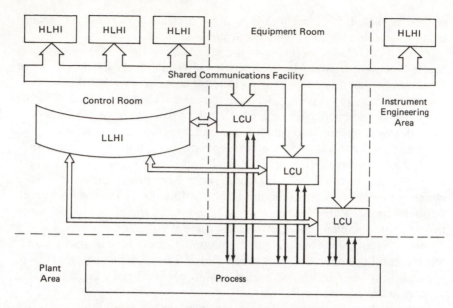

Figure 6.2. Geographically Centralized Control Configuration

interface fails. A high-level human interface is located in the instrument engineer's area so that control system monitoring and analysis can be done without disturbing plant operations. This type of installation is typical of early distributed control system configurations in which equipment location and operator interface design followed conventional practices.

Figure 6.3 shows a fully distributed control system configuration. In this case, each LCU is located in the plant area closest to the portion of the process that it controls. Associated low-level human interface equipment (if provided) is also located in this area. The control room and instrument engineering areas contain high-level human interface units, which are used to perform all of the primary operational and engineering functions. The low-level units are used only as manual backup controls in case the high-level equipment fails or needs maintenance. This configuration takes advantage of two areas of equipment savings that result from a totally distributed system architecture: (1) reduction in control room size (by eliminating panelboard equipment), and (2) reduction in field wiring costs (by placing LCUs near the process).

These examples of system configurations illustrate the point that human interface equipment in a distributed control system must be designed to meet a wide range of applications:

1. Large as well as small systems;
2. Centralized equipment configurations (often used in retrofit instal-

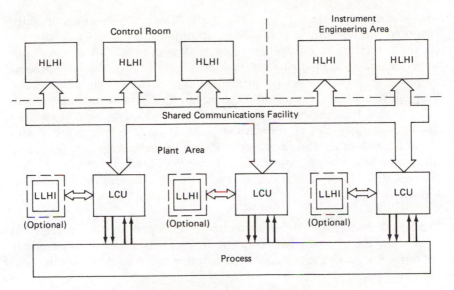

Figure 6.3. Geographically Distributed Control Configuration

lations made long *after* original plant construction) as well as distributed ones (likely in "grass roots" installations made *during* plant construction);

3. Variety of human interface philosophies, ranging from accepting CRT-only operation to requiring panelboard instrumentation in at least a backup role.

This chapter and the next provide an overview of the major issues to consider when evaluating or designing human interface equipment in a distributed control system. As in the previous chapters, the discussion will not be a detailed analysis but instead will address only the significant points; the references will permit the reader to go into any selected area in greater depth. This chapter discusses operator interface requirements and design issues; Chapter 7 will deal with instrument engineer interfaces. Section 6.2 summarizes the key requirements of an operator interface system; Sections 6.3 and 6.4 describe and evaluate alternative design approaches to implementing these requirements for the low-level and high-level operator interfaces, respectively.

6.2. OPERATOR INTERFACE REQUIREMENTS

Despite the continuing trend toward increased automation in process control and less reliance on the operator, the basic responsibilities of the operator have remained largely the same in the last fifty years. Most of the changes have come in the relative emphasis on the various operator functions and the means provided to accomplish them. As a result, the operator interface in a distributed control system must allow the operator to perform tasks in the following traditional areas of responsibility: process monitoring, process control, process diagnostics, and process record keeping. In addition, it is important to design the operator interface system using human factors design principles (also called *ergonomics*) to ensure that the operator can perform these tasks in an effective manner with minimum risk of confusion or error. The following paragraphs provide a discussion of the key functional requirements in each of these areas. References 6.1–6.8 give additional information on advances in operator interfaces.

Process Monitoring.   A basic function of the operator interface system is to allow the operator (whether one or more) to observe and monitor the current state of the process. This function includes the following specific requirements:

1. The current values of all process variables of interest in the system must be available for the operator to view at any time. This includes both continuous process variables (e.g., flows, temperatures, and pressures) and logical process variables (e.g., pump on/off status and switch positions). The operator must have rapid access to any variable, and the values displayed must be accurate and current. If the information provided is not valid for some reason (e.g., a sensor has failed or has been taken out of service for maintenance), this condition should be readily visible to the operator.
2. Each process variable, rather than being identified by a hardware address only, must be identifiable by a "tag" or name assigned by the instrument engineer; a descriptor that expands on and describes the tagged variable must be associated with the tag. The tag and descriptor give the variable a meaning relative to the process; an example might be to label a certain temperature with a tag of TT075/B and a corresponding descriptor "COLUMN TEMPERATURE 75 IN AREA B."
3. The value of the process variable must be in engineering units that are meaningful to the operator, and those units must be displayed along with the variable values. In the temperature example just given, the engineering units might be in degrees Fahrenheit or Celsius.
4. In many cases, the operator is interested in variables that are functions of or combinations of the basic process variables being measured (e.g., an average of several temperatures, a maximum of several

flows, or a computed enthalpy). The operator must have these computed variables available at all times in the same formats as the basic variables (i.e., tags, descriptors, and engineering units).

Another monitoring function of the operator interface is to detect abnormalities in the state of the process and to report them to the operator. In its simplest form, this is the familiar function of alarming. Some of the specific requirements of this function are the following:

1. The control and computing hardware in the distributed system identifies the alarm statuses of individual variables in the process. The operator interface system must report these statuses to the operator in a clear manner. Types of alarms for each variable—such as high, low, and deviation (from a nominal value)—must be differentiated clearly. True alarms must be differentiated from indications of process equipment status that do not denote an abnormal condition requiring operator action.
2. The operator interface must also report similar alarm statuses for computed variables.
3. The operator interface must either display the alarm limits along with the process variable or make them easily accessible to the operator.
4. When the system has detected an alarm condition, the interface must alert the operator to this condition in unambiguous terms and require the operator to acknowledge the existence of the alarm.
5. If the system detects multiple alarm conditions within a short time period, the operator interface must inform the operator that multiple alarms have occurred, preferably with some indication of the priority of the various alarm conditions.
6. In some processes, "abnormal operation" can be detected only by looking at a combination of several process variables and noting if this combination is within an allowable region of operation. In this case, the operator interface system must provide an appropriate mechanism to allow the operator to view this multivariable alarm status condition and interpret it properly.

When monitoring the process, an operator is interested in not only the *current* value of a process variable but also its *trend* in time. This gives the operator an idea of the direction in which the process is moving and whether or not there is trouble ahead. For this reason, the operator interface system must provide the operator with fast access to the recent history of selected (not necessarily *all*) process variables in the plant; these variables are called *trended variables*. Some specific requirements in trending are that:

1. It must be possible to group the trended variables by related process function as well as by similarities in time scale of interest. For example, it might make sense to group all temperatures that are associated with a particular portion of the process.
2. The trend graph must clearly label the engineering units, time increments, and absolute time of day of the trended variables.
3. The operator must be able to obtain a precise reading (in engineering units) of both the current value as well as past values of the trended variable.
4. If at all possible, the same graph displaying the trend should also show auxiliary information that would help the operator evaluate the status of the trended variable. This information might include the nominal value of the variable, the set point of the associated control loop, the allowed range of the variable, or the allowed rate of change.

Process Control. The process *monitoring* capabilities just described provide the necessary information for the operator's primary function—process *control*. The following specific operator interface requirements come under the category of process control:

1. The operator interface must allow the operator to have rapid access to all of the continuous control loops and logic sequences in the process control system.
2. For each continuous control loop, the interface must allow the operator to perform all of the normal control functions: changing control modes (e.g., automatic, manual, or cascade), changing control outputs in manual mode, changing set points in automatic mode, and monitoring the results of these actions.
3. The interface must allow the operator to perform such logic control operations as starting and stopping pumps or opening and closing valves. If interlocking logic is included in these operations, the interface must allow the operator to observe the status of the most recently requested command, the current logic state of the process, and the status of any permissives (interlocking signals) that may be preventing execution of the requested command.
4. In the case of a batch control sequence, the operator interface must allow the operator to observe the current status of the sequence and to interact with it to initiate new steps or halt the sequence, as required.

5. In both the continuous and sequential control cases, the interface system must allow the operator to have access to and be able to manipulate the control outputs despite any single-point failure in the equipment between the operator interface and the control outputs.

Process Diagnostics. Monitoring and controlling the process under normal operating conditions are relatively simple functions compared to operation under abnormal or hazardous conditions caused by failures in plant equipment or in the instrumentation and control system. The operator interface system must provide enough information during these unusual conditions to allow the operator to identify the equipment causing the problem, take measures to correct it, and move the process back to its normal operating state.

The first step in this sequence is to determine whether it is the instrumentation and control equipment that is causing the problem. To this end, the distributed control system should provide the following diagnostic features and make the results of the diagnostic tests available to the operator:

1. Ongoing tests and reasonableness checks on the sensors and analyzers that measure the process variables of interest;
2. Ongoing self-tests on the components and modules within the distributed control system itself: controllers, communication elements, computing devices, and the human interface equipment itself.

These diagnostic features also are essential to aid the work of the instrumentation engineer. Chapter 7 will discuss diagnostics from that point of view.

Historically, diagnosing problems within the process itself has been a manual function left to the operator. Operator interface systems have been designed to display *all* of the available process information (both relevant and irrelevant), and the operator has had to sort it all out and come up with the right diagnosis. This was not a bad approach when the operator had to contend with small processes, those characterized by only a few hundred process variables. More recently, however, processes have grown to such a size that describing them takes 5,000–10,000 process variables (many of which may be strongly interacting). It has become extremely difficult for an operator to identify the source and nature of a fault in an item of process equipment in this environment. A conventional alarming system, for example, may indicate the most immediate failure symptom but provide few clues as to the original source of the alarm condition. As a result, diagnostic functions that automatically detect process faults are now often required in distributed control systems. These functions may include:

1. *First-out* alarming functions, which tell the operator which alarm in a sequence occurred first;
2. Priority alarming functions, which rank the current alarms by their importance to process operation, allowing the operator to safely ignore the less important ones, at least temporarily;
3. More advanced diagnostic functions that use a combination of alarming information and data on process variables to identify the item of failed process equipment and (in some cases) the mode of failure.

Many of these advanced alarming and diagnostic functions are application-oriented ones that the designer must configure for the specific process of interest; however, the distributed control system must support the implementation of these functions.

Process Record Keeping. One of the more tedious duties that operating people in a process plant must perform has been to *walk the board*; that is, to take a pencil and clipboard and periodically note and record the current values of all process variables in the plant. Depending on the process, the frequency for doing this has ranged from once an hour to once every several hours. This logged information, along with the trend recordings obtained automatically, serves as a useful record of plant operating status during each shift. The record-keeping burden has increased significantly in recent years due (in part, at least) to governmental reporting requirements related to pollution monitoring, product liability, and worker safety regulations.

Record-keeping was one of the first functions to be automated using conventional computer systems. In state-of-the-art distributed control systems, this function often can be implemented in the operator interface system without the use of a separate computer. Specific record-keeping requirements include the following:

1. *Recording of short-term trending information*—The earlier section on process monitoring described this requirement.
2. *Manual input of process data*—The operator must be able to enter manually collected process information into the system for record-keeping purposes. This information includes both numeric data and operator "notes" or journal entries.
3. *Recording of alarms*—These are logged on a printer, a data storage device, or both, as they occur. Often, the return-to-normal status

and operator acknowledgments must also be logged. The information recorded includes the tag name of the process variable, the time of alarm, and the type of alarm (high, low, or deviation). There must also be a mechanism that allows convenient review of the alarm information.

4. *Periodic records of process variable information*—The values of selected variables are logged on a printer, data storage device, or both, on a periodic basis: every few minutes or every hour, depending on the dynamics of the variable. The operator or instrument engineer may decide to store an averaged value over the sampling period instead of the instantaneous value.

5. *Long-term storage and retrieval of information*—The alarms and periodic logs as described above are accessible for short periods of time, commonly, for a single eight-hour shift or a single day. In addition, the same information, or a smoothed or filtered version of it, must be stored on a long-term basis (months or years). The system must include a mechanism for easy retrieval or "instant replay" of such information.

6. *Recording of operator control actions*—Some process plants require the actions of the operator affecting control of the process to be recorded automatically. These include changes in control mode, set point, manual output, or logic command. Clearly this recording function must be implemented in such a way that the operator cannot deactivate it.

Guidelines for Human Factors Design. In the past, equipment used for operator interfacing has often been designed more for the convenience of the equipment vendor or architect-engineer than for ease of use by the operator. In recent years, it has become clear that a small investment made in the proper design of human interfacing equipment pays handsome dividends: fewer operator errors (which can cause plant downtime or damage to equipment), less operator fatigue (which can cause a loss in productivity), and more efficient use of operating personnel. Compiling an exhaustive list of requirements in the area of human factors design is beyond the scope of this chapter. (For such a list, see References 6.32–6.45, for example.) However, some general design guidelines for designing operator interface systems for industrial control include the following:

1. Consider the full range of expected operator population (e.g., male and female, large and small, right-handers and left-handers).
2. Take into account common minor disabilities in operators (e.g., color blindedness and nearsightedness).

3. Design the system for operators, not for computer programmers or engineers.
4. Allow rapid access to all necessary controls and displays.
5. Arrange equipment and displays to make sense from an operational point of view; cluster with respect to process unit, functional operation, or both.
6. Make consistent use of colors, symbols, labels, and positions to minimize operator confusion.
7. Do not flood the operator with a lot of parallel information that is not structured in any way; the information should be prioritized, organized in a meaningful manner, and reported only when it changes significantly.
8. Ensure that the operator's short-term memory is not overtaxed when performing a complex sequence of operations: provide aids such as operator guides, menus, prompts, or interactive sequences for assistance in these operations. These aids are particularly important in stressful situations, during which short-term memory is not a reliable source of operating information.
9. As much as possible, design the system to detect and filter out erroneous operator inputs; when an error occurs, the system must tell the operator what the input error was and what to do next.
10. Make sure the control room environment (e.g., light, sound levels, and layout) is consistent with the selection and design of the control room equipment.

In some respects, these guidelines may only seem to state obvious, common-sense design principles; however, a glance at existing operator interface designs shows that these principles are very often violated, either for design expediency or through ignorance of these ergonomic issues. In later sections of this chapter, discussions of operator interface design features will include commentary on the degree to which these features meet the intent of the guidelines.

6.3. LOW-LEVEL OPERATOR INTERFACE

As the introduction to this chapter indicated, the low-level operator interface (LLOI) in a distributed control system is connected directly to the LCU and is dedicated to controlling and monitoring that LCU. This contrasts with the high-level operator interface (HLOI), which can be associated with multiple LCUs and is connected to them through the shared communication facility. LLOIs are used in a variety of applications, in some cases in conjunction with high-level operator interfaces (HLOIs) and in others in *place* of them. In some applications, all operator functions are performed through the HLOI and no low-level interface is required except during emergency or failure conditions. There are a number of motivations for using an LLOI:

1. It provides an interface that is familiar to operators trained to use panelboard instrumentation, since it is usually designed to resemble that type of instrumentation.
2. It is usually less expensive than an HLOI in small applications (say, less than 50 control loops).
3. It can provide manual backup in case the automatic control equipment or the HLOI fails.

LLOI instrumentation usually includes the following devices: control stations, indicator stations, alarm annunciators, and trend recorders. In some distributed control systems, the vendor offers exactly the same type of instrumentation as used in his conventional analog and logic control systems. More often, however, the vendor supplies *smart* (microprocessor-based) instrumentation, which offers the user functionality beyond that available in conventional panelboard instrumentation. The following paragraphs describe several of these smart devices. References 6.38 and 6.43 provide many helpful suggestions regarding the proper ergonomic design of this type of operator interface.

Continuous Control Station. One type of panelboard instrumentation used in process control systems is the manual/automatic station associated with a continuous control loop. The stations discussed here are *split* stations; that is, they are separate from the LCU. Figure 6.4 illustrates a typical version of a smart continuous control station in a distributed control system. As in the case of most conventional control stations, this one has bar graph indicators that display the process variable ("PV"), associated set point ("SP"), and the control output as a percent of scale ("OUT"). In addition, however, the smart station includes a shared digital display to provide a precise reading of each of these variables in engineering units. The units used are indicated in an accompanying digital display or are printed on a removable label (in this example, "DEGF" or "%"). The shared digital display also can be used to indicate the high and low alarm limits ("HI ALM" and "LO ALM") on the process variable when selected by the operator. Pushbuttons allow the operator to change the mode of control (e.g., manual, automatic, or cascade) and to ramp the set point ("SET") or control output ("OUT"), depending on the mode. Usually, both fast and slow ramping speeds are provided for the convenience of

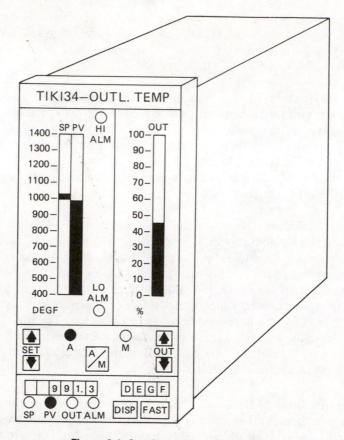

Figure 6.4. Continuous Control Station

the operator. Other indications the control station often provides include any alarms associated with the process variable being controlled and an indication of the operational status (whether "healthy" or not) of the associated LCU.

To minimize requirements for spare parts, one basic control station should be used for all types of associated control loops: standard PID, cascade, ratio, or bias. The station can be customized through the configuration of options in the electronics (using jumpers or switches) and on the front plate indicators and switches (using different overlays or faceplates as appropriate).

To be effective as a manual backup station in addition to its role as a single-loop operator interface, the control station must be connected directly to the control output section of the LCU or to the associated field termination panel. In this arrangement, a "hard" control output (e.g., a

4–20 ma signal) generated by the station can pass directly to the process as a backup control signal in case the LCU fails or is undergoing maintenance. The direct connection also allows the process variable input to come into the station for indication to the operator during manual control. To keep the control output from going through a step change in value when the backup mode is initiated or concluded (automatic bumpless transfer), the station and the LCU must be aware of each other's nominal control output signal. These signal values and other useful information (such as alarm and diagnostic status signals) are often sent over a direct serial communication link between the LCU and the station. (See Figure 4.8 and the discussion in Section 4.2.5 for more details.)

Manual Loader Station. Some applications use the HLOI as the primary control station and don't require a full-blown continuous control station for each loop. However, a device is still needed to hold the 4–20 ma control output signal if the LCU fails or is taken off-line for maintenance or other reasons. In this situation, a simple manual loader station is a low-cost alternative to the continuous control station for the purposes of backup. The manual loader station is plugged in at the same point as the continuous control station but only allows the operator to run the loop in manual mode. Sometimes the process variable is displayed; more often it is not. Any balancing of the control output to accomplish bumpless transfer to or from backup is accomplished manually.

Both the continuous control station (if used for backup) and the manual loader station should be powered from a different supply than that used for the LCU, to ensure continuous backup in case of an LCU power failure.

Indicator Station. If the operator must be able to monitor process variables *not* associated with control loops, a panelboard indicator station can be provided as a part of the LLOI family of products. The indicator station is similar to the control station in that it provides both bar graph and digital numeric readouts of the process variables in engineering units. Of course, an indicator station requires no control push buttons. However, it often provides alarming and LCU diagnostic indications, as does the continuous control station.

Logic Station. Figure 6.5 illustrates a control station for a logic control or sequential control system. It consists simply of a set of pushbuttons and indicating lights that are assigned different meanings (through labels) depending on the logic functions being implemented. This type of station is used to turn pumps on and off, start automatic sequences, or provide permissives or other operator inputs to the logic system. In some systems,

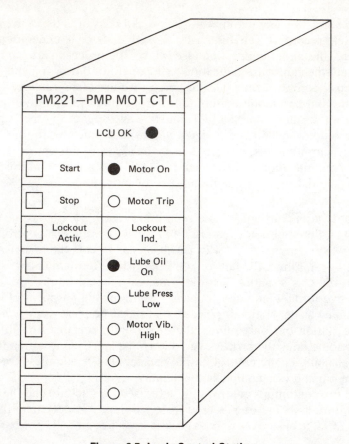

Figure 6.5. Logic Control Station

the logic control station performs a manual backup function similar to that performed by the continuous control station in case of a failure of an LCU. More often, however, the logic station acts simply as a low-cost operator interface; if the LCU fails, the logic outputs revert to their default or safe states, as described in Section 4.2.4.

Smart Annunciators. Alarm annunciators in distributed control systems are often microprocessor-based, providing a level of functionality beyond the capability of conventional hard-wired annunciator systems. These smart annunciators can provide such functions as:

1. *Alarm prioritization*—The annunciator differentiates between status annunciation and true alarms (and how critical the alarms are);

2. *Annunciation and acknowledgment mode options*—The operator receives a variety of audible and visible alarm annunciation signals (e.g., horns, buzzers, flashing lights, and voice messages). A range of alarm acknowledgment and silencing modes also can be provided.

3. *First-out annunciation*—The annunciator displays the first alarm that appears within a selected group.

4. *Alarm "cutout"*—The annunciator suppresses an alarm condition if other specified status conditions are fulfilled.

The last function is valuable in minimizing meaningless "nuisance" alarms, a problem that References 6.14 and 6.36 describe in some detail. For example, if a pump fails and triggers an alarm, the pump-failed status signal can be used to lock out other related alarms such as "low flow" or "pump speed low," since they are not meaningful given the failed operating status of the pump.

Of course, the four alarm logic functions previously listed also can be accomplished within the LCUs in the distributed system itself; however, in some applications it may be convenient to incorporate the functions externally in the annunciators.

Chart Recorders. Although conventional round chart or strip chart recorders are often used to record process variables in a distributed control system, digital recorders which use microprocessors are becoming more cost-effective and popular. The *digital recorder* gathers trend data in its memory and displays the data to the operator using a liquid crystal panel or other flat display device. For hard-copy output, the recorder uses an impact- or heat-type of printing mechanism instead of pen-and-ink to record the information. In some models, the recorder draws the chart scales as it is recording, so that plain paper instead of chart paper can be used. The recorder often provides such functions as automatically labeling time and range of variable directly on the chart, using alphabetic or numeric characters. Also, each process variable can be recorded using a different symbol or color to allow the operator to distinguish between the variables easily. Because of the flexibility of the printing mechanism and the memory capabilities of the recorder, intermittent printing of the process variables can supplement the display output without losing any of the stored information.

Selection of Station Components. To a considerable degree, the type of display and pushbutton components selected determines the reliability and ease of use of the LLOI equipment. This equipment must be designed to meet the exacting needs of the process control application; components that are suitable for home or office environments may not be at all appropriate in a process plant or factory. Some of the requirements the designer should meet include the following:

1. Displays and pushbuttons should be sealed against the atmosphere to avoid contamination (from dirt or corrosive gases, for example);
2. Displays should be selected for high visibility in the expected ambient light environment;
3. Each pushbutton when depressed should provide tactile (touch) feedback to the operator to minimize potential errors.

A variety of display types has been developed for industrial use. The workhorse of the discrete display world is the light-emitting diode (LED). This component type is used in on/off status, bar-graph, and alphanumeric displays. It is quite suitable in most applications. However, bar-graph displays tend to be somewhat low in resolution when composed of LEDs rather than other display components. Gas-discharge and gas-plasma displays provide high-resolution and high-visibility bar graphs. The declining cost trend for these devices has made them an attractive display alternative to LEDs. Liquid crystal displays (LCDs) are very flexible and have been used in a wide variety of display configurations (mixtures of bar graphs, alphanumerics, and status displays). However, LCDs are not as visible as LEDs or gas-discharge displays, especially in low ambient lighting situations.

In the operator input area, the two most common types of push-button and switch inputs are:

1. *Spring-loaded plungers*—This component, often used in typewriter-like keyboards, can make use of a number of different switch-sensing mechanisms—magnetic, optical, or capacitive, for example. It is not used very often in panelboard equipment since its mechanical configuration makes it difficult to isolate the sensing mechanism from the environment.
2. *Membrane or dimple switches*—These are inexpensive mechanical switching components that come in a flat configuration suitable for direct mounting on a printed circuit board. An overlay sheet of mylar or plastic protects the switch assemblies from the environment. If packaged properly, they provide tactile feedback to the operator when depressed.

There are many other types of displays and switches suitable for use in panelboard equipment. For a survey of these types and their relative advantages and disadvantages, consult references such as 6.21 and 6.25.

Application in Distributed Systems. In the early installations of distributed control systems, both suppliers and users were concerned whether the operating personnel in the plants would accept the new technology. This involved two aspects of the new technology: (1) using microprocessors to implement closed-loop control functions, and (2) using new human interface hardware such as CRTs as the primary operating tool. As a result, those responsible for many of these installations took a "belt and suspenders" approach to the design of operator interface equipment by providing *both* panelboard instrumentation and CRT consoles. Operators were first trained to use the panelboard-type equipment, then were gradually weaned from it in favor of the CRT consoles. As the next section of this chapter will discuss, few industrial users now have any hesitation in providing CRT consoles as the primary operator interface tool. The LLOI equipment described in this section does, however, find continuing application in small control systems and as a backup mechanism for critical process control loops.

6.4. HIGH-LEVEL OPERATOR INTERFACE

In contrast with the low-level operator interface described in the previous section, the high-level operator interface in a distributed control system is a shared interface that is not dedicated to any particular LCU. Rather, the HLOI is used to monitor and control the operation of the process through any or all of the LCUs in the distributed system. Information passes between the HLOI and the LCUs by means of the shared communications facility, as described in Chapter 5.

While the LLOI hardware resembles conventional panelboard instrumentation, HLOI hardware uses CRT or similar advanced display technology in console configurations often called video display units (VDUs). The HLOI accepts operator inputs through keyboards instead of the switches, push-buttons, and potentiometers characteristic of conventional operator interface panels. Other digital hardware prints, stores, and manipulates information required in the operator interface system. This section will discuss many of the issues involved in the design of the HLOI; References 6.9–6.14 provide additional information on these issues.

In general, the use of microprocessor-based digital technology in the design of the HLOI system allows the development of a hardware configuration that departs radically from the design of panelboard-based operator interfaces. This configuration provides the user with several significant advantages over previous approaches:

1. Control room space is reduced significantly; one or a few VDUs can

replace panelboards several feet to 200 feet in length, saving floor space and equipment expense.

2. One can design the operator interface for a specific process plant in a much more flexible manner. The hardware operations peculiar to panelboard design and implementation (e.g., selecting control stations and cutting holes in panels) are eliminated. Instead, CRT display formats define the key operator interface mechanisms. One can change these formats during startup and duplicate selected information displays wherever necessary. Being able to do this leads to a much more usable operator interface configuration than conventional approaches.

3. Using microprocessors permits cost-effective implementation of functions that previously could be accomplished only with expensive computers. These include color graphic displays that mimic the organization of the process; information presented in engineering units; and advanced computing and data storage and retrieval functions.

However, one must take great care in designing the HLOI to achieve these benefits while minimizing any negative effects or concerns on the part of the operating personnel. It became evident during the early introduction of this technology to the marketplace that operators accept properly designed HLOIs very quickly. This is especially true of younger operators who have been preconditioned and pretrained by video games and personal computers.

6.4.1. Architectural Alternatives

All high-level operator interface units in distributed control systems are composed of similar elements: operator display; keyboard or other input device; main processor and memory; disk memory storage; interface to the shared communication facility; and hard-copy devices and other peripherals. However, the architectures of the various HLOIs on the market vary significantly depending on the way in which these common elements are structured.

Figure 6.6 shows one architecture commonly used in computer-based control systems and early distributed systems. In this architecture, there is a single central processing unit (and associated random-access memory) that performs all of the calculations, database management and transfer operations, and CRT-and-keyboard interfacing functions for the *entire* HLOI system. A separate communications controller interfaces the central processor with the shared communications facility.

There are several advantages to this configuration. First, there is a single

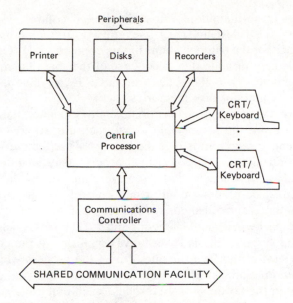

Figure 6.6. Centralized HLOI Configuration

database of plant information that is updated from the communication system. As a result, each of the CRTs has access to any of the control loops or data points in the system. This is desirable, since it means that the CRTs are all redundant and can be used to back each other up in case of a failure. Another advantage is that the peripherals can be shared and need not be dedicated to any particular CRT/keyboard combination. This can reduce the number of peripherals required in some situations.

The disadvantages of this configuration are similar to those of all centralized computer systems:

1. It is an "all eggs in one basket" configuration, and so is vulnerable to single-point failures. In some cases, redundant elements can be provided; but this approach can lead to complex peripheral-switching and memory-sharing implementations.
2. Any single-processor, single-memory configuration has limitations on the number of loops and data points it can handle before its throughput or memory capacity runs out. In many operator interface systems of this type, the display response times are long and the size of system that can be handled is severely limited.
3. The centralized architecture is not easily scalable for cost-effectiveness: if it is designed properly to handle large systems, it may be too expensive for small ones.

Because of these limitations, most distributed control systems use a decentralized HLOI design. That is, several HLOI units provide the operator interface for the entire system. In this context, an HLOI *unit* refers to a single element or node that makes use of the shared communication facility. Each unit may include one or more CRTs, keyboards, or peripherals such as printers or disk memories.

When the operator interface is distributed in this manner, the issue arises of how to partition the responsibilities of each unit to cover the entire process. Usually, each unit is designed to be cost-effective when monitoring and controlling a relatively small process (say, 400 control loops and 1,000 data acquisition points). However, this means that several of these units must be used to monitor and control a larger process (say, 2,000 control loops and 5,000 data acquisition points). For example, five units of the capacity indicated (400 loops and 1,000 points) could just cover the 2,000-loop system. In this case, however, if one of the control units failed, the operator interface for one-fifth of the process would be lost. To avoid this situation, the HLOI units usually are configured for significant overlap in the portions of the process each unit covers. Figure 6.7 illustrates a two-to-one overlap configuration, in which three HLOI units control and monitor a 600-loop process. With this approach, the loss of any single HLOI unit does not affect the capability of the operator interface system to control the process.

Overlap obviously is not an issue if each HLOI is designed to be large enough to accommodate *all* of the points in an installation (say, 5,000 to

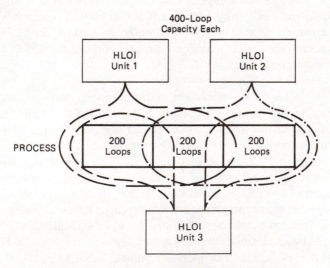

Figure 6.7. Overlap in HLOI Scope of Control

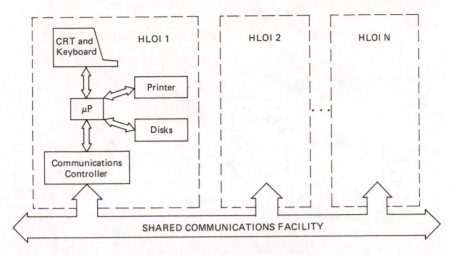

Figure 6.8. Fixed HLOI Configuration

10,000 points). This design approach results in a more expensive version of an HLOI than one designed to handle a smaller number of points. However, in this case each HLOI unit is capable of backing up any other unit in the system.

The first versions of distributed HLOI systems introduced to the marketplace had a relatively fixed configuration of elements, such as that shown in Figure 6.8. That is, a single HLOI unit consisted of a communications controller, main processor, CRT and keyboard, and associated mass storage. The only option for the user was whether to include a printer or other hard-copy device. Because of this fixed configuration of elements, the scope of control and data acquisition of the HLOI unit also was fixed.

Later versions of HLOI units have been designed to be modular: the user can buy the base configuration at minimum cost or expand it to handle a larger number of control loops and data points. Figure 6.9 shows one example of a modular HLOI configuration. The base set of hardware in this case is a communications controller, main processor, single CRT and keyboard, and mass storage unit. However, the system is designed to accommodate optional hardware such as:

1. One or more additional CRTs to allow monitoring of a portion of the process (for example) while the primary CRT is being used for control purposes.
2. Additional keyboards for configuration or backup purposes.
3. Hard-copy devices such as printers or CRT screen copiers.

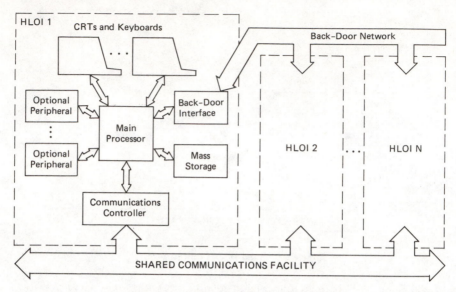

Figure 6.9. Modular HLOI Configuration

4. Additional mass storage devices for long-term data storage and retrieval.
5. Interfaces to trend recorders, voice alarm systems, or other external hardware.
6. Interface ports to any special communication systems such as back-door networks to other HLOI units or diagnostic equipment.
7. Backups to critical HLOI elements such as the main processor, communications controller, or shared memory.

The modular approach to HLOI unit design significantly improves configuration flexibility. The user can select the base configuration for small applications and add the optional hardware as the user sees fit. Of course, the performance of the main processor and other hardware must be adequate to provide the display update and response capability required, even with the maximum size hardware configuration.

Figure 6.10 shows a more detailed block diagram of the modular HLOI configuration. Usually, an internal bus is used to allow communication of information among the modular elements in the HLOI. Note that this configuration uses a direct memory access (DMA) port to allow the communications controller to transfer data directly into the shared memory of the HLOI. The other elements of the HLOI then can obtain access to this information over the internal bus.

6.4.2. Hardware Elements in the Operator Interface

Since the HLOI system is based on digital technology, many of the hardware elements that go into the system are similar to those used in other portions of the distributed control system (e.g., the microprocessors and the memory and communications components). However, the performance requirements of the HLOI place special demands on its elements; also, the on-line human interface functions performed by the HLOI require display and input hardware that is unique to this subsystem. An exhaustive survey of HLOI hardware requirements and alternatives is beyond the scope of this chapter; rather, some of the key factors to consider in selecting or evaluating operator interface hardware are summarized. References 6.21–6.31 provide additional information.

Microprocessor and Memory Components. The high-level operator interface is the most complex subsystem in the distributed control hierarchy. As a result, the microprocessors used in its implementation must

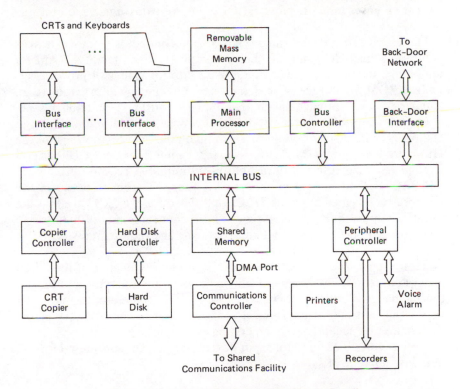

Figure 6.10. Modular HLOI Configuration in Detail

be faster and more powerful than microprocessors used elsewhere in the distributed system. The microprocessor hardware selected for use in the HLOI in commercially available systems tends to have the following characteristics:

1. It uses one or more standard 16- or 32-bit microprocessors available from multiple vendors; these are not single-sourced special components.
2. Its processors are members of a family of standard processors and related support chips.
3. It is designed to operate in a multiprocessor configuration, using a standard bus for communication between processors and an efficient real-time operating system as an environment for application software.

The last characteristic is important, since to accomplish the desired computing and data control functions at the speeds required by the real-time operating environment, most HLOI configurations must use multiple processors.

The HLOI requires the same types of semiconductor memory devices as used in the LCUs and the shared communications facility: RAM for temporary storage of changing data (e.g., current values of process variables); ROM for storage of predetermined, unchanging information (e.g., standard display formats and computational algorithms); and nonvolatile, alterable memory for storage of data that changes only infrequently (e.g., custom graphic display formats). The nonvolatile memory options for the HLOI are the same as those discussed in Chapter 2 for the LCU: battery-backed RAM, electrically erasable programmable read-only memory (EEPROM), and bubble memory. The main differences between the memory requirements for the HLOI and those for the LCU are that the HLOI requires shorter access times and greater amounts of memory to meet its high performance and large data storage requirements.

Operator Input and Output Devices.   The primary function of the HLOI subsystem is to allow communications between the operator and the automatic portions of the distributed control system. Therefore, the particular data input and output devices selected are vital to the usability of the system and its acceptance by operating personnel.

A great variety of operator input devices have been considered for use in industrial control systems:

1. *Keyboard*—There are two kinds of keyboard in use: the conventional electric typewriter type and the flat-panel type;

2. *Light pen*—This device allows a person to "draw" electronically on a CRT screen. In industrial control systems, the light pen is more often used by the operator to select among various options displayed on a CRT screen.
3. *Cursor-movement devices*—These allow the user to move a *cursor* (position indicator) around on a CRT screen. Types of devices used include joy sticks (such as those used in video games), track balls (imbedded in a keyboard), and the "mouse" (a hand-held device that the operator moves around on a flat surface).
4. *Touch screens*—There are CRTs with associated hardware that allows the user to select from menus or to "draw" on the screen by directly pointing with a finger.
5. *Voice-input devices*—These devices allow a user to speak directly to the HLOI and be understood. They are most useful for specific commands such as selecting displays or acknowledging alarms.

Many of these devices were originally developed for use in other applications, such as military or aerospace systems or in terminals for computers or computer-aided design systems. In evaluating these devices, the designer of an industrial control system must remember that the needs, background, and training of an operator in a process control environment differ substantially from those of an astronaut, military aviator, or engineer. For example, the use of hand-held devices such as light pens or mice in industrial applications has been criticized on the grounds that operators prefer *not* to use any devices that require a separate operation—removal from or return to storage—for their use. As a result, the most popular input device technologies in industrial control systems are keyboards and touch screens. The next section will discuss these in more detail.

As with input devices, several types of display and output devices have been considered for use in HLOI systems:

1. *CRTs*—This still is the dominant technology in the area of operator displays; CRTs come in either color or monochrome versions.
2. *Flat-panel displays*—These include gas plasma, vacuum fluorescent, liquid-crystal, and electroluminescent displays; most are monochrome only.
3. *Voice-output devices*—Usually these are used to generate alarm messages that the operator will hear under selected plant conditions. The messages can be prerecorded on tape or computer-generated by voice synthesizer.

In industrial distributed control systems, the CRT has been and continues to be the predominant visual display device used in HLOI systems. Some flat-panel display devices have been used in aerospace and military applications (see Reference 6.30); however, in general they have not yet reached the point of development at which their performance–cost ratio seriously threatens that of the CRT. The main features that differentiate the various CRTs on the market include:

1. Size of screen;
2. Number of colors available;
3. Resolution of pixels on the screen;
4. Character-oriented versus bit-mapped displays.

A screen size with a 19–20″ diagonal is adequate for most purposes; occasionally special-purpose consoles that include a large amount of panelboard equipment use a 25″ screen. Ideally, the design of the HLOI should accommodate a range of CRT sizes, ranging from 19″ to 40″. Most video display units employ a range of eight to 16 colors. An operator generally finds it difficult to discriminate among a larger number of colors.

The third feature listed above can be thought of as the graininess of the displays generated on a particular CRT screen. Each display is, of course, composed of a large number of individual *pixels* (dots) that are controlled by a processor in the VDU. The display will be quite *grainy* if the number of pixels per square inch is small. A larger number of pixels per square inch results in a better-quality display. A medium-quality, 19-inch CRT might have an array of 640 by 512 pixels; higher-quality CRTs might have twice the number of pixels in each direction—say, 1280 by 1024. Of course, the computing requirements (and therefore the cost) on the display processor go up significantly as the density of pixels increases.

The fourth feature refers to the method by which the display processor controls the pixels to form images on the CRT screen. In *bit-mapped* designs, the on/off status and the color of each pixel are controlled by the processor on an individual pixel basis. In *character-oriented* designs, the pixels are grouped into rectangular clusters (usually eight high by six wide) called characters. Each character depicts a letter, a number, or a special graphical symbol. In this approach, the on/off status and the color of the pixels in each type of character are controlled by the processor on a character-by-character basis instead of on an individual pixel basis. Figure 6.11 illustrates these two approaches to display generation. The upper portion of the figure shows typical characters that are defined and used in combination to create a complete display. The lower portion of the figure shows a segment of a display created using the bit-mapped approach.

It is clear from the figure that the two approaches will produce similar quality results if only alphabetic or numeric information has to be displayed. However, there can be a significant difference in appearance when

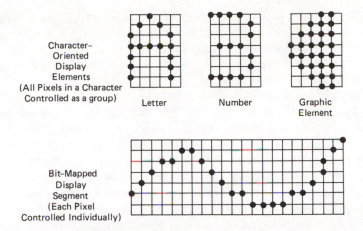

Character-
Oriented
Display
Elements
(All Pixels in a Character
Controlled as a group)

Letter Number Graphic
Element

Bit-Mapped
Display
Segment
(Each Pixel
Controlled Individually)

Figure 6.11. Two Types of Display Construction

generating displays such as trend graphs or piping and instrumentation drawings. The character-oriented approach requires that individual characters be linked together to form the graphic display. If the types of characters available match those needed to construct the desired display, the result will be acceptable; otherwise, the display will look ragged. On the other hand, the increased flexibility and generality of the bit-mapped approach allows a smooth picture to be drawn in almost all cases.

The advantage of the character-oriented approach is that it simplifies the hardware and software requirements on the display processor, resulting in a relatively low-cost product. The bit-mapped approach is relatively expensive since it requires significantly more computing power. As a result, HLOI systems have more frequently used the character-oriented technique. This situation is changing rapidly, however; with the emergence of special graphical processing chips as auxiliaries to the main display processors, the cost of computing power continues to go down. Each user or designer must select the level of performance that is appropriate to the application, keeping in mind the ever-present trade-off with regard to cost of the HLOI.

Peripherals. In addition to the processing, memory, input, and display devices required to perform the basic operator interface functions, the HLOI configuration must include the following additional peripheral devices to implement the full range of functions:

1. *Fixed disk drives*—This type of mass memory uses nonremovable memory media to store large amounts of information that must be accessed rapidly (such as standard and graphical display formats) or

to provide a location for temporary storage of historical data. One example of such a memory device is the *Winchester disk,* a magnetic memory disk with a capacity in the 5–100 Mbyte range. Another is the *read/write optical disk,* which is used for even higher density storage (500–1,000 Mbytes).

2. *Removable mass memory*—This type of mass memory, typified by the *floppy disk,* uses removable memory disks for storage of information that is to be downloaded to other elements in the distributed system (such as control configurations, tuning parameters, and custom programs). It also can be used for long-term storage of small quantities of historical data; *magnetic tape* can be used for large quantities. *Read-only optical disks,* such as those in commercial video applications, are useful for storage of large amounts of unchanging information, such as text used in operator guides.

3. *Printers and plotters*—At least one printer is required to implement the logging and alarm recording functions. The printer can also provide a hard copy of the CRT displays; or a separate printer can be dedicated to that function. A *black-and-white dot matrix printer* is the most prevalent type used, since it can implement either function. *Pen plotters, ink-jet printers,* or *thermal transfer printers* can provide full-color hard copies of CRT displays. (See Reference 6.27 for a survey of these devices.) Since these devices tend to be slow, it is important that the HLOI be designed so that the keyboard and CRT are active and available to the operator while the printing or plotting process is going on.

Modular Packaging Approach.   A few suppliers of distributed control systems provide their HLOI units in a split configuration, in which a table-mounted package houses the CRT and keyboard and a separate cabinet is used to mount the driving electronics and peripherals. However, most vendors use a modular packaging approach, which provides the user with maximum configuration flexibility without requiring the use of any separate furniture. Figure 6.12 shows an example of such a family of modules that can be used to form an integrated HLOI unit. In this family, the base module houses a CRT, a keyboard, driving electronics, and mass memory peripherals. Together they form a stand-alone, single-CRT HLOI unit. The following additional modules can be added to expand the capabilities of this base unit:

1. *CRT module*—For additional display:
2. *Alarm panel module*—For dedicated alarm indicators in addition to those provided on the CRT;

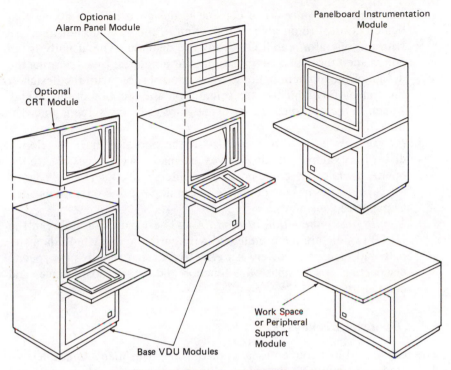

Optional
Alarm Panel Module

Panelboard Instrumentation
Module

Optional
CRT Module

Work Space
or Peripheral
Support
Module

Base VDU Modules

Figure 6.12. Family of HLOI Modules

3. *Panelboard instrumentation module*—To provide a space for mounting trend recorders, indicators, manual backup stations, telephones, and other auxiliary equipment.
4. *Work space module*—To provide a place for operator documentation and large peripherals such as printers or plotters.

Many versions of this modular approach to packaging have been brought to the marketplace, and no two are exactly alike. However, the well-designed versions have a number of characteristics in common:

1. *Good anthropometric design*—Attention is paid to the height, positioning, and orientation of the CRT and keyboard arrangement so that it is suitable for long-term use by the full range of operational personnel and in the operating positions expected (i.e., seated, standing, or both). Ideally, the design allows for adjustment of the arrangement to suit an individual's preferences (as is done in the case of a tilt steering wheel in an automobile, for example).

2. *Elimination of glare*—The console is designed in such a way that lighted control room objects reflecting in the CRT do not interfere with the operator's ability to view the displays. This usually is accomplished through a combination of approaches: by integrating the design of the ambient lighting in the control room with the design of the console; by adjusting the orientation and location of the display screen in the console; and by using glare-reducing screens to cover the CRT face.

3. *Easy accessibility of peripherals*—If the operator must use floppy disks, for example, the disk drives are made easily accessible to the operator while in a seated position. Printers and copiers are designed for ease of use and maintenance (including routine operations such as paper replacement).

4. *Simple interconnection of modules*—The various modules in the HLOI system are interconnected with wiring to carry both data signals and electrical power. An effective design requires no special engineering to accomplish this function and uses standard cables and connectors.

6.4.3. Operator Displays

The panelboard in a conventional control room uses many square feet of dedicated instruments to provide the operator with the information and mechanisms needed to control the plant. In theory, the operator has simultaneous access to all of these instruments at one time, since they all are physically located in the same room. In practice, of course, the operator must move about the room to be able to see the indicators and manipulate the various stations needed to control the plant. The video display unit in an HLOI system, in contrast, provides a "window" to the process that allows the operator to see only a relatively small amount of information at any one time on one or more CRT displays. The operator is able to monitor and control the whole process only by calling up a number of these displays, which usually are arranged in a fixed logical structure or hierarchy. If this display structure and the associated display access mechanisms are designed properly, the HLOI will provide the operator with much faster access to the needed information than is possible by moving around a panelboard (see Reference 6.8). If they are designed poorly, however, the operator will view the HLOI as an impediment to access of this information and a step backwards from the "good old days" of panelboard operation. This section describes some of the elements that go into a well-designed structure of CRT displays in an HLOI system. The next section will discuss display access mechanisms in the context of operator input hardware.

Typical Display Hierarchy.   The flexibility of CRT display technology makes it possible to conceive a great number of different display structures that would be appropriate for industrial control systems. Since the introduction of distributed control systems in the mid-1970s, however, a *de facto* standard display hierarchy has evolved over the years through the pioneering efforts of Dallimonti (6.2) and others after him (see References 6.4–6.8). A typical version of this hierarchy, illustrated in Figure 6.13, is composed of displays at four levels:

1. *Plant level*—Displays at this level provide information concerning the entire plant, which (if large enough) can be broken up into several areas of interest.
2. *Area level*—Displays at this level provide information concerning a portion of the plant equipment that is related in some way, e.g., a train of separation processes in a refinery or a boiler-turbine-generator set in a power plant.
3. *Group level*—Displays at this level deal with the control loops and data points relating to a single process unit within a plant area, such as a distillation column or a cooling tower.
4. *Loop level*—Displays at this level deal with individual control loops, control sequences, and data points.

With some variations, the VDUs that most distributed control system vendors offer follow this general structure. (Some vendors provide an

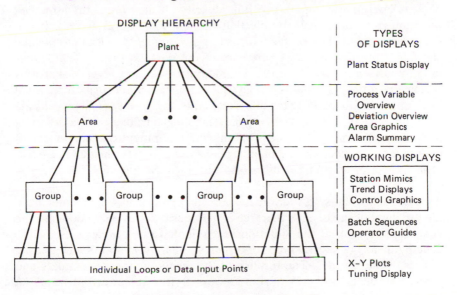

Figure 6.13. Typical Display Hierarchy

option that allows the user to define a customized display hierarchy and the allowed movements within the hierarchy.) There are several types of CRT displays that generally are associated with each level, and these will be described in the following paragraphs.

This general display structure is attractive from several points of view. First, it covers the full range of detail of information that is likely to be of interest to the operator, from overall plant conditions to the status of each loop in the plant. Also, it allows for the grouping of available information in a way that matches the structure of the process itself. Finally, it provides a mechanism that allows the operator to form a mental model of the relationships between the various pieces of information in the plant. This is similar to the mental model of a panelboard that develops in the mind of an operator after gaining experience with its layout. After a period of weeks or months, the operator no longer has to refer to the labels on the panelboard to find a particular instrument, but moves to it instinctively. Similarly, a meaningful display structure such as the one shown in Figure 6.13 allows the operator to learn to move from one display to the next in a smooth and efficient manner.

Plant-Level Displays. Typically, at the top level of this structure is a single type of plant status display (perhaps consisting of several pages), as Figure 6.14 illustrates. This display summarizes the key information needed to provide the operator with the "big picture" of current plant conditions. This example shows the overall production level at which the plant is operating compared to full capacity. It also indicates how well the plant is running (e.g., by plotting efficiency of energy usage). In addition, some of the key problem areas (e.g., equipment outages or resource shortages) are displayed. A summary of the names of the various areas in the plant serves as a main *menu* (index) to the next level of displays. At the top of the plant-status display is a status line of information provided in all operating displays. This line shows the current day of the week, the date, and the time of day for display labeling purposes. In addition, it provides a summary of process alarms and equipment diagnostic alarms by listing the numbers of the plant areas in which outstanding alarms exist. (The subject of alarming is discussed further in Section 6.4.5.)

Area-Level Displays. After obtaining a summary of the plant status from the top level of the display hierarchy, the operator can move down to the next level to look at the situation in a selected plant area. This can be done by means of several types of displays; Figure 6.15 shows a composite of four of these types. The top line of the display is the system date and status line described previously. The upper left quadrant illustrates an

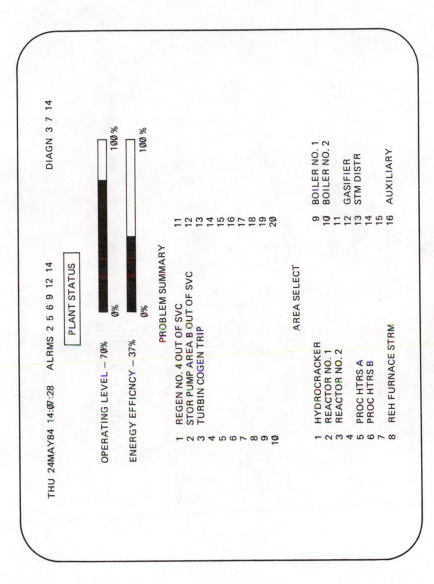

Figure 6.14. Example of a Plant Status Display

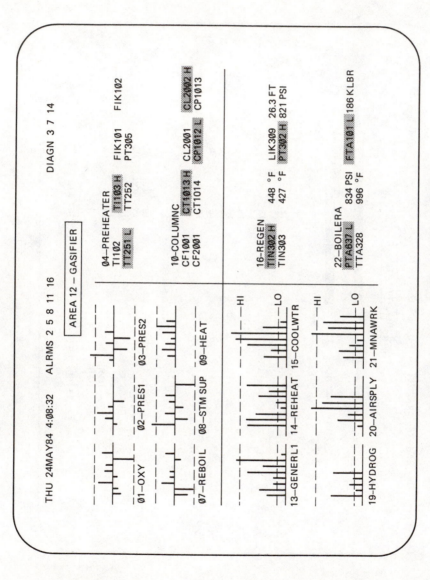

Figure 6.15. Examples of Area Overview Display

area display type known as *deviation overview,* which displays in bar graph form the deviation of key process variables from their corresponding set points. The deviations are usually normalized to reflect a percentage of total span, and are clustered into a number of groups within each area. If the absolute value of deviation exceeds a predetermined level (e.g., 5 percent of span), the process variable enters a deviation-alarm status condition and the bar graph for that variable changes color. This approach to overview display derives from the *green-band concept* in conventional analog instrumentation, in which the manual-auto stations for continuous control loops are arranged side by side in a row on the panelboard. For each loop, if the process variable is within a small percentage of the set point, the analog pointer for that variable remains hidden behind a green band on the station face. The operator then can determine which loops are upset by simply scanning the row of stations and seeing which pointers are outside the green band. The deviation overview display provides the operator with the same information in a CRT display format.

The lower left quadrant of Figure 6.15 shows a variation of this approach in which a bar graph indicates the absolute value of the process variable instead of its deviation from set point. Some versions of this display also show the set point and the high and low alarm limits on the process variable. When one of these limits is exceeded, the bar graph changes color as in the case of the deviation display. This method is more general than the previous one in that it accommodates the alarming of process variables that are *not* used in control loops as well as those that are.

The two display types just described essentially mimic the analog portions of a conventional panelboard. The upper right-hand quadrant of Figure 6.15 shows another approach to the area overview display. Here the tag numbers of the various loops and process variables are arranged in clusters by group. If the point associated with a particular tag is *not* in alarm, its tag number is displayed in a low-key color. If it *does* go into alarm, it changes color and starts flashing to get the attention of the operator. Underlining also can be used under the tag number, so that a color-blind operator still can see the alarm state clearly. This format of an overview display is similar to that of an alarm annunciator panel in a conventional panelboard.

The lower right-hand quadrant shows a variation of this display. In addition to the tag number itself, the current value of the process variable is displayed in engineering units to the right of the tag. This provides the operator with information on the values of the key variables in a group in addition to their alarm status.

In some implementations of area overview displays, several of these approaches may be intermixed in a single display. Also, two other types of area-level display often are provided:

1. *Area graphics display*—This display is similar to a piping-and-instrumentation diagram (P&ID) or mimic panel used on conventional panelboards to illustrate the process equipment and its associated instrumentation. It usually is designed to provide the same type of information that other area displays give: alarm status and perhaps current values of key process variables. The capabilities and use of graphics displays are discussed in more detail later in this section.
2. *Alarm summary display*—This display is simply a listing of the most current alarms that are still outstanding in the area. Its format is similar to that of an alarm log produced by a computer, and would include the following information on the points in alarm: tag number and description of point in alarm, time of alarm, type of alarm (e.g., deviation, high, and low), current value of point, and current alarm status (e.g., in alarm or not in alarm, returned to normal, acknowledged or not acknowledged).

Group-Level Displays. The displays at the plant and area levels of the hierarchy in Figure 6.13 are designed to provide the operator with information on the alarm and operational status of the key process variables in the plant. To perform control operations, however, it is necessary to use the displays at the next lower level in the hierarchy—the group level. As in the case of the higher-level displays, many of the display formats at the group level are patterned after the layout of panelboard instrumentation designed to accomplish similar functions. Figure 6.16 shows one example of a typical group display. Mimics of manual and automatic stations for continuous control loops occupy the upper left-hand corner of the display. These mimics include all of the elements contained in a similar panelboard station: bar graphs showing values of set point, control output, and process variables; manual, automatic, and cascade mode indicators; high and low alarm levels; and other information as needed for the type of station implemented. (The next section will discuss the mechanisms that allow the operator to interact with these stations.) The upper right section of Figure 6.16 shows indicator stations that let the operator view (but not control) selected process variables. Also in this section is a logic station that allows the operator to perform logic operations such as opening and closing valves, as well as starting or stopping sequential control sequences (e.g., for batch processes). The bottom half of the display is devoted to plotting the trends of one or more process variables as a function of time, mimicking the operation of a trend recorder on a panel-

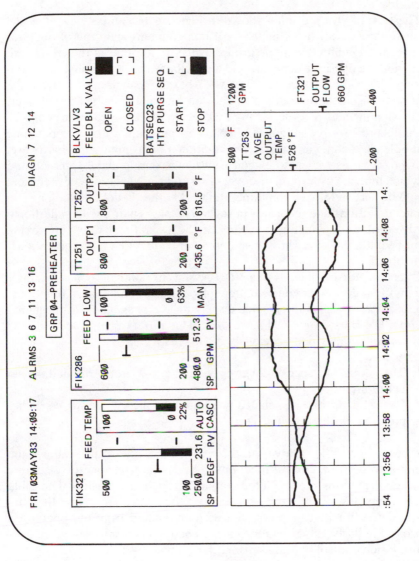

Figure 6.16. Example of a Group Display

board. In some operator interface systems, each screen "page" of a group display can use only one type of station or trend recorder; others provide much more flexibility by allowing the user to mix and match the types on each display.

The type of group display shown in Figure 6.16 can be viewed as the equivalent of a section of panelboard in a conventional type of operator interface. Switching from one group display to another is the equivalent of having the operator move around a panelboard to accomplish the monitoring and control functions. The CRT-based "panelboard" offers the user some significant benefits over the conventional panelboard, however. First, stations and recorders can be added to or removed from the CRT "panelboard" by reconfiguring displays rather than cutting or patching real holes in a panel and procuring additional instrumentation hardware. This provides a significant flexibility advantage during initial plant startup, at which time the user often discovers that additional stations or recorders would be very helpful in plant operations. Another benefit is that one can duplicate stations and recorders in several displays without any additional hardware. This duplication capability can be a significant aid to improving plant operations—one whose cost could not be justified in a conventional panelboard.

Of course, the capabilities of a VDU permit the configuration of operator displays that go well beyond simple replacement of panelboard functions. One example of this is the graphic display for a piping-and-instrumentation diagram (P&ID), shown in Figure 6.17. This differs from the area level P&ID display described previously in two respects:

1. The scope of process covered is smaller—a group rather than an entire area.
2. Control capability is included in addition to the monitoring capability provided in the area P&ID.

The controller station shown on the right side of the display allows the operator to perform control functions. The operator is able to select one of the control loops shown on the graphic through one of several possible mechanisms described in the next section; the controller station then becomes active for that loop and can be manipulated from the operator's console. Similarly, a logic station can be used to perform a sequence control or batch control operation using the graphic display.

It should be noted that in some systems, selected controller stations or logic stations on a particular console can be designated as *monitor only:* the operator cannot perform any control actions but can only monitor the station variables on the display. This capability is useful in ensuring that

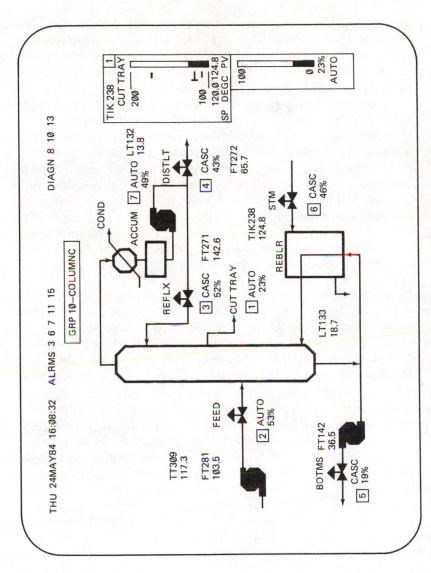

Figure 6.17. Example of a Control Graphics Display

operator control actions are coordinated when the consoles are physically distributed in several locations in the plant.

Two other types of displays also have proved useful at the group level:

1. *Batch control displays*—These are menu-oriented displays that allow an operator to observe the progression of a batch recipe (such as that shown in Figure 3.7 in Chapter 3) and interact with the sequence: start it, stop it, provide permissives to allow it to continue, and so forth. This class of displays also allows the operator to diagnose problems in executing a sequence, such as identifying the part of the process that is preventing the sequence from continuing.

2. *Operator guides*—These are advisory displays that provide the following kinds of information to the operator: problems diagnosed by the automatic system, suggested alternative courses of action in an emergency, or step-by-step startup and shutdown procedures for a piece of plant equipment. These displays may combine alphanumeric and graphic information. One can think of them as CRT-based substitutes for a set of plant operating manuals. They differ from manuals in that they can take current plant conditions into account as well as simply provide standard operating procedures to the operator.

Loop-Level Displays. The displays at the group level are the operator's primary working displays. The operator uses a few types of displays dealing with single loops or data points for control and analysis purposes. Figure 6.18 shows one example, the *X–Y operating display*. Here one process variable is plotted as a function of another to show the current operating point of this pair of variables. The operator then can compare this operating point against an alarm limit curve or an operating limit curve. In the example shown in the figure, the combination of temperature and pressure for a particular portion of the process may be critical to safety. Therefore, this pair of variables is made available to the operator in the X–Y format shown. If this pair can be controlled directly, manual/automatic stations also can be included in the display for direct operator manipulation. This approach to control and display is not possible using standard panelboard instrumentation. The CRT format makes it feasible and cost-effective.

Figure 6.19 shows an example of a *tuning display,* another single-loop display that is of use to both operating personnel and instrumentation engineers. This display includes several elements that make the tuning function possible:

1. A "fast" trend-plotting capability;
2. A manual/automatic station to allow the operator to control the loop;

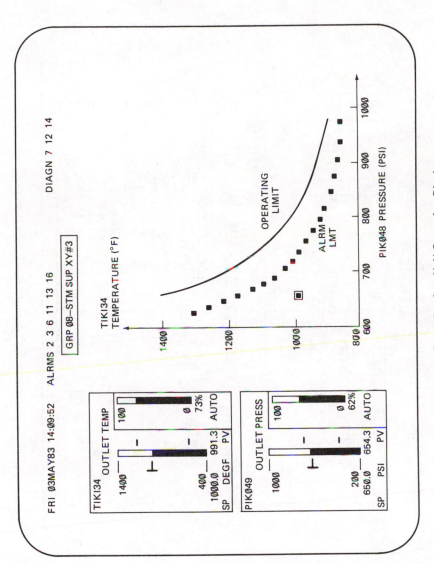

Figure 6.18. Example of an X–Y Operating Display.

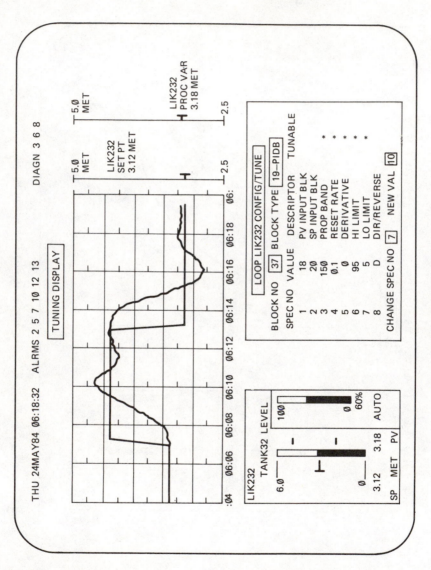

Figure 6.19. Example of a Tuning Display.

3. A list of the tuning parameters (e.g., proportional band, reset rate, and derivative rate) associated with the loop.

The trend graph is used to plot set-point changes (in automatic mode), manual control output changes (in manual mode), and the resulting responses of the process variable being controlled. Based on these responses, the operator or instrumentation engineer can make on-line adjustments to the tuning parameters to improve the performance of the control loop. This example of integrating control, trending, and tuning functions is one illustration of the ability of the CRT-based operator interface to provide the operator with a very usable and convenient tool for plant operation.

Graphics Displays.   The concept of user-generated custom graphics displays was introduced above in the context of their application to P&IDs. Operators have accepted the graphics P&ID display both for monitoring the process at the area level of display and for controlling the process at the group level. This type of display helps an operator (especially an inexperienced one) maintain an accurate mental image of the effect that any control actions will have on the process, thereby minimizing errors that could have an adverse effect on its operation. This is especially important given the typical situation in a process plant with regard to operating personnel: high turnover, minimal opportunity for training, frequent reassignments, and steady increase in workloads. It is difficult for an operator to maintain a good mental model of the process under these conditions; as a result, graphic aids to visualization of the process are very helpful, both at the area and the group level of displays. Process mimic diagrams have been used in the layout of panelboard instrumentation in the past; however, they have proved to be too expensive, space-consuming, and difficult to update as the process changes. The graphics approach to generating control-oriented P&IDs has been very effective in overcoming these difficulties while retaining the benefits of the mimic concept.

The graphics display capabilities provided in most HLOI systems can be used to generate a variety of displays other than P&IDs. The types of displays generated are limited only by the imagination of the user. Typical graphics display features include:

1. *Static fields*—These provide a background for the dynamic portion of the display. They include labels, symbols, and other elements that do not change.
2. *Data fields (in engineering units)*—These display process information that is updated automatically.
3. *Dynamic display elements*—These change size, color, or shape as a function of changing process conditions (e.g., line drawings, process

equipment symbols, bar graphs, or pie charts). They can include both user-defined elements and other elements (e.g., station faces, trends, or process equipment symbols) that are provided as a part of the standard display product.

4. *Ability to build a graphics display that is several times larger than a single CRT screen*—The operator uses a mechanism to pan across this display or "zoom" in on portions of interest.

References 6.15–6.20 provide additional suggestions regarding the proper design of graphics displays.

Design Considerations for Displays. Whether evaluating standard display formats or configuring custom graphics displays, the user of an HLOI system needs to be aware of the qualities that differentiate good from bad displays. Of course, this evaluation can be very subjective, since there are no hard and fast rules in this new area of human interface design. However, as References 6.32–6.45 describe in detail, guidelines to keep in mind during such an evaluation include the following:

1. Displays should not be cluttered, but kept as simple as possible. Often, displays are designed to cram as much information as possible on one screen; this is counterproductive if it confuses rather than helps the operator. Some systems solve this problem by allowing the operator to select between a simple version and a detailed version of the same display. The simple version is used for most operations; the operator presses a detail key to get more information when needed.

2. Displays should not be overly "flashy" or have light-colored backgrounds. Such displays may look impressive at demonstrations and trade shows but can be very tiring and annoying to an operator who must sit and look at them all day while trying to run a plant.

3. As described previously, the top line or two of each display should contain common information of interest to the operator, such as the date and time of day as well as an overview of the alarm status situation. The bottom line or two of each display should be reserved for communications (e.g., prompts or error messages) between the HLOI system and the operator.

4. Color should be used in a consistent way throughout all displays to minimize operator confusion; for example, certain colors should be reserved for the static portions of the display, dynamic fields in the display, or alarming information. If at all possible, the color conventions of the industry in which the system is being applied should

be followed. The user should be able to select or change colors in both standard and custom displays to meet the needs of the application.

5. Color should not be the sole means for communicating with the operator in the case of critical functions such as alarming. The incidence of color-blindedness among the operator population is too great to permit this approach. Instead, other mechanisms such as blinking or underlining should supplement color to ensure that proper communications takes place.

As in the case of other guidelines in the human factors area, these common-sense rules appear to be obvious but often are neglected in actual practice.

6.4.4. Design Considerations for Operator Input

The CRT in a high-level operator interface unit is the primary way the automatic control system transmits information to the operator. The HLOI also must provide a way for the operator to input the following types of information into the automatic system:

1. *Display-select commands*—To allow the operator to move about the display hierarchy described in the previous section;
2. *Cursor-movement commands*—To allow the operator to move a cursor (position indicator) from place to place on any one display;
3. *Control-input commands*—To allow the operator to interact with the station mimics and other control-oriented displays in the hierarchy;
4. *Data inputs*—To allow the operator to enter numeric information (e.g., set points and measurement values obtained manually) into the automatic control system.

As mentioned in Section 6.4.2, there are a variety of hardware devices that can implement this input function. The one device that is common to all commercially available HLOI systems is one version or another of an operator's keyboard. In more recent years, the CRT touch screen has developed into a cost-effective and reliable device for operator use. Devices such as light pens and "mice" have been found to be less suitable for two reasons: (1) they are more prone to failure in an industrial environment, and (2) they must be stored and retrieved from some location within the console.

Figure 6.20 illustrates the use of a touch screen as an operator input device. (See References 6.25 and 6.28 for more information on touch

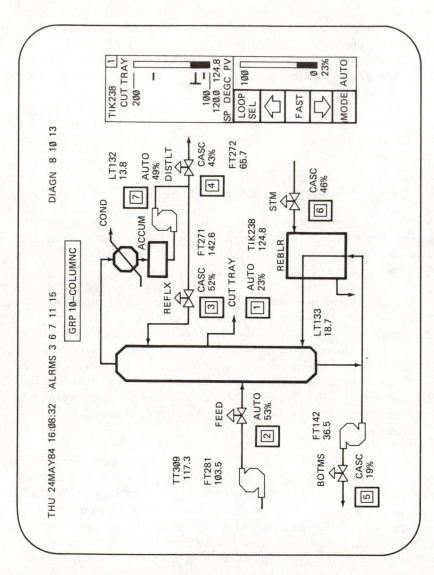

Figure 6.20. Example of Touch Screen Operation.

screens.) A fine grid of sensing areas on the CRT screen allows the HLOI to sense the touch of the operator's finger on any portion of the screen. The grid of sensing areas usually is implemented using one of two approaches: (1) an array of infrared emitters and receivers located on the periphery of the CRT tube, or (2) a pattern of transparent touch wires, thin-film conductors, or capacitance-sensing panels overlaid on the screen itself. The HLOI relates the screen location of the operator's touch to the corresponding segment of the display on the screen. In this example, one can use the touch screen both to select and to manipulate a control loop. To do this, the operator need only touch the loop-select segment of the display ("LOOP SEL" on right-hand side) then touch the desired control loop on the P&ID graphic. At this point the control station on the right side of the display becomes active, and the operator can change modes, raise and lower set points, and perform other functions by touching the relevant portion of the station mimic display. This is done in the same way as in operating a physical station on a panelboard.

There are two design considerations to keep in mind when evaluating or designing the layout of a touch screen and the corresponding CRT displays for use as an operator input device:

1. The spaces between the keys or control segments on the CRT must be large enough to meet the needs of a "gloved hand operator" described by Herb (6.12).
2. Audible feedback (such as a beep or tone) must be provided to confirm that the operator has depressed a control segment on the CRT. This feature is essential to minimizing operator errors.

While useful, the touch screen is not adequate by itself to provide the operator with the full range of input functions needed in an HLOI. It is most convenient for implementing cursor-movement and control-input functions. A keyboard usually is necessary for display-select commands and data inputs. Two versions of keyboard hardware are in common use: (1) the conventional push-button type of keyboard found in electric typewriters; or (2) the flat-panel type using membrane switches or similar hardware to implement the push buttons under a flat layer of mylar. Generally, the flat panel type is preferred for use in industrial control systems because of its ruggedness. The layer of mylar protects the key contacts from a contaminated atmosphere and eliminates the infamous "coffee-spill problem." Because of the limited key action that the flat-panel type allows, it is not suited to touch typing or other fast operations. However, since most operator actions do not require extremely fast action, the flat-panel approach is quite acceptable in this application. Just as in the case of the touch screen, audible feedback to push-button operations helps to minimize errors. In the case of the keyboard, proper selection of keyboard components also can provide tactile feedback to the operator.

The layout of the flat-panel keyboard is crucial to ensuring its ease of use in an industrial operating environment. Since the operator is *not* a typist or computer technician, providing a general-purpose typewriter-like keyboard is not appropriate. Instead, the keyboard should be partitioned into dedicated functional areas. Figure 6.21 is an example of such partitioning. The following paragraphs summarize the purpose and layout design of each of these areas.

Display Select Area.   As its name implies, this keyboard area allows the operator to select a particular display of interest within the hierarchy. In some cases, this selection can be done using the touch screen on the CRT; in others, using the keyboard is more convenient. The keys in this area should allow the operator to move to any display in the hierarchy with a minimum number of keystrokes (two or three at most). The operator should have the option of moving either by making selections from menus or by calling up the area, group, or loop by name or number.

One means for providing the operator with a flexible input capability (for display selection or other purposes) is through the use of *soft keys*. These are selected keys in the keyboard whose assigned functions can change depending on the current display on the screen. One approach to implementing this concept is to mount a set of blank keys on the keyboard as close as practicable to the CRT display area. The current display then defines the operational meaning of these keys through messages or symbols displayed near the corresponding keys. Another approach is to mount a small CRT or flat-panel display in the keyboard area and overlay it with

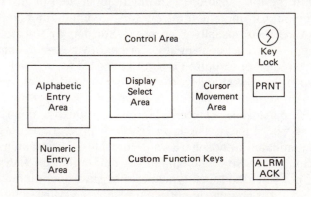

Figure 6.21. Typical Partitioning of a Keyboard.

touch-sensitive sensors. Then the "keys" shown on the display can be labeled dynamically, depending on the particular human interface situation.

The advantage of the soft-key approach is that it can reduce the number of dedicated function keys required on the keyboard. However, the use of soft keys also has been criticized on the grounds that in crisis situations the operator may become confused over their function when moving quickly from one display to another.

Alphabetic and Numeric Entry Areas.   In the process of calling up various displays by name or identification number, it may be necessary for the operator to enter alphabetic and numeric information into the system through the keyboard. As mentioned previously, a process operator is not a typist and therefore is likely to enter this information through the hunt-and-peck method. To make this as painless as possible, the standard QWERTY typewriter keyboard layout is *not* used, since its configuration has no recognizable pattern as far as the average operator is concerned. Instead, the keys in the alphabetic entry area usually are laid out in alphabetic order. Very often, the numeric entry area is configured like the keypad on a touch-tone telephone, since the operator is likely to have some familiarity with that arrangement.

Cursor Movement Area.   After selecting a particular display, very often it is necessary for the operator to move a cursor around the display to perform certain operations (such as activating a control station or selecting an item from an on-screen menu). In the cursor movement area of the keyboard are *arrow* keys for moving the cursor in the direction indicated. Some keyboard implementations replace the arrow keys with such devices as a joy stick, a track ball, or a mouse. However, the arrow keys have been preferred in most vendor offerings for reasons of reliability and cost.

Control Area.   To control the process through the HLOI, the operator first selects a particular loop for manipulation or a logic operation for initiation through one of the mechanisms described in preceding sections. Depending on how the operator interface system is designed, the operator then works through the CRT touch screen or through the control area of the keyboard to execute the control operation. In either case, the operator input system accommodates the following continuous control actions: selecting manual, automatic, or other modes (e.g., cascade, ratio, or supervisory control); increasing or decreasing the set-point value or control-output value in either a slow or fast mode; and entering a desired set-point or control-output value in engineering units. Except for the last action, these functions are the same as those available using panelboard instrumentation. In the case of a logic or sequencing operation, the operator input system allows execution of start, stop, and permissive commands. These are usually simple push-button operations and can be implemented using either the touch screen or the keyboard.

The layout of the control area of the keyboard varies widely from one distributed control system to another. In some systems, the layout is similar to that of the vendor's corresponding panelboard instrumentation. This is an advantage in applications that include both panelboard instrumentation and an HLOI, since it minimizes operator confusion when moving from one human interface device to another. In some layouts, only one set of control operation keys is provided for multiple loops. The operator first selects the loop to be controlled and then works through that set of keys. In other systems, multiple sets of control operation keys are provided to match the layout of a particular group display (e.g., eight sets of control keys for an eight-loop group display). After selecting the group, the operator can manipulate any of the loops in the group at the same time without having to select each loop first. No conclusive ergonomic results have been obtained to determine which approach is better; the multiple-loop method provides slightly faster access to loops within the same group, at the expense of cluttering up the keyboard with a larger number of keys.

Some vendors mount panelboard instrumentation in the keyboard itself to serve as the control input hardware. The intent is to provide the operator with familiar hardware, but in practice this approach leads to keyboards that are large and cumbersome. In addition, the operator then must switch back and forth between this panelboard instrumentation and the rest of the keyboard, which can cause confusion. The more prevalent practice is to keep the keyboard as simple and consistent as possible to minimize such confusion.

Miscellaneous Keyboard Functions. In addition to the dedicated functional areas just described, there are several other operator functions that the keyboard hardware must accommodate. Many distributed control system vendors are now offering a set of keys that the user can configure to perform custom functions. These keys can provide direct call-up of a selected set of displays critical to the particular process. Direct call-up bypasses the normal display hierarchy, giving the operator faster access to these displays. Keyboard hardware used to implement other miscellaneous operator interface functions include the following:

1. *A print key*—This allows the operator to obtain a hard copy of any display that is currently on the screen. The print function must be

designed in such a way that the CRT and keyboard are still active while the printing process is going on;

2. *An alarm acknowledge key*—This allows the operator to inform the HLOI that he or she has recognized a particular alarm situation and acknowledges it;

3. *A key lock*—This sets the status of the console to one of three modes: (a) *off-line*, in which console reconfiguration and maintenance functions are performed; (b) *operational*, in which the normal operator functions are activated; or (c) *engineering*, in which control system tuning and modification can be accomplished.

6.4.5. System Design Issues

The hardware elements and the display capabilities described in the previous subsections combine to form a total high-level operator interface *system*, which the operator uses to perform the functions summarized in Section 6.2: monitoring, control, diagnostics, and record keeping. The methods used in implementing many of these functions have already been described in the preceding paragraphs in the context of particular hardware elements and display types. The following subsections discuss other implementation issues involving the total operator interface system.

Distributed Database Considerations. The database associated with each point (control loop, analog input, or digital input) in a distributed control system consists of the current value of that point along with a great deal of auxiliary information. Some of this information relates to the identification of the point in the system, such as the following:

1. Physical hardware address of the point (cabinet, module, or input channel);
2. Classification of point (analog or digital);
3. Tag name and descriptor (if any) associated with the point;
4. Engineering units associated with the point.

Other information relates to the monitoring, alarming, and trending functions performed on the point:

1. High and low alarm limits;
2. Alarm status (not in alarm, in high alarm, in low alarm, or returned to normal);
3. Alarm acknowledgment status (alarm acknowledged or not acknowledged by the operator);

4. Past values of the point (used in trending);
5. Computed functions of past values of the point (e.g., average value, maximum value, minimum value, and smoothed or filtered value over some time period).

Each vendor's distributed control system stores this database for each point in different locations. In many systems, the local control unit stores only the hardware address and the current value of the point in engineering units. The other information is distributed throughout the system in higher-level devices such as the HLOI units or computers. This distributed approach to the structuring of the database has a number of negative consequences, including the following:

1. If there are multiple HLOIs that display the same set of points (which is usually the case), *each* HLOI must store the tag name, descriptor, alarm limits, and other information associated with each point. This is expensive in terms of memory requirements on the HLOI.
2. Each HLOI must compute the alarm status for each point, since each interface must display this status. This procedure is expensive in terms of computing requirements on the HLOI.
3. If the operator changes an alarm limit for a point, he or she must either change it manually in all HLOIs or there must be a mechanism to change the corresponding alarm limits automatically in the other HLOIs. The latter leads to complications if, for example, one of the HLOIs is temporarily off-line.
4. The same problem as in item 3 holds for alarm acknowledgments.

A better approach is to store *all* of the information associated with a point in the same LCU as the point value itself. Then there is a single location that all HLOIs and other devices in the system can query for this information. This approach also implies that such computational functions as alarm checking and averaging must be done in the LCU. This used to be impractical to implement due to the limited memory and computational resources of the LCUs. With the continuing reductions in cost and increases in performance of the hardware in the LCUs, this approach has become feasible.

One result of performing the trending and alarming functions in the individual LCU is that each LCU must then keep track of the time of day. Since the HLOI units must sort out and display trend and alarm data from a large number of LCUs in a consistent manner, each data point must be tagged with its associated time of occurrence. The mechanism for providing synchronized time clocks in each LCU varies from system to system. The simplest approach is to have one high-level element in the system maintain the master time base. That element can periodically update the other clocks in the system by sending messages over the shared communications facility (for example).

Alarming. In conventional control rooms, the operator relied on the annunciator panel to provide timely information on alarms in the system. The design of the HLOI has replaced this panel with an alarming function distributed among the hardware in the distributed control system and among the displays in the HLOI. As described in the previous paragraph, the alarm-checking function is often performed by the LCU, which then makes the alarm status of each point available to other elements in the distributed system. Usually there is one display or set of displays in the HLOI dedicated to the alarming function. It generally takes the form of a chronological list of the previous N alarms. In large systems, a complete HLOI unit can be dedicated to displaying this set of alarms. If the HLOI includes several CRTs, one of them can display this alarm list.

However, it is important that the operator be made aware of the alarm status of the plant on *each* display in the HLOI system, since at any particular time he or she may be working with and concentrating on a display *other* than the alarm display. For this reason, in each operating display in the HLOI the top line is usually a time/date/alarm summary, as described in Section 6.4.3. The design of each display also incorporates alarming functions by giving the alarm status, alarm type, and (sometimes) the alarm limits along with the value of each point.

When a point first goes into alarm, its new alarm status usually is signaled when the tag name of the alarmed point changes color and starts to blink. Often an audible signal such as a bell or a tone accompanies the visible change in alarm status. When the operator acknowledges the alarm, the blinking stops and the audible signal is silenced but the color change on the display remains as long as the point is in alarm. In some systems, the alarm status of each point can be placed into one of several levels of priority when the system is first configured. This priority level is displayed along with the alarm status itself, usually through the color of the alarm indication.

The mechanism used for acknowledging alarms differs from one distributed system to another. An alarm acknowledgment key is always included in the keyboard, but the scope of the alarm points acknowledged by the keystroke ranges from a single point to all the points in the area being displayed. Usually the design forces the operator to move to a group display that includes the point in alarm before the system will accept the operator's acknowledgement. This mechanism is intended to force the operator to review the nature of the alarm and act accordingly instead of simply hitting the acknowledge button as a reflex action to silence the audible signal.

References 6.14 and 6.36 provide additional information on alarm management in distributed control systems.

Trending.   The data storage and retrieval capabilities of the HLOI system provide the operator with much more flexibility and accuracy in trending than ever possible with conventional strip chart or round chart recorders. Of course, many implementations of the HLOI provide an analog output capability that can be used to drive conventional recorders. However, the real benefits of advanced trending accrue when trend data are stored digitally within the distributed control system (either in the LCUs, in the HLOI unit, or in a separate trending box). The following trending features are commonly available in state-of-the-art distributed control systems:

1. Trend data for each point are stored at a resolution the user selects to match the dynamics of the point being trended (e.g., once a second for flows, once every 30 seconds for temperatures).
2. The operator receives the data in graphical form by means of CRT displays designed to look like conventional trend graphs (as described in Section 6.4.3.). Usually, each display can share trend graphs of several points.
3. The data shown on the CRT screen at any one time are usually a small fraction of the data available in storage. This allows the operator to pan through the data or zoom in on the portion of time that is of particular interest. Of course, the maximum time resolution achievable in the use of these functions is limited by the frequency of data collection originally specified for the point.
4. The amplitude of the trend graph can usually be changed on-line by the operator to magnify the graph, making it easier to read. Of course, the resolution of the particular CRT used will limit the amplitude resolution of the trends. Also, a digital readout usually is provided to display the value of the point at any time along the trend graph, along with a cursor function that allows the operator to select the time to which the digital readout applies.
5. Pressing the print-display key produces a hard copy of the trend graph.
6. In addition to providing the operator with trend displays preconfigured to include certain points, some systems have a "wild card" display that allows the operator to select a unique set of trends that are of particular interest to him.

Trend data are usually stored in the distributed system elements for only a limited amount of time (typically 10 to 12 hours) to allow some overlap between operator shifts. The long-term data storage and retrieval function (described in the following subsection) provides storage over a longer period of time.

Long-Term Data Storage and Retrieval. This feature is the process control equivalent of the flight recorder, which commercial and military aviation uses to store selected data points as a function of time and which allows later review for investigative or historical purposes. For example, this information can be quite valuable for determining the root cause of an equipment failure, for analyzing the dynamic characteristics of a process, or for providing proof of a product's proper manufacture. The information stored commonly includes a record of key process variables, alarms, and operator actions (for example) as a function of time. Traditionally, this feature has been implemented using a computer. The significant expansion of processing and memory capabilities in an HLOI unit has made it feasible and cost-effective to implement this feature in the HLOI itself.

In its basic form, long-term data storage and retrieval involves the following sequence of operations:

1. A sequence of process data points or events over a selected time period is recorded.
2. Each data point is labeled with the appropriate tag name, engineering units, and time at which it was recorded.
3. The sequence is written onto a memory medium, such as a floppy disk or magnetic tape, that can be removed from the HLOI and placed in storage.

As a minimum, the long-term data storage and retrieval implementation in a high-level operator interface must allow the operator to run an "instant replay" of selected data sequences on the HLOI in the form of trend graphs. Other features to consider in evaluating or designing a long-term data storage and retrieval system are:

1. *Compatibility with on-line displays*—To minimize operator confusion, the HLOI should allow the replay of long-term storage data by means of the same trend displays used for on-line trending. It should not be necessary to take the HLOI off-line to perform the replay function.
2. *Tabular format capability*—In addition to allowing replay in a trend graph format, the HLOI should be designed to permit display of the

data in a tabular format. As a minimum, this format should include the tag name of the point, the time associated with the point value, and the point value itself in engineering units. It also should be possible to produce a hard copy listing of selected time sequences of points in long-term storage.

3. *Data storage format*—The format of data storage on the floppy disk or magnetic tape should allow computers or digital devices *other* than the vendor's HLOI to read and manipulate the data. In many cases, the off-line data analysis operations that must be performed require the use of a general-purpose digital computer. Convenience in accessing the data is essential.

4. *Density of data storage*—Data compression techniques should be used to maximize the amount of information stored on a single floppy disk or magnetic tape cartridge or cassette. This will minimize the amount of human interaction (i.e., disk or tape loading and unloading) required to support the long-term storage function. The operator or instrument engineer should not have to be involved in this function any more often than once a day. Appropriate prompts and alarms must be provided to ensure that the magnetic medium is replaced on schedule and that no data are lost.

In some distributed control systems, the long-term data storage and retrieval feature is *not* included in the HLOI. Rather, it is implemented in a separate device, sometimes called a *process historian,* which gathers data using the plant communications facility.

Logging. The third record-keeping function (in addition to trending and long-term data storage and retrieval) that distributed control systems provide is logging. The primary objective of the logging function is to produce a hard-copy record of process data and events on a printer. Like the long-term storage and retrieval function, logging traditionally has been implemented in a computer system. In current distributed control systems, logging is implemented either in the high-level operator interface or in a separate process historian.

Logging functions fall into two categories: periodic and event-driven. A *periodic log* is simply a printed record of the values of a particular process point or points at regular time intervals. Many early computer systems performed this data-logging function. It was mainly successful in generating reams of printout paper that was rarely looked at again unless a process problem developed. The periodic logging function has largely been supplanted by long-term data storage and retrieval. Recording the information on magnetic media has proved to be much more efficient than producing hard copy.

Most hard-copy logging functions are now *event-driven,* and include the following examples:

1. *Process alarms*—High, low, and deviation alarms are logged when they occur; often, operator acknowledgments and alarm return-to-normal conditions also are logged.
2. *Equipment alarms*—The failures of devices (e.g., sensors, transmitters, and controllers) within the instrumentation and control system often are detected through on-line diagnostics and are recorded on a hard-copy log.
3. *Operator control actions*—Controller mode changes, set-point and control-output changes, sequence initiations, and other control actions performed by the operator often are logged. Some systems also allow the operator to store notes or journal entries that explain or expand on the record of his or her actions.
4. *Sequence-of-events (trip) logs*—In many distributed control systems, dedicated devices called *sequence-of-events recorders* monitor the occurrence of discrete events (e.g., switches opening or closing or a variable exceeding a limit) dealing with a major piece of plant equipment. If this equipment fails or is tripped off-line, the recorder remembers the sequence of events that led to the failure or trip event. If the recorder is integrated into the distributed control system (instead of being a stand-alone device), the sequence can be transmitted to the logging device for recording on the logging printer.

One of the issues involved in implementing the logging function is what format the log printout should use. Usually, the vendor provides a standard format that includes the time the logged event occurred, the type of event that occurred, and the appropriate tag number or device number associated with the event. Some logging systems allow the user to customize this format to his or her own needs; others are not as flexible.

In most distributed control systems, at least one printer is dedicated to the logging function. This approach minimizes the mixing of log printouts with other system functions, such as hard copy of CRT displays and printing of data from long-term storage.

This concludes the review of operator interface design issues in distributed control systems. The discussion in Chapter 7 moves to the design of human interfaces for instrument engineers and other support personnel.

REFERENCES

Advances in Operator Interfaces

6.1 Dallimonti, R., "Future Operator Consoles for Improved Decision-Making and Safety," *Instrumentation Technology,* vol. 19, no. 8, August 1972, pp. 23–28.

6.2 Dallimonti, R., "New Designs for Process Control Consoles," *Instrumentation Technology,* vol. 20, no. 11, November 1973, pp. 48–53.

6.3 Stewart, C.R., "Operator Interface in Distributed Microprocessor Control System," Instrument Society of America International Conference, Houston, Texas, October 1976.

6.4 Sheridan, T.B., "Theory of Man–Machine Interaction as Related to Computerized Automation," in *Man–Machine Interfaces for Industrial Control,* Kompass, E.J., and Williams, T.J., eds., Control Engineering, Barrington, Illinois, 1980.

6.5 Hedrick, J.L., and Pageler, E.L., "Effective Operation System Characterization with an Interactive Colorgraphics Operator Console," Instrument Society of America International Conference, Houston, Texas, October 1980.

6.6 Jones, D.D., Agrusa, R.L., and Doyle, C.L., "The Future of Operator Interfaces to the Power Plant," 25th ISA Power Instrumentation Symposium, Phoenix, Arizona, May 1982.

6.7 Browngardt, R.P., and Johnson, R.K., "Microprocessor Driven Displays for the Industrial Power House," Instrument Society of America International Conference, Houston, Texas, October 1983.

6.8 Krigman, A., "Operator Interfaces: Mirror, Mirror on the Wall," *InTech,* vol. 32, no. 4, April 1985, pp. 55–58.

Operator Interface Design Issues

6.9 "Selecting CRT-based Process Interfaces," *Instrumentation Technology,* vol. 26, no. 2, February 1979, pp. 28–33.

6.10 Dallimonti, R., "Principles of Design for Man-Machine Interfaces in Process Control," in *Man–Machine Interfaces for Industrial Control,* Kompass, E.J., and Williams, T.J., eds., Control Engineering, Barrington, Illinois, 1980.

6.11 Redrup, J.L., Jr., "System Design Considerations for a Real-Time Man–Machine Interface," Third Annual Control Engineering Conference, Rosemont, Illinois, May 1984.

6.12 Herb, S.M., "Technology Improves Process Control Displays," *Instruments & Control Systems,* vol. 57, no. 5, May 1984, pp. 45–49.

6.13 Bailey, S.J., "From Desktop to Plant Floor, a CRT is the Control Operator's Window on the Process," *Control Engineering,* vol. 31, no. 6, June 1984, pp. 86–90.

6.14 Schellekens, P.L., "Alarm Management in Distributed Control Systems," *Control Engineering,* vol. 31, no. 12, December 1984, pp. 60–64.

Graphic Displays

6.15 Friedewald, W., and Charwat, H.J., "Design of Graphic Displays for CRTs in Control Rooms," *Process Automation,* no. 1, 1980.

6.16 Weber, R., et al., "Graphics-based Process Interface," *Chemical Engineering Progress,* vol. 78, no. 1, January 1982, pp. 50–53.

6.17 Lieber, R.E., "Process Control Graphics for Petrochemical Plants," *Chemical Engineering Progress,* vol. 78, no. 12, December 1982, pp. 45–52.
6.18 Instrument Society of America, "Graphic Symbols for Process Displays," Draft Standard ISA–dS5.5, February 1984.
6.19 Manuel, T., "Computer Graphics," *Electronics,* vol. 57, no. 13, June 28, 1984.
6.20 DeVries, E.A., "Improving Control Graphics," *Hydrocarbon Processing,* vol. 64, no. 6, June 1985, pp. 69–71.

Operator Interface Hardware

6.21 Morris, H.M., "Pushbutton Keyboards Let Man 'Talk' to Controls," *Control Engineering,* vol. 28, no. 11, November 1981, pp. 85–88.
6.22 Miller, W., and Suther, T.W., "Display Station Anthropometrics: Preferred Height and Angle Settings of CRT and Keyboard," *Human Factors,* vol. 25, no. 4, 1983, pp. 401–408.
6.23 Borrell, J., "Industry Review: Graphics Terminals," *Digital Design,* vol. 14, no. 2, February 1984, pp. 42–50.
6.24 Castellano, J.A., "Trends in Flat Information Display Technology," *Digital Design,* vol. 14, no. 5, May 1984, pp. 122–131.
6.25 Flynn, W.R., "Control Panels: From Pushbuttons to Keyboards to Touchscreens," *Control Engineering,* vol. 31, no. 6, June 1984, pp. 79–81.
6.26 Mokhoff, N., "Thirty-Two Bit Micros Power Workstations," *Computer Design,* vol. 23, no. 6, June 15, 1984, pp. 97–112.
6.27 Watkins, H.S., and Moore, J.S., "A Survey of Color Graphics Printing," *IEEE Spectrum,* vol. 21, no. 7, July 1984, pp. 26–37.
6.28 Comerford, R., "Pointing-Device Innovations Enhance User/Machine Interfaces," *EDN,* vol. 29, no. 5, July 26, 1984, pp. 54–66.
6.29 Switzer, C., "Display Technologies for Control Applications," *Instruments & Control Systems,* vol. 58, no. 2, February 1985, pp. 49–53.
6.30 Peterson, R.E., Jr., "Flat-Panel Displays Beat CRTs for Military Systems," *EDN,* vol. 30, no. 8, April 11, 1985, pp. 77–88.
6.31 "Special Report on Display Technologies," *IEEE Spectrum,* vol. 22, no. 7, July 1985, pp. 52–73.

Human Factors Issues

6.32 Miller, R.B., "Response Time in Man-Computer Conversational Transactions," in *AFIPS Conference Proceedings,* Fall Joint Computer Conf., San Francisco, CA, Dec. 1968; pub. by AFIPS Press, Arlington, Va., 1969, vol. 33, pt. 1, pp. 267–277.
6.33 Edwards, E., and Lees, F.P., *The Human Operator in Process Control,* Halsted Press, New York, 1974.
6.34 Rouse, W.B., "Design of Man-Computer Interfaces for On-Line Interactive Systems," *Proceedings of the IEEE,* vol. 63, no. 6, June 1975, pp. 847–857.
6.35 Dallimonti, R., "Human Factors in Control Center Design," *Instrumentation Technology,* vol. 23, no. 5, May 1976, pp. 39–44.
6.36 Kortlandt, D., and Kragt, H., "Ergonomics in the Struggle Against 'Alarm Inflation' in Process Control Systems," *Journal A,* vol. 19, no. 3, 1978, pp. 135–142.

6.37 Shneiderman, B., "Human Factors Experiments in Designing Interactive Systems," *Computer,* vol. 12, no. 12, December 1979, pp. 9–19.

6.38 Sheridan, T.B., "Human Error in Nuclear Power Plants," *Technology Review,* vol. 83, no. 2, February 1980, pp. 22–33.

6.39 Geiser, G., "Ergonomic Design of Man–Machine Interfaces," Sixth IFAC/IFIP Conference on Digital Computer Applications to Process Control, Dusseldorf, Germany, October 1980.

6.40 Rijnsdorp, J.E., "Important Problems and Challenges in Human Factors and Man–Machine Engineering for Process Control Systems," in *Chemical Process Control 2,* Proc. of Engineering Foundation Conference, Sea Island, GA, January 1981; pub. by United Engineering Trustees, New York, New York, 1982, pp. 93–110.

6.41 Rouse, W.B., "Human-Computer Interaction in the Control of Dynamic Systems," *Computing Surveys,* vol. 13, no. 1, March 1981, pp. 71–99.

6.42 Herbst, L., and Hinz, W., "Control Room Design and Human Engineering in Power Plants," IAEA Interregional Training Course on Instrumentation and Control of Nuclear Power Plants, Karlsruhe Nuclear Research Center, Federal Republic of Germany, October–November 1982.

6.43 Singer, J.G., and Reeder, G., "A Human Factors Review of a Nuclear Plant Control Room," *ISA Transactions,* vol. 22, no. 1, 1983, pp. 59–72.

6.44 Shirley, R.S., "Human/Process Interfaces: Making Them Easy to Use," *Instrumentation Technology,* vol. 31, no. 8, August 1984, pp. 55–58.

6.45 *Computer–generated Display System Guidelines,* vols. 1 and 2, Interim Report EPRI NP–3701, Electric Power Research Institute, Palo Alto, California, September 1984.

7
ENGINEERING INTERFACES

7.1. INTRODUCTION

Chapter 6 discussed in detail the human interfaces that allow the plant operator to monitor and control the process. As mentioned in the introduction to that chapter, the functions that the plant's instrument and control system engineer performs are usually quite different and separate from those that the operator performs. (This separation arises due to standard plant practices or even union contracts, which spell out the responsibilities of each group of workers.) Because of this, many vendors of distributed control systems provide an engineering interface that is totally independent of the operator interface. Other vendors recognize that there are many common features and functions that both the operator and engineering interfaces require. As a result, these vendors combine the functions in a single set of hardware, but allow the hardware to take on different "personalities" depending on its current user.

As in the case of the operator interface, vendors normally provide the user a choice between two levels of engineering interface hardware:

1. Low-level, minimum-function devices that are inexpensive and justifiable for small systems;
2. High-level, full-function devices that are more powerful (and expensive), but which are needed and justifiable for medium- and large-sized distributed control systems.

This chapter describes both of these levels of engineering interface. Section 7.2 summarizes the basic requirements that any engineering interface system must meet. Section 7.3 describes and analyzes representative design approaches taken by vendors to meet these requirements for the low-level interface, and Section 7.4 does the same for the high-level interface. Many of the references at the end of chapter 6 provide additional information on engineering interfaces.

7.2. ENGINEERING INTERFACE REQUIREMENTS

In the past, defining and setting up a monitoring and control system consisting of conventional discrete analog and sequential modules has involved a tremendous amount of engineering labor. The instrument engineers (either the vendor's or the end user's) had to select and procure the control and data acquisition modules, mount them in cabinets, and do a significant amount of custom wiring between modules. Then the engineers had to test and check out the entire system manually prior to field installation. Similarly, they had to select operator interface instrumentation, mount it in panelboards, wire it up, and test it. They had to prepare documentation for the entire configuration of control and operator interface hardware and the corresponding control logic diagrams, usually from manually generated drawings. When errors in the control system were found, new modules had to be obtained, wiring redone, and documentation laboriously updated.

As pointed out in earlier chapters, the introduction of distributed control systems has simplified tremendously the process of engineering a control system. A small number of general-purpose, microprocessor-based modules have replaced dozens of dedicated-function hardware modules. The use of shared communication links has reduced or eliminated custom intermodule wiring. Control system logic has been expressed in function block logic diagrams instead of hardware schematics. CRT-based operator consoles have replaced huge panelboards filled with arrays of stations, indicators, annunciators, and recorders. As a result of these simplifications in the architecture of industrial control systems, the process of *engineering* such a system has become simpler in a corresponding manner.

However, a significant amount of engineering work is still necessary to put a distributed control system out into the field. Special hardware has been developed as a part of the distributed control system architecture to make this process as painless as possible. This *engineering interface hardware* must perform functions in the following categories:

1. *System configuration*—Define hardware configuration and interconnections, as well as control logic and computational algorithms;
2. *Operator interface configuration*—Define equipment that the operator needs to perform his or her functions in the system (as described in Chapter 6), and define the relationship of this equipment with the control system itself;
3. *Systen documentation*—Provide a mechanism for documenting the system and the operator interface configuration and for making changes quickly and easily;

4. *System failure diagnosis*—Provide a mechanism to allow the instrument engineer to determine the existence and location of failures in the system in order to make repairs quickly and efficiently.

The following sections will discuss these requirements in detail along with a number of general requirements that do not fall into any of these categories.

General Requirements. Like the operator interface devices described in Chapter 6, the engineering interfaces in a distributed control system must be designed for the appropriate class of users of the equipment. These ergonomic requirements and several other requirements dealing with the specific functions of the engineering interface are as follows:

1. *Access security*—The engineering interface defines and modifies the control logic and tuning parameters (among other items) of the process control system. Therefore, the system must include a security mechanism to keep unauthorized users from getting access to the system configuration through the engineering interface.
2. *Ergonomic design*—The instrumentation and control engineer using the engineering interface equipment is likely to have more technical training than the process operators; however, the engineer often will not have a computer hardware or software background. Therefore, the engineering interface should be designed to accept inputs through an interactive prompt-and-response sequence, rather than through entering of data tables or program statements. Data input formats should be in a form understandable to a process instrumentation engineer, not to a computer expert (no octal or hexadecimal data formats, please). If the distributed control system has more than one type of engineering interface, there should be consistency of user interactions from one device to the other.
3. *Data reasonableness and consistency*—As much as possible, the engineering interface system should be able to check an engineer's inputs for reasonableness and for consistency with previously entered information. If there is a problem, the system should advise the engineer of the situation and provide prompts that allow the engineer to correct the problem. In addition, it should not be necessary to enter the same information into the system more than once (e.g., an engineer should not have to enter an alarm limit once for alarming and again for trending). Also, the engineering interface system should keep track of the information entered to ensure consistency. If more than one engineering interface device is in use in the system at the

same time, there must be a mechanism in the system to make sure that changes made by one such device are picked up by the others. Finally, if the engineering inputs for several related pieces of hardware and control logic must be consistent (e.g., in defining parameters for a controller, an operator station, a termination unit, and a PID control algorithm), the system itself should provide a check of consistency and notify the user of any errors.

4. *User convenience*—The engineering interface devices must be designed for convenient use. For example, it should not be necessary to shut the control system down in order to connect or disconnect the engineering interface to the system. Similarly, the devices should be designed for easy storage when not in use.

5. *Cost-effectiveness*—The cost to the user of the engineering interface must be small when compared to the total installed cost of the control system.

System Configuration Requirements. Setting up any process control system requires a certain amount of manual work: determining control system requirements, selecting and procuring hardware, physically assembling the various modules and other elements into cabinets, and connecting external wiring between transmitters and field termination points in the control cabinets. However, the introduction of distributed control systems has made it possible to automate quite a number of system configuration functions. The degree of automation depends on the level of sophistication of the engineering interface equipment used.

Whatever the level, the engineer must perform the following system configuration functions (as a minimum) in implementing a distributed process control system:

1. The engineer must define the *addresses* of input and output points in the system with respect to their location in the shared communications facility (e.g., by identifying the point number within the module, the module number within the cabinet, and the cabinet number within the communication hierarchy). This is equivalent to assigning telephone numbers (by area code, exchange, and number) to people in a country so that you know where to reach them.

2. The engineer must define the tag names and associated descriptors that humans will use to identify certain (not necessarily all) points in the system, and relate these tags to the hardware addresses. (It is much more convenient for a human to describe a thermocouple input point as "TT106—Reflux Temperature" than as point number 27–5–18.")

3. The engineer must define any signal conditioning that needs to be

done with the input points in the system: e.g., linearization, zero and span shifting, or conversion to engineering units. Similar conditioning functions may need to be defined for control outputs to compensate for nonlinear control drive characteristics, for example.

4. The engineer must select, configure, and tune the control and computational algorithms in the system. Data to enter and verify include PID and other control algorithms, tuning constants, alarm limits, logic sequences, batch control recipes, and high-level language statements (e.g., in BASIC or FORTRAN). The engineer also must select any auxiliary functions that the system is to perform on certain points, such as trending, logging, and long-term data storage and retrieval.

5. When the implementation of the control and computational algorithms in item (4) requires transmitting data through the shared communications facility, the engineer must define the linkages from one element to another.

After the data described in this list have been entered into the system, there must be a mechanism to verify that the engineer performed the data entry process correctly.

Of course, the LCUs and DI/OUs in the distributed control system must store these data during on-line operation. It is also desirable that the engineering interface provide a mass memory facility that stores a complete duplicate of this database. Such a facility allows the distributed system to be configured before the actual system hardware becomes available. The facility also supports easy maintenance of the system after it has been started up.

Some distributed control systems provide more than one type of engineering interface device. All such devices in the system should be capable of reading and writing to the same type of mass memory in order to provide full compatibility of engineering operations throughout the system.

Requirements for Operator Interface Configuration. Configuring the control and computational functions of the distributed control system is only part of engineering a process control system. An equally important aspect of the job is selecting and configuring the operator interfaces to the system. The degree of support for this that the engineering interface can provide depends on how the operator interface system is implemented—through panelboard instrumentation or through VDUs. Ideally, the engineering interface should support at least the following functions:

1. It should allow the engineer to select and define the devices and mechanisms the operator will use in running the process. These include hardware such as control stations, indicators, recorders, mimic

panels, alarm indicators and related devices (or their equivalent in CRT displays).
2. It should relate the operator interface devices or displays to the control and instrumentation hardware in the field. This includes labeling the devices or displays with the tags, descriptors, and engineering units appropriate to the process points being controlled or monitored.

As in the case of configuring the control and computational functions, it is desirable that the engineering interface have a mass memory device to allow storage and later recall of the operator interface configurations.

Documentation Requirements. Documenting the hardware configuration and functional logic diagrams of an industrial process control system is one of the most painful and costly aspects of engineering the system. In conventional control systems, almost all of this documentation is accomplished manually. Distributed control systems that include engineering interfaces can change this situation significantly. In these systems the instrumentation engineer enters the bulk of the configuration information through the engineering interface and stores it in a mass data storage facility. For this reason a great potential clearly exists for automating the documentation function. This potential can be realized if the engineering interface meets the following requirements:

1. The engineering interface system must include a hard-copy device such as a printer to support the documentation function.
2. The documentation system must support both tabular and graphical data formats. The formats must be adjustable so that the user can adhere to the company's in-house documentation conventions.
3. One of the most difficult tasks of the instrumentation engineer is to keep track of field changes to the control system. The documentation function in the engineering interface must handle these changes as well as handle the original engineering design.
4. As much as possible, the documentation process should be automatic, requiring no special actions on the part of the instrumentation engineer. Experience has shown that documentation will not be done if it is too much trouble.

Diagnosis of System Problems. As described in detail in Section 4.2.3., the increased intelligence of the individual devices in a distributed control system allows them to implement self-diagnostic algorithms and report any failures directly to the maintenance personnel in the plant. The engineering interface unit is one of the key mechanisms by which this failure information is reported to the instrumentation and control system engineer. The engineering interface unit can also be a very useful tool in debugging and troubleshooting control logic.

To support the diagnosis of system problems, the engineering interface system must meet the following requirements:

1. There must be mechanisms that allow the instrumentation engineer to identify any failed devices in the system down to the level of repairable elements. These include modules, sensors, power supplies, and communication devices.
2. If a partial failure of an element occurs, there must be a mechanism that allows the instrumentation engineer to determine the severity and nature of the partial failure in order to identify the best course of action to solve the problem.
3. There must be mechanisms to expedite troubleshooting of control systems during initial check-out as well as during on-line operation. These mechanisms must be applicable to continuous, sequential, and batch control systems.

Diagnosis of *process* problems is not within the scope of the engineering interface system. This diagnosis is important, but it is an application-oriented function implemented within the distributed control and computing system itself.

7.3. LOW-LEVEL ENGINEERING INTERFACE

As mentioned in the introduction to this chapter, the low-level engineering interface (LLEI) is designed to be a minimum-function, inexpensive device whose cost is justifiable for small distributed control systems. It also can be used as a local maintenance and diagnostic tool in larger systems. Some vendors of distributed control systems do not offer such a device as a part of their product family, but only provide the high-level engineering interface (HLEI). Such systems can suffer from a cost disadvantage in small applications (say, less than 50 control loops), since it is difficult to justify an HLEI in that size of system. Conversely, the LLEI may not be needed in larger applications that rely primarily on the HLEI to implement engineering interface functions.

This section describes the various possible approaches to designing the LLEI to meet the requirements listed in Section 7.2. The order of the subsections follows the same sequence as the requirements.

7.3.1. General Description

The low-level engineering interface is usually a microprocessor-based device designed either as an electronic module that mounts in a rack or as a hand-held portable device (see Figure 7.1). To minimize cost, the device usually is designed with a minimal keyboard and alphanumeric display so that the instrument engineer can read data from and enter data into the device. Some LLEIs use small CRTs or flat-panel displays to implement the human interface. However, these are more expensive and are more closely akin to the high-level devices discussed in Section 7.4. Some versions of the LLEI must connect directly to and communicate with only one local control unit or data input/output unit at a time. More sophisticated versions can connect to a local branch of the shared communications facility and are able to communicate with any one of several LCUs or DI/OUs in adjacent cabinets or areas of the plant. In either case, the LLEI can be connected or disconnected while the LCU or DI/OU is powered and in operation; it is not necessary to shut the process down. Some devices include interfaces to low-cost peripherals, such as a printer (for documentation purposes), or a mass memory device, such as a tape cassette or microfloppy diskette (for storage of configuration data).

In general, the LLEI is a dedicated device that is *not* used for operational purposes. Therefore, when it is not needed for engineering use, it can be

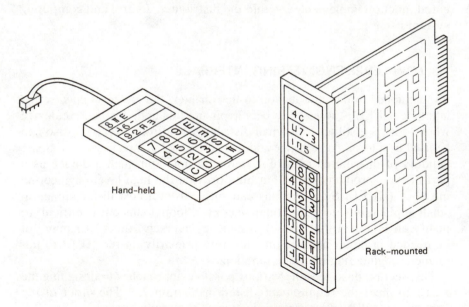

Figure 7.1. Examples of Low-Level Engineering Interfaces.

disconnected from the distributed control system and locked up for safe-keeping. This keeps the control configuration and tuning constants secure from alteration by unauthorized personnel.

Because of the minimal display and user input capabilities built into the LLEI, the interaction between user and device is often not as *user-friendly* as it is between user and high-level device. There is usually heavy reliance on using code words, symbols, or dedicated function keys to implement man-machine communications in the low-level device. The engineer generally has to document the input data on configuration forms first, then enter the data through the interface. However, the entry of data can be designed to take place in an interactive request-and-response manner. The interface device can also make some basic reasonableness and consistency checks on data entries and input sequences and give the engineer error messages when it detects a problem. The displays and input keyboard can be made flexible enough so that instrument engineering personnel can enter and read out data in engineering units that they understand.

7.3.2. System Configuration

When the system provides only an LLEI, the hardware in the system is selected and configured manually. To simplify this task, most vendors of distributed systems provide a *systems engineering guide* or similar document that leads the user in a step-by-step manner through the hardware configuration procedure. In this situation, the primary purpose of the LLEI is to provide a tool for configuring the algorithms in the system controllers (i.e., entering control strategies, setting tuning parameters, selecting alarm limits, and so forth).

Some low-level interfaces have a removable mass memory device (such as a small cassette, diskette drive, or magnetic strip) incorporated in their designs for storage of control configurations. When connected to a power supply, the engineer can then use the interface to develop and edit control strategies even if the controller itself is not connected. All that is required is that the configuration limitations of the target controller be stored in the engineering interface device. The availability of mass memory also makes it possible to download control configurations into the target module from the engineering interface, or conversely to "upload" the configurations from the controller. This function is very convenient when it is necessary to install a control configuration in a spare controller used to replace a failed controller.

In general, the LLEI is not designed to support generation and editing of high-level language programs such as BASIC and FORTRAN. A separate terminal or HLEI is required to provide this capability.

7.3.3. Operator Interface Configuration

As discussed previously, the distributed control systems that require only a low-level engineering interface generally are small ones involving a limited number of control loops. In this type of system, the operator interface also is simple, usually consisting of a small number of dedicated panelboard instrumentation devices (with no shared CRT-based console). Therefore, all configuration of the operator interface is done manually. As in the system configuration process described in Section 7.3.2, the vendor may supply documentation and forms to help the user select and define the stations, indicators, and other operator interface devices used in the system.

As in the case of all panelboard instrumentation, the connections between the stations and indicators and the controllers in these small systems are established through the manual process of hard wiring or cabling. Assigning tags to the control loops and system inputs and labeling the stations and indicators with these tags and the corresponding engineering units also are manual operations. These tasks can be very time-consuming and prone to error. Also, changes are difficult to make, since there is a significant lead time involved in procuring the new panelboard hardware, cabling, and labels needed to implement the changes.

7.3.4. Documentation

In a small system that requires only a low-level engineering interface, the vendor usually provides the user with very little or no help in automating the process of documenting the hardware and control configurations. All documentation is a manual process, sometimes with the help of standard forms in the system engineering guide.

When changes are made to a system of this type in the field after initial start-up, documenting these changes is a manual process that can be haphazard. It requires great discipline for the user organization to ensure that these field changes are tracked and identified accurately.

7.3.5. Diagnosis of System Problems

The LLEI, since it is not always connected to the distributed control system and often is not even located in the control room, provides little help in the way of notifying the operator of hardware failures in the control system. The operator must rely on the self-diagnostic capabilities of the distributed equipment itself to detect and make known the failure to the operator. Failures of this equipment generally are indicated at the control cabinets through alarm lights on the individual pieces of equipment. The failures are alarmed in the control room either through a conventional annunciator panel or through indications on the panelboard instrumentation.

However, the LLEI can be very useful in helping the instrumentation and control system engineer identify the specific location and nature of the failure. For example, the LLEI can interrogate a controller or other element that has failed; the element, if it still can communicate, can report on the specific problem that caused the failure through the engineering interface. Also, the instrument engineer can use the LLEI as a *digital voltmeter* to trace through the control logic and identify problems. Some LLEIs are equipped with a verify function that allows an automatic comparison of the actual configuration in the controller with the correct one stored in the interface's mass memory. This function can be very helpful in checking out a controller during initial start-up and in making sure the configuration hasn't changed after it has been in use in the field for some time.

7.4. HIGH-LEVEL ENGINEERING INTERFACE

The high-level engineering interface allows a user to reap the full benefits of the flexibility and control capabilities of a distributed control system while minimizing the system engineering costs associated with such a system. Although more expensive than the low-level version, this device is extremely cost-effective when used in conjunction with medium- to large-scale systems because of the significant engineering cost savings it can provide.

7.4.1. General Description

In most commercially available distributed control systems, the HLEI is implemented in the form of a CRT-based console, or VDU, similar to the high-level operator interface unit described in Chapter 6. Generally, the internal architecture of the VDU is modular, using multiple microprocessors, as shown in Figure 6.10. This approach provides a significant amount of flexibility in accommodating hardware options for engineering purposes (e.g., special keyboards or printers). Since there is a significant amount of commonality in the hardware in both kinds of VDUs, the description of hardware elements given in Section 6.4.2 also applies to the engineer's VDU. Like the operator's VDU, the engineering console can interact with any other element in the distributed system through the shared communications facility.

Dual-Console Functions. In a few distributed systems, the engineering console is a specialized device that is dedicated to the engineering function. In most offerings, however, the engineering console can also be used as an operator's console; a key lock on the console implements the switch between the two console "personalities." The first position permits only operator functions (e.g., display selection, control operations such as mode selection and set-point modification, and trend-graph selection). The second position allows engineering functions (such as control logic configuration, modification and tuning, and system documentation) as well as operator functions. Some systems provide a third key-lock position that allows the user to perform tuning operations but does not allow the user to modify the control logic structure. Implementing dual console "personalities" in a single piece of hardware is very cost-effective for the user, since the engineering functions are needed only during initial system start-up and occasionally thereafter when system modifications are made. During the other periods of time, the hardware is put to good use as an operator's console. However, the console is always connected to the system and is conveniently available when engineering functions need to be performed. The incorporation of a key lock ensures that the system configuration is secure while allowing authorized plant personnel access to the system.

Special Hardware Required. As indicated by the list of requirements in Section 7.2, engineering functions are much more oriented towards data entry and documentation than are operator functions. Because of this, the hardware requirements for an engineering console are somewhat different than those for a console used strictly for operations. One major difference is in the keyboard provided for the user. The operator's console uses a flat-panel, dedicated-function keyboard for ruggedness and simplicity of operation. The engineer's console, however, requires a general-purpose keyboard to promote speed of data entry and to support a wider range of human interface functions. This keyboard usually is a push-button type whose keys are laid out either in the traditional QWERTY configuration found on most typewriters or in the more recent Dvorak configuration (a human-engineered version that repositions the letters to promote faster touch typing). The vendor may supply additional special-purpose keys to allow the user to select special characters, symbols, and colors employed in generating control configurations and displays. To further simplify the process of building custom color-graphic CRT displays, some vendors also provide a digitizer tablet and stylus, a light pen, or other device as auxiliary hardware for the engineering console. (A digitizer tablet is a touch-sensitive pad on which the engineer enters information using the stylus.) This hardware supplements the cursor keys, touch screens, and other human interfacing hardware supplied with the operator's console. When the plant operator is using the console, the special keyboard or auxiliary hardware usually is stowed away in a storage location. Only when the console's personality is changed to become an engineer's console is this hardware brought out. In addition to this auxiliary hardware, some vendors also supply special color-graphic printing or plotting devices, which allow more sophisticated system documentation to be generated than is possible with the standard printer that comes with an operator's console.

Portable Engineering Interface.   Some distributed control system vendors offer a CRT-based engineering interface device that is a compromise between the full-function engineering console and the minimum-function low-level device described in the previous section. Usually, this is a portable unit that includes a bulk memory device such as a floppy disk or cassette tape drive for storage of system configuration data. This unit generally is designed to plug into and interface with a single LCU or cabinet. It can be very useful and cost-effective device for certain system configurations. However, its design will not be discussed here since its functions are a subset of those implemented in the HLEI console.

7.4.2. System Configuration

Because of its computational, display, and data storage capabilities, the HLEI can play a major role in automating the process of configuring a distributed control system. The entire database that defines the configuration of the hardware, control structures, and computational algorithms of the distributed system can be stored in the HLEI. For example, the following information dealing with the system hardware configuration can be entered by means of an interactive dialog between the engineering interface and the instrument engineer:

1. Number, type, and location (relative to the shared communications facility) of each hardware module in the LCUs and DI/OUs in the distributed system;
2. Definition of any hardware options (such as expansion hardware, jumper positions, or switch settings) selected on each module;
3. Definition of each input point (by type and hardware address) in each of the hardware modules;
4. Number, type, and location of all operator and engineering consoles in the system;

5. Number, type, and location of any other devices in the system that communicate using the shared communications facility (e.g., computer interfaces, and special logging or computing devices).

While the instrumentation engineer enters most of this information manually, the HLEI can acquire some of the data (such as the addresses and types of devices using the shared communications facility) automatically. It can do this by means of a sequence of broadcast messages through the communications facility asking any devices that are listening to identify themselves and transmit any configuration information that they have. When implemented, this approach can save a substantial amount of the engineer's time and effort and cut down dramatically on the number of configuration errors introduced. In either case, once this information is entered in the system, the engineer uses the HLEI to make reasonableness and consistency checks on the information, save it on a mass memory medium, and document it in a printed format. During normal operation, this information is not used anywhere else in the distributed system. It is saved to document the hardware configuration installed in the plant for the instrument engineer's use and for downloading in case of hardware failure and replacement.

In addition to this hardware-related information, the engineering interface is also used to store information dealing with the control and computational functions of the system. At a minimum this information includes the following:

1. Point tags and associated tag descriptors, engineering unit definitions, and related point addresses;
2. Logic state descriptors (e.g., on/off, and run/stop) that correspond to digital points in the system.
3. Control algorithms implemented in each of the LCUs;
4. Signal conditioning and linearization algorithms implemented in the DI/OUs;
5. Communications linkages needed to transfer information among the control and computational algorithms in different LCUs and DI/OUs in the system using the shared communications facility;
6. High-level language computational algorithms implemented in the LCUs.

Control and Computational Logic Configuration.   One of the major benefits of using an HLEI in a distributed control system is that it simplifies the process of configuring the control and computational logic in the system. As described in the previous section, configuration using the low-level interface can be a somewhat tedious process involving the use of code numbers and names during the procedure. The high-level console provides one or both of the following control logic configuration capabilities:

1. A fill-in-the-blanks function in which the instrument engineer interacts with the console through a sequence of prompts and responses to configure the control logic in the system.
2. A graphics capability in which the instrument engineer draws the control configuration on the screen with a light pen or on a digitizer tablet with a stylus. This capability is similar to that provided in computer-aided-design (CAD) systems, and allows the user to define the control logic using a familiar function block format (see Section 2.3 for a definition of function blocks). After laying out the basic control structure graphically, the instrument engineer can define the parameters associated with the function blocks through an interactive sequence similar to that mentioned in item (1).

While both approaches are quite user-friendly, the instrument engineers generally prefer the second. One significant advantage of the graphics procedure is that it allows the engineer to visualize the control system structure more clearly than is possible using other approaches. In addition, the graphics approach leads directly to control logic documentation that also is in an easily readable, graphical format. Finally, checking out and debugging control logics are easy to accomplish using the graphics format if the graphics display shows the current values of the process variables at the output of each function block while the control logic is being executed. Using this display capability, the instrumentation engineer can easily work through the control logic to track down any problems with the control configuration. If the logic diagram is too large for all of it to show on a single display screen, the CRT display system can include a pan or zoom capability that allows the engineer to move easily through the logic diagram to find the problem.

After the instrument engineer has configured the control logic, he or she must tune the control parameters in the logic to match the dynamic characteristics of the process being controlled. To determine these dynamic characteristics, the engineer must make a number of tests on the process by perturbing it with set-point or control output changes and observing the resulting behavior of the process. Then the engineer changes the tuning parameters accordingly and repeats the perturbations to check that the performance is as expected.

This tuning process can be tedious if the operational and engineering displays provided by the HLEI are not laid out properly. In some designs, the engineer would be forced to start with an operational display containing a station mimic to accomplish the perturbations, switch to a trend display to observe the dynamic behavior of the process, and finally go to an engineering display to adjust the tuning parameters. The engineer might have to repeat this sequence several times until the tuning parameters are adjusted satisfactorily. A much better approach is to provide a unified tuning display such as that shown in Figure 6.19. This approach allows the engineer to accomplish all of the operations in the tuning process from one display without having to move back and forth among two or more different displays.

The last configuration function that the HLEI must accommodate is allowing the instrument engineer to enter, debug, and check out high-level language routines (e.g., in BASIC or FORTRAN) in the LCUs. To perform that function, the engineering interface must take on another personality: it behaves like a smart terminal to any one of the LCUs. When the interface is in this mode, the engineer can enter programs through the keyboard, download them over the shared communications facility to the LCU, debug them, and check them out through the interface. In this mode, the interface implements the utility software functions itemized in Section 3.6.2. This capability eliminates the need to have a separate terminal connected directly to the LCU for purposes of program checkout.

Storage of Configurations.   As described previously, one of the basic functions of the HLEI is to provide the engineer with a tool for configuring the control logic and computational algorithms in the target hardware (i.e., the LCUs) that will execute the algorithms. However, the HLEI can be used to perform additional useful functions if it includes a mass memory facility that allows duplicate storage of this configuration information. The mass memory facility is generally implemented using one or more types of storage media: floppy disk, hard disk, magnetic tape, bubble memory, or optical disk. The additional functions that configuration storage allows include the following:

1. The engineer can use the interface to configure the control logics and computational algorithms *without* the presence of the target LCUs. In this situation, the configurations are stored directly into the mass memory of the interface. Of course, the interface must be aware of the limitations of the target LCU (in terms of memory size and computational speed, for example) and ensure that the configurations entered do not exceed these limitations. After storage, the engineer can then download the configurations at a later time to the

LCUs once this hardware becomes available. This feature can dramatically cut the time necessary to deliver a control system, since the job engineering can begin and the control logics can be configured and stored long before the actual target hardware is available.

2. The HLEI can be used to verify that the engineer has correctly entered the control logic and algorithms into the LCU and that they have not been altered; the HLEI does this by performing a bulk comparison of the logic in the LCU with that stored in the mass memory. Any mismatches are displayed for the engineer, who can correct them immediately.

3. If an LCU or other element of the system fails, it can be replaced by a new element. The appropriate control and computational algorithms can then be downloaded from the mass memory to the new or repaired element. This results in a very short mean time to repair for that element and a minimum downtime of the function performed by that element.

4. The engineering interface also should support the uploading of database information from a hardware device to the interface. This capability helps in documenting functions performed by modules or elements that are removed from service or moved from one control system to another.

7.4.3. Operator Interface Configuration

The engineering interface operations discussed in the previous sections dealt with the configuration of the elements of the distributed control system *external* to the operator interface (e.g., the LCUs and the communication system). When a high-level operator interface of the type described in Chapter 6 is used in the distributed system, there must be a mechanism that allows the instrument engineer to configure or change its display structures and parameters in a convenient manner. In most distributed control systems, this mechanism is the high-level engineering interface. This device allows the engineer to change the layout of the series of displays that make up the "panelboard" used to control plant operations.

For maximum flexibility, the engineering interface must be designed in such a way that it can configure *any* HLOI in the distributed control system. That is, the system should be able to download displays and display hierarchies configured on one engineer's console to any other operator's console in the system over the shared communications facility. This capability implies that displays configured for one operator's console can be duplicated on other consoles without the need for people physically transporting magnetic storage media (e.g., floppy disks) from one console to another.

The first step in configuring an HLOI is to structure a hierarchy of displays such as the one shown in Figure 6.13. This includes specifying the following information as a minimum:

1. Number of areas in the plant and their identifying tag names and descriptors;
2. Number of groups in each area and the tag names and descriptors for each area;
3. Assignment of control loops and input points to a group or to multiple groups;
4. Types of displays to be used at each level, whether preformatted displays or custom graphics;
5. Linkages between displays in the hierarchy (i.e., the paths that the operator must follow in moving from one display to another; these linkages are prespecified in some systems and configurable in others;
6. Assignment of points in the system to the special functions of the operator console: trending, alarming, logging, and long-term data storage and retrieval; specification of the parameters involved in each special function (e.g., trend periods, logging formats, and data storage frequency).

Most distributed systems provide a simple menu structure with interactive displays to make it convenient for the instrument engineer to enter this information into the engineering interface.

The next step in configuring an HLOI unit is to define the individual displays in the hierarchy. If the operator interface keyboard contains user-defined keys, the engineer must also define the functions of these keys and link them to the appropriate elements of the displays for which they are active.

Laying out and defining the standard, preformatted displays described in Section 6.4.3 is a relatively simple process. Generally, the HLEI provides a CRT-based template for each preformatted display type that allows the engineer to "fill in the blanks" in the template to define the desired options in each display.

Defining and laying out graphics displays is a more challenging task, since they are usually completely user-configurable and do not follow any standard format. Of course, the vendor's display hardware imposes limitations on the structure of these displays, such as resolution, number of colors available, pixel control method (character oriented or bit-mapped), special characters and symbols, and so forth. Usually, the vendor provides

a graphics display engineering kit that spells out these limitations and helps
the user to sketch each display on a special grid form before entering it
into the engineer's console. In laying out each display, the engineer must
enter the following information as a minimum:

1. *Graphic symbols*—The engineer must define the new graphic symbols
   to be used in the operator interface displays. Usually, the system
   vendor supplies a base set of symbols that represent standard items
   of process equipment. These include symbols for piping, valves,
   pumps, and so forth. The ISA standard given as Reference 6.18 provides a typical list of these symbols. However, each user generally
   has a need to configure additional symbols that are appropriate to
   the particular application. The symbol library is expanded to include
   these new symbols along with the standard ones; they are then also
   available for incorporation in the user's displays.
2. *Static background elements*—These are elements in the display (both
   graphic and alphanumeric) that do not change with time. These usually include the major items of process equipment, the interconnecting
   piping, the equipment labels, and engineering unit identifiers. The
   information required for each element includes its shape, size, and
   color.
3. *Dynamic graphics elements*—These are the graphics elements in the
   display that change to reflect corresponding changes in the process.
   For example, pumps may change color when they are turned on and
   off; piping may change color when it contains fluid; the displayed
   levels of fluid in tanks may move up and down to reflect actual fluid
   levels; bar graphs may change to depict temperature profiles. Or the
   actual symbols may change. For example, one symbol may represent
   a closed valve and another symbol an open valve. In each case, the
   dynamic element must be linked to the corresponding tag that defines
   the process state represented by the graphics element. For instance,
   the engineer can link a tag representing a digital process input to the
   graphics element illustrating an open or closed valve. In addition to
   the tag definition, the engineer must specify *how* the dynamic element
   will change (e.g., in shape or color) in response to the change in tag
   state and enter this information into the definition of the display.
4. *Dynamic alphanumeric elements*—The engineer must also define and
   link these to the corresponding tags. These elements include alphabetic labels that change color, wording, character size, or brightness
   as a function of process conditions. They also include numeric values
   or logic states that the VDU updates to reflect changes in the process
   variables represented by the corresponding tags. Alarm conditions

can be indicated by color changes or by having the VDU place the element into a blinking condition. Usually, there are limits to the number of dynamic elements that a single graphics display can include; 200 to 400 elements is a typical range.

5. *Control stations*—If the graphics display structure supports continuous or sequential control operations (or both), the engineer must define the controllable elements in the graphic display and label them with tag numbers, reference numbers, or both. This allows the operator to call up the appropriate control stations on the graphics display and connect them to these controllable elements.

6. *"Poke points"*—If the operator's console provides a touch screen input capability, the display specification will include the definition of *poke points* or fields that will be sensitive to operator inputs. As in the case of the dynamic display elements, the engineer must link each poke point to the corresponding tag that represents a push-button input from the operator.

The mechanisms provided for entering this information vary widely from one vendor's system to another. In all cases, the user should have to do no programming. The engineer enters data and draws the displays through keyboard entries, light-pen movements, touch-screen inputs, or operations involving a stylus and digitizer tablet, depending on the type of engineering interface hardware provided with the system.

Whatever physical hardware the vendor supplies, it is extremely important that the mechanism provided for defining and editing the graphics displays be well documented and simple for the engineer to use. The following features have been found to be very useful in such a mechanism:

1. *Special symbol definition*—The engineer should be able to create special symbols in a simple graphical manner without having to build them on a character-by-character basis. The engineer should be able to draw them directly on the CRT and be able to review and edit the results immediately.

2. *Graphics drawing and editing aids*—It should be possible for the user to draw, modify, and erase commonly used graphics elements such as lines, boxes, and circles as a part of the symbol definition without having to construct them from scratch.

3. *Symbol modification*—The system should allow the user to expand, shrink, move, or rotate all symbols to a size and orientation that is appropriate for a particular display. The system should automatically take care of the details (e.g., selecting the proper graphics characters) involved in implementing these operations.

4. *Macro symbol operations*—The system should allow the user to define a portion of an existing graphic display as a *macro symbol,* and then edit and replicate it as desired in other displays or portions of the same display. This can save a significant amount of time in the display creation process.

5. *Display transportability*—The system should allow the user to create a display on an HLEI and then transmit it to any high-level operator interface in the distributed system using the shared communications facility; similar transportability must be provided for the symbol library to allow its use by multiple HLEIs in the same system.

6. *Expanded display definition*—In some systems, the apparent size of each graphics display can be defined to be larger than the size of the CRT screen. The operator then can pan across the display or zoom in and out to be able to see the whole display at one time or portions of it in more detail. The engineering interface must allow the engineer to define the limits of this expanded display and determine the mechanisms by which the operator moves from one portion of the display to another (e.g., continually or in discrete segments).

The specific mechanisms provided for configuring the graphics displays vary significantly from one distributed control system to another. In evaluating the tools provided by several vendors for display configuration, the user should consider selecting one or more displays as representative of the application. The user can then use the time and effort required to construct these displays as measures of the quality of the configuration tools that are supplied.

7.4.4. Documentation

As mentioned in the previous sections, the high-level engineering interface is a tool that can significantly reduce the amount of time required to configure a control system and its associated operator interface. It also can provide the user significant benefits in the area of documentation. After the configuration process has been completed, all information defining the hardware, control logic, computational algorithms, and displays for the system is stored in mass memory in the engineering interface. As mentioned previously, this makes it possible to completely automate the process of documenting this information in a hard-copy format. Ideally, the intelligence and printing and plotting hardware in the HLEI should be designed to generate the following documentation automatically:

1. Lists of hardware modules in the distributed system, including their location by number of LCU or DI/OU;

2. Documentation of the control configuration and associated tuning parameters for each LCU, in both listing and graphic formats showing the control system structure; listing includes any high-level language programs or batch control recipes executed in the LCUs;
3. Listing of the tags in the distributed system, along with the associated tag descriptor information and the hardware addresses of the physical inputs or module outputs that correspond to these tags;
4. Listing of the special operator interface functions that are associated with each tag, such as trending, logging, and long-term storage and retrieval functions;
5. Definition of the operator displays in the system, including a drawing of the display hierarchy, a listing of the displays in the hierarchy, and a printout of the formats of each display.

In all cases, it should not be necessary for the engineer to obtain hard-copy documentation only by printing CRT screen displays; the documentation should be available through reports generated by the printing and plotting equipment associated with the HLEI system.

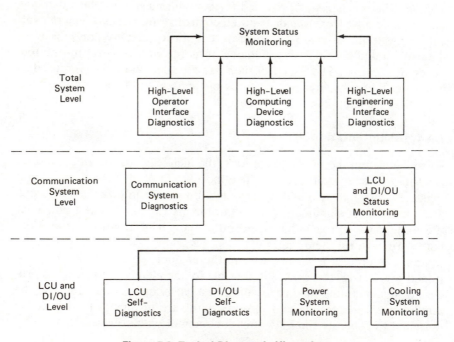

Figure 7.2. Typical Diagnostic Hierarchy.

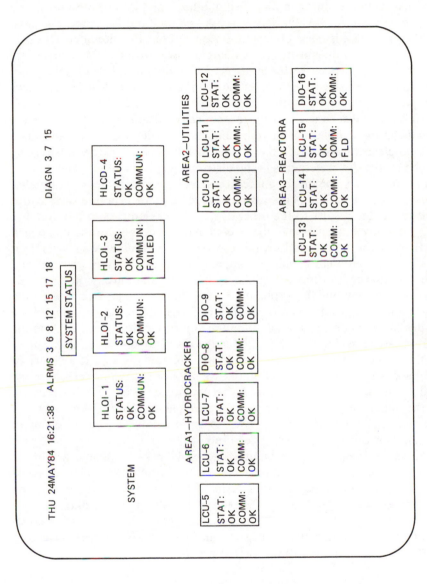

Figure 7.3. Example of a Diagnostic Display.

7.4.5. Diagnosis of System Problems

In addition to its other functions, the HLEI can be an invaluable aid to the instrument engineer in diagnosing failures and other problems in the distributed control system hardware. As pointed out in Chapter 4, most of this hardware is microprocessor-based and has the intelligence to perform on-line self-diagnostics to evaluate its own "health." When a failure or other problem occurs, this hardware is aware of it and reports the problem to the higher-level elements in the distributed system. Figure 7.2 shows a typical diagnostic hierarchy. At the lowest level, the LCUs and DI/OUs perform diagnostics such as those itemized in Table 4.1, and report the results up through the shared communications facility. The communication system elements also check their own "health" and provide status reports to the system-level elements in the distributed system—the high level operator interfaces, engineering interfaces, and computing devices. Finally, these system-level elements also execute their own on-line diagnostics and report the results to the other system-level elements in the system.

As described in Chapter 6, the overall diagnostic status of the equipment in the system is indicated on the top line of each display in the HLOI system. If a problem develops, an equipment status alarm goes off and the operator or instrument engineer can call up a hierarchy of diagnostic displays to pinpoint the problem. Figure 7.3 shows an example of the highest level of display in this hierarchy. This display shows a *map* of the nodes or drops on the shared communications facility; these contain the major hardware elements that exist in the distributed system. Any failure in the elements within a node are reported on this display. If a failure or problem is identified at this level, the operator or instrument engineer can call up the next lower level of display to determine the cause of the problem in the individual module or element within a node. Through this method, the user can trace the failure down to an individual hardware element, which then can be replaced or repaired.

Since the information on failures and problems is available within the distributed system through this diagnostic hierarchy, it can also be logged on a printer and saved in a long-term data storage file. This allows the user to accumulate statistics on the rates and modes of failure of the various pieces of hardware in the distributed system. This information is essential to planning a cost-effective strategy for maintaining a spare-parts inventory and in providing inputs to an overall program for managing plant maintenance.

8
OTHER KEY ISSUES

8.1. INTRODUCTION

The subject of distributed control systems for industrial applications is extremely broad-ranging and not possible to cover completely in a single volume. The previous chapters provided only an introduction to the major topics central to the evaluation and design of distributed control systems: controller hardware and software, communications, and human interfaces. The references listed at the end of these chapters gave additional details in each technical area.

This chapter will provide brief overviews of several other technical areas that have a significant impact on the performance and cost-effectiveness of a distributed control system. The first section will review the current evolution in implementing high-level computing, control, and human interfacing functions in distributed control systems. The next two sections will discuss the major issues regarding packaging the hardware to meet the needs of a distributed system configuration and the design of the electrical power system for that hardware. Finally, the last section of the chapter describes some of the future developments expected to occur in the architecture, hardware, and functional capabilities of distributed control systems.

8.2. IMPLEMENTATION OF HIGH-LEVEL FUNCTIONS

This section first reviews the recent trend of moving the implementation of high-level functions out of centralized computers and distributing it among dedicated microprocessor-based computing devices and other elements of the distributed system. Then, the current role of general-purpose computers in a distributed control system and the approaches used in interfacing the computers with the rest of the system are summarized. References 8.1–8.5 provide additional information on the role of computers in distributed control systems.

8.2.1. Distribution of High-Level Functions

All industrial monitoring and control systems of more than minimal complexity have to perform a great number of functions beyond those of simple regulatory and sequence control. These high-level functions include:

- "advanced" control (e.g., adaptive, feedforward, and optimizing control algorithms)
- implementation of high-level languages
- complex calculations (e.g., performance calculations, linear programming algorithms, matrix manipulations, and Fourier transforms)
- long-term storage and retrieval of process data for historical purposes
- color-graphic displays
- logging of process data on printers
- advanced alarming functions (e.g., multi-leveled alarming, alarm suppression or "cutout" algorithms, and alarm prioritization)
- economic process optimization and other supervisory control algorithms

Systems having the hybrid system architecture shown in Figure 1.2 and those with the early distributed control architectures have implemented these functions exclusively in a general-purpose computer. In most of these systems, the computer has been a device separate from the regulatory and sequence control subsystems, interacting with these subsystems by means of data transfers over an appropriate interface. In other systems, the computer has played the more central role of a "host," on which the rest of the distributed system depended for management of the system data base and coordination of all data communications.

In both of these architectures, the computer executes all of the functions virtually simultaneously through the use of a sophisticated operating system that allows orderly sharing of the available computer resources among the functions. As shown in Figure 1.4, the architecture of distributed control systems also has accommodated the use of a general-purpose computer by providing a computer interface device, which allows the computer to interact with the other devices in the system over the shared communications facility.

While effective in some applications, using a general-purpose computer to implement *all* high-level functions in an industrial control environment has several disadvantages:

1. As the number of functions implemented in a single mainframe increases, the complexity of the resulting software system must go up

exponentially to handle the increased competition for processor time and other shared resources. This leads to an undesirable dependence (from the point of view of the user) on computer software specialists to make changes in the system and to keep it running.

2. In terms of response time and throughput, the performance of the computer system degrades as the number of implemented functions increases.

3. The computer system is not scalable; that is, it is very difficult for the user to purchase only the minimum number of functions needed in a cost-effective manner while retaining the option to add functionality at a later date.

In recent years, a distributed computing approach has superseded to a great extent this centralized approach to implementing high-level functions. The distribution of these high-level functions has become feasible as powerful 16-bit and 32-bit microprocessors and their associated memories and support chips have been introduced to the marketplace. These hardware developments have increased the capabilities of the local control units and the high-level human interface devices in the distributed system while allowing them to remain cost-effective. In addition, it has become feasible to design microprocessor-based devices that are dedicated to performing selected high-level computing and control functions. As a result, an increasing number of these functions are being moved out of the computer and distributed into other elements in the distributed system as Figure 8.1 illustrates. Because of this trend toward functional distribution, in many applications there is no longer a need to include a general-purpose computer in the distributed control system architecture. When it is required, the computer can be dedicated to only the most complex and application-specific tasks.

8.2.2. Implementation in Distributed System Elements

As shown in Figure 8.1, many of the high-level functions are now being performed in the high-level human interface devices in the more advanced distributed control system offerings. These functions include:

- color graphics displays
- high-resolution trending on CRTs
- long-term data storage and retrieval
- advanced logging capabilities
- high-level language implementation
- graphics-based control system configuration

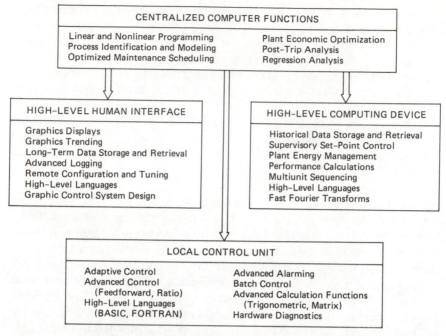

Figure 8.1. Distribution of High-Level Functions

Other advanced functions are being implemented in high-performance versions of the LCUs in the distributed control system:

- advanced control algorithms (adaptive controls, optimizing controls)
- batch control algorithms
- advanced alarming algorithms
- high-level language packages

8.2.3. Implementation in Dedicated Computing Devices

In addition to moving the functions previously performed by a computer into existing distributed control system elements as just described, many vendors are also creating new microprocessor-based elements dedicated to performing specialized high-level functions. These high-level computing devices, shown in the generalized distributed system architecture in Figure 1.4, are differentiated from general-purpose computers in that they are (1) manufactured by the distributed control system vendor, (2) integrated into the shared communications facility provided by the vendor, and (3) designed to be used by instrument engineers, not computer specialists. Typical examples of these devices are as follows:

1. *Historical storage device*—This device collects data from the rest of the distributed system and stores the information on disk, tape, or other memory media. Information is stored in an organized format for ease of later retrieval. Usually, the device uses data compression techniques to minimize the amount of storage capacity required.

2. *Logging device*—This is responsible for collecting data and printing the data on hard-copy devices such as high-speed printers and X–Y plotters. This device also implements computational functions related to logging, such as calculating averages, maxima, minima, totals, and filtered versions of process variables.

3. *Graphical control configuration device*—This device allows the instrument engineer to configure and tune control systems using a graphical computer-aided design (CAD) approach. With this device, the engineer can draw the control configuration on a CRT screen and set tuning parameters without going through a laborious "fill in the blanks" procedure.

4. *Computing device*—A computing device allows the user to develop and run custom programs in a high-level language such as BASIC, FORTRAN, or PASCAL. It differs from a general-purpose computer in that the interface between the user programs and the distributed system is already provided in the form of database locations or standard subroutine calls. The computing device includes the software and peripherals needed to debug, monitor, and save programs.

While there are many advantages of the distributed approach to implementing high-level functions, there also are a number of potential pitfalls. The potential user of such a distributed *computing* and control system must evaluate the system carefully to ensure that a distributed architecture does not create a whole new set of problems. Some of the issues to consider are:

1. *Consistency of functional implementation*—In the distributed computing approach, many of the same functions are implemented in several different elements in the system. This implementation should be consistent from one element to another so that the user is not confused. For example, both an LCU and a high-level computing device (HLCD) may provide a high-level language capability. The language dialect and program development facilities should be con-

sistent in both implementations so that the user can move easily from one to another.

2. *Consistency of data base and computations*—Several high-level devices may be performing the same operations (e.g., averaging, alarming, or filtering) on a set of process data. Care must be taken to ensure that the data used by each device are consistent and that the operations are performed in the same way. Otherwise, it is possible to generate confusing information; for example, a calculated point might go into alarm and be saved on the historical storage device but (due to minor timing or computational differences) never show up on the operator's console.

3. *Compatibility with the shared communications facility*—In the centralized computer configuration described earlier, the computer uses a certain percentage of the capacity of the shared communications facility to read a single process point. Once it has done this, however, it performs a number of operations (e.g., display, averaging, and alarming) on the same data point without using any additional communications resources. On the other hand, in a distributed computing configuration, each computing device uses the shared communications facility to obtain an update on each process point. The need of the distributed computing devices to exchange information on the results of their computations generates additional traffic. This increased level of message traffic can create a problem unless the bandwidth of the communications facility is designed to take it into account.

None of these potential problems is an insurmountable obstacle to implementating high-level system functions using a distributed computing approach. However, one should keep them in mind when evaluating a system based on a distributed computing architecture.

8.2.4. General-Purpose Computers in Distributed Systems

The advantages in flexibility, modularity, and user-friendliness of the distributed approach to implementing high-level control and computing functions were noted in the previous section. However, the general-purpose computer may well have a role to play in a distributed control system depending on the background of the user and the needs of the particular application. Some of the issues that would motivate a user to include a general-purpose computer in a distributed control system are:

1. *Software investment*—The user already may have invested considerable time and resources in software packages that run on a specific

computer. The cost of converting these packages to a form that would run in a particular vendor's distributed computing environment may not be worth the benefits.

2. *Specialized language requirements*—The user's application may be implemented most readily by means of a software language that is not available in the systems provided by the distributed control vendors. Examples include LISP for expert system (artificial intelligence) applications and COBOL for business applications.

3. *Extensive computational requirements*—The speed and memory requirements of a particular application may preclude the use of microprocessor-based devices. Some examples of large computing applications of this type include modeling large dynamic systems (e.g., water resources and weather patterns), running large linear and nonlinear programs, and identifying the dynamics of high-order systems.

4. *Personal computer for small systems*—Some digital control applications require some high-level functions but are too small in scope to justify the purchase of any high-level computing or human interface devices from the control system vendor. In many of these situations, a personal computer can provide the functions required (typically, a few data acquisition, logging, and computational functions).

Because of the diversity of hardware and software products available in the marketplace, no attempt will be made here to characterize the functions or structure of a general-purpose computer used in conjunction with a distributed control system. However, there is one function that is common to all such computers: interfacing with the distributed system for purposes of data transfer. The next subsection will discuss the characteristics of such an interface.

8.2.5. Computer Interface Design Issues

To accomplish its functions as an integral part of a distributed control system, the general-purpose computer (or computers) must be able to acquire data *from* as well as transmit data *to* the other elements in the system. To meet this requirement, most distributed system vendors provide at least one port, or *gateway,* out of the shared communications facility for an external device such as a general-purpose computer to use. This is the computer interface device (CID) shown in Figure 1.4.

Some of the key requirements on a CID are as follows:

1. It must be able to handle all of the types of messages transmitted over the shared communications facility. These include analog and

digital inputs from the process, variables associated with control loops, control configuration and tuning data, and the operational status of all the hardware in the distributed system.

2. Information must travel across the interface at the speeds required by the computer to perform its functions, consistent with the ability of the shared communications facility to provide this information.

3. Time delays across the interface must be small in order to maintain the accuracy and timeliness of the data.

4. The computer time and memory required to support interface operations must be minimal.

5. Similarly, support of the interface should not place undue demands on the shared communications facility.

6. The interface must be able to support the full range of general-purpose computers used for industrial control, not just the computer favored by the vendor of the particular distributed control system in question.

There are a number of issues to consider in evaluating or designing a computer interface. These include the form of the interface (serial or parallel), the speed of the interface (in bits per second), and the degree of decoupling desired between the operations of the computer and those of the shared communications facility.

The following discussion defines three examples of typical interfaces between a computer and a distributed control system and describes their properties. There are a number of other variations that could be considered, but these three are adequate to illustrate the major issues. Block diagrams of the interfaces (which for brevity are called simply types A, B, and C) are shown in Figures 8.2, 8.3, and 8.4. The characteristics of the three interfaces are compared in Table 8.1.

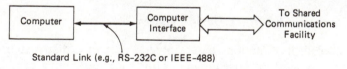

Standard Link (e.g., RS-232C or IEEE-488)

Figure 8.2. Computer Interface—Type A

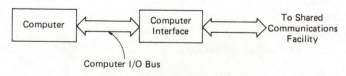

Computer I/O Bus

Figure 8.3. Computer Interface—Type B

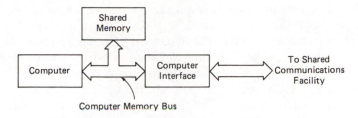

Figure 8.4. Computer Interface—TypeC

In all cases, the interfaces are assumed to be intelligent (i.e., each uses one or more microprocessors) and to contain the hardware and firmware needed to interface with the shared communications facility of the distributed control system. The differences in the interfaces are in the mechanisms by which the computer obtains access to and interacts with the shared communications facility.

The type A interface (Figure 8.2) is designed as follows:

1. The hardware interface to the computer conforms to some recognized interface standard (e.g., a serial RS–232C link or a parallel IEEE 488 link).

Table 8.1. Comparison of Computer Interface Approaches

	INTERFACE A	INTERFACE B	INTERFACE C
Type of interface	Serial	Parallel	Parallel
Relative speed of interface	Low	Medium	High
Computer-specific hardware required?	No	Yes	Yes
Computer-specific software required in interface?	No	No	Yes
Interface-specific software required in computer?	Yes	Yes	No
Allows computer to talk directly to communications facility?	No	Yes	No
Offloads computer communication functions?	Yes	No	Yes
Relative cost	Low	Low	High

2. The computer interface is responsible for maintaining an up-to-date database of the information to be transferred to or from the shared communications facility. This database is set up as a table or list of values to which the computer can read or write. The computer interface takes care of all of the transactions on the shared communications facility needed to maintain the table of values.

3. The computer is "master" of the interface: it initiates all data transmissions to, and requests for data from, the interface.

The type A computer interface has a number of desirable characteristics. Its primary advantage is that using the standard hardware interface allows it to communicate with a wide range of computers. (Of course, a software driver that supports that interface must be installed in the computer.) Also, the use of a data table as the intermediary between the computer and the communications facility effectively decouples the operation of the two entities. Therefore, the computer cannot monopolize the communications facility to the detriment of the other elements using that facility. Finally, this type of computer interface is relatively inexpensive. The disadvantage to type A is that the speed of the data flow across the interface is limited by the speed of the serial or parallel standard link. In the case of an RS–232C port, for example, this maximum speed is 19,200 bits/sec. One can use multiple computer interfaces, of course, to increase both the rate of data transfer and the number of points that the computer can access. In many cases this speed limitation is not a problem since the computer often cannot service more information than that provided by two or three interfaces running in parallel.

The type B computer interface (Figure 8.3) is characterized by the following design features:

1. This interface also uses a data table as the intermediary between the computer and the communications facility. Also, this interface handles all of the communications facility transactions required to update the table or to transmit new values from it to other elements in the distributed system.

2. The hardware link between the computer and the interface is the computer's I/O bus; therefore, from the point of view of the computer, the computer interface looks like a peripheral device (such as a printer or CRT).

3. As in type A, the computer is the "master" of the interface, controlling transfers of data read from or written to the interface.

The primary advantage of type B over Type A is that the data transactions over the computer's full parallel I/O bus can take place at a significantly higher speed than possible over a bit-serial or byte-serial link. In this case, the main bottleneck to transfers across the interface is likely to be the computer interface hardware itself or even the speed of the shared communications facility. Another advantage is that the type B interface is likely to be not much more expensive than type A. On the negative side, the type B design does not offload the computer any more than does the type A version. The computer CPU has to be involved in every interface transaction, just as in type A. However, the primary disadvantage of the Type B structure is that the hardware and software in the computer interface and the driver software in the computer itself must all be designed around the I/O bus of the computer in question. While there are some bus standards in existence, most computer vendors use their own design in this area. This implies that there must be a unique interface hardware and software design for each type of computer used in the distributed system.

The type C computer interface design (Figure 8.4) has the following characteristics:

1. It is the same as the previous two interface types with regard to servicing the shared communications facility: it handles all of these transactions independently from the computer's operations.
2. On the computer side, the interface consists of direct memory access (DMA) hardware that interfaces to the memory bus of the computer. Instead of a data table in the memory of the computer interface itself, a shared memory accessible by both the computer and the computer interface over the memory bus provides the intermediary data storage.
3. In this design, the computer views the interface to the distributed system as a portion of its random-access memory. The computer does not get involved in the transmission of data to or from the interface at all.

From the point of view of performance, the structure of the type C interface has significant advantages over types A and B. If the interface is designed properly, the speed of data transfer across the interface is likely to be limited only by the throughput of the shared communications facility, not by any of the other elements in the chain. In addition, the computer is completely decoupled from the interface operations, so its resources are fully available for its other required functions. Also, the computer requires no special driver software since it views the interface simply as a portion of its memory. However, the type C interface has the same major disadvantages as Type B: its design is specific to the particular computer in question and so its hardware and software must be customized for each application. The other disadvantage of the type C interface is that it is likely to be more expensive than the other two (due to the cost of the hardware required to achieve the high data transfer speeds over a full parallel memory bus).

Any one of these computer interface designs may be quite suitable and appropriate in a particular situation. It is up to the designer or evaluator of the interface to select the interface that best meets the needs of the application in a cost-effective manner.

8.3. PACKAGING ISSUES

The packaging elements in an industrial control system include the cabinets, enclosures, and mounting racks used to hold the active electronic equipment, and any cooling equipment or other hardware used to protect the electronics from the ambient environment. These packaging elements must be designed to:

1. Ensure that the environment surrounding the active electronic equipment is within the allowed operating specifications, given the possible ambient conditions in the environment external to the cabinet (this may include a wide range of temperature, humidity, vibration, and other conditions);
2. Protect the active equipment from access by unauthorized personnel and from other disturbances;
3. Allow authorized operating and maintenance personnel to gain convenient access to the active equipment;
4. Be as cost-effective as possible for the full range of environmental conditions and for the size of the system encountered in the intended applications.

For industrial control systems characterized by the hybrid system architecture shown in Figure 1.2 or the central computer system architecture shown in Figure 1.3, the packaging design problems to solve have been relatively straightforward. In these configurations, all of the process control and computing hardware is located in the control room and equipment room areas. As a result, the packaging for this hardware traditionally has been designed for the single set of relatively mild environmental conditions that are characteristic of these areas. Also, since all of the hardware is in one location, a standard size of equipment cabinet (typically 7 ft. high) could be used in a wide range of applications. Only rarely would a centralized system be so small as to require less than one cabinet; large systems could be housed in multiple standard cabinets.

The problem of designing an effective packaging approach is more challenging in the case of the distributed control system architecture shown in Figure 1.4. In addition to the control room and equipment room environments characteristic of the centralized systems, the packaging in a geographically distributed control system must be designed for the wide range of environments encountered in industrial process plants. Very often selecting the proper packaging approach is critical to the cost-effectiveness of the system as a whole and to the feasibility of distributing its elements geographically throughout the plant.

This section of the chapter will first summarize the packaging requirements for each of the three areas (control room, equipment room, and distributed plant locations). Then it will review and analyze some of the common design approaches taken to meet these requirements. The discussion will concentrate primarily on issues that are pertinent to distributed control systems; topics common to centralized systems will not be covered in any detail. References 8.6–8.11 provide additional information on packaging-related issues.

8.3.1. Control Room Environment

The type of equipment housed in a control room in an industrial plant includes human interface equipment such as panelboard instrumentation and operator video consoles; it may also include computer hardware and its associated peripherals. Cabinet-mounted control hardware usually is *not* located in the control room, with the possible exception of interfaces between the process control system and the computer, the operator interface equipment, or both.

Generally, the control room has a benign environment since it is designed for the comfort of operators as well as the protection of this hardware. Typical specifications that define the control room environment are as follows:

- *Temperature*—50°F to 80°F;
- *Thermal shock*—1°F per minute;
- *Relative humidity*—20% to 80%, noncondensing;
- Negligible requirements relative to vibration, shock, dust, or corrosive atmosphere.

In light of these relatively mild specifications, standard commercial-grade equipment can generally be used in the control room without any special protection for it. However, there must be sufficient air flow in the electronics enclosures and cabinets to keep the inside temperatures below

70°C (158°F), the limit of most commercial components. Following the National Electrical Manufacturers Association (NEMA) classification of enclosures given in Reference 8.6, a NEMA 1 enclosure ("General Purpose, Indoor") is quite adequate to protect the electronic equipment in a control room environment. Standard mass memory media, such as floppy disks and hard disks, and display hardware, such as CRTs, can be used without concern about dust or vibration. Standard panelboard instrumentation, such as operator stations, indicators, switches, and trend recorders, require no special considerations for packaging design.

Because of this benign environment, the cost of the hardware used in the control room can be minimized at the expense of maintaining the controlled environment (normal heating and air conditioning costs). Since there is only one central control room in the plant and its size is limited, this expense is usually not excessive.

8.3.2. Equipment Room Environment

As its name implies, the equipment room is designed to provide a central location suitable for housing the bulk of the control and data acquisition equipment used in an industrial process automation system. A look inside a typical equipment room reveals row upon row of standard-sized, floor-mounted cabinets that are arranged to allow front access (and sometimes rear access) to the internal electronic hardware, power supplies, and field termination panels. Field wiring is routed to the termination panels through either the top or bottom of the cabinets.

Generally, the environment in the equipment room (sometimes called the *relay room* from pneumatic control terminology) is not controlled as closely as in the control room itself. However, the equipment room usually is situated indoors, not far from the control room, in a location that provides some protection from the outdoor environment. A typical set of specifications that define the equipment room environment is as follows:

- *Temperature*—32°F to 110°F;
- *Thermal shock*—5°F per minute;
- *Relative humidity*—10% to 90%, noncondensing;
- *Dust*—Mild, nonexplosive, nonconducting;
- Negligible requirements relative to vibration, shock, or corrosive atmosphere.

While these specifications cover a wider range of operating conditions than those identified for the control room, they are not so harsh as to place extraordinary demands on the ingenuity of the packaging designer.

Commercial electronic hardware can generally be used in this environment as long as it is protected by industrial-grade enclosures. Usually, NEMA 2 ("Dripproof, Indoor") or NEMA 12 ("Industrial Use—Dust Tight and Drip Tight, Indoor") enclosures are quite adequate to protect the electronics from the mild dust conditions and occasional liquid splashes that are characteristic of this environment. The following normal industrial packaging practices can be used in this application:

1. Standard cabinets should be full size (approx. 7 ft. high), with all components 19 in., rack-mountable (including electronics racks, power supplies, cooling hardware, and termination panels). Top-lifting brackets should be provided for shipment.
2. Cabinets should be floor-mounted, with optional top or bottom entry of field wiring. Cabinets should be provided in either an individual configuration or a ganged configuration with protected channels for wiring between cabinets.
3. Cabinets should allow either front access only or both front and rear access to internals. The doors should have locks.
4. Field termination panels should be located either in the same cabinets as the electronics or (as an option) in separate cabinets to allow early shipment and hookup of field wiring to termination panels. The cabinets should have adequate space for the full complement of field wiring. There should be convenient grounding points for electronic shielding.
5. Dependence on active cooling (e.g., fans) should be minimal. Low-maintenance dust filters should be provided if ambient air is to be introduced to the cabinet for cooling purposes. If the system requires active cooling, there should be redundant cooling fans in each cabinet plus remote alarming of cooling fan failure.

These packaging design approaches are intended to protect the standard electronic hardware from the somewhat harsh environment of the equipment room at minimal cost. This approach eliminates the costs of providing heating and air conditioning for the equipment room, at the expense of a somewhat higher cost of packaging compared to standard commercial practice.

8.3.3. Distributed Plant Environment

The control room and equipment room environments described in the previous subsection are relatively consistent and do not vary a great deal from one industrial plant to another. On the other hand, the environmental conditions surrounding control hardware that is geographically distributed around the plant can vary considerably. The environment can range from a relatively controlled indoor location (similar to the equipment room) to a totally uncontrolled outdoor location that is exposed to the elements. In early installations of distributed control systems, users built small sheds, or *blockhouses,* to house the distributed hardware and create an environment similar to that in the equipment room. This approach was effective in protecting the distributed equipment, but the cost of building and maintaining these blockhouses diluted the benefits of distributing the control hardware (e.g., savings in dedicated wiring runs and reduced control room and equipment room space). More recently, prefabricated modular shelters (see Reference 8.11, for example) have been used as a lower-cost alternative to the blockhouse in industrial installations. The most desirable approach is to use control hardware that has been designed to operate in the distributed environment without requiring this special protection. Of course, the incremental cost to the user of this *hardened* equipment must not exceed that of the blockhouse or modular shelter approach.

A typical set of specifications that characterize such a worst-case distributed environment is as follows:

- *Temperature*—0°F to 130°F;
- *Thermal shock*—5°F per minute;
- *Relative humidity*—5% to 95%, noncondensing;
- *Dust*—Heavy dust environment that is nonexplosive but may contain flammable or conductive particles (e.g., coal or alumina dust);
- *Corrosive atmosphere*—Containing hydrogen sulfide, sulfur dioxide, or chlorine (for example);
- *Other conditions that are application-specific*—For example, vibration, seismic environment, water, salt spray, blowing sand, and fungus.

Note that these environmental specifications do not include applications in *"hazardous locations,"* which are defined by the National Electrical Code as containing flammable or explosive gases, vapors, dust, or fibers. This is a specialized environment that calls for specific features in the design of the system electronics, cabling, and packaging subassemblies beyond the level to be discussed here. (See Reference 4.15 for information on design for hazardous locations.)

The severe environmental specifications just listed place constraints on the design of the distributed control hardware that are well beyond normal commercial or industrial practice. One approach to meeting these specifications is to design specialized control hardware specifically for the remote environment. This would involve using high-temperature, *Mil-spec* (military specifications) electronic components, providing conductive heat sinking for the electronics, and designing specialized packaging to withstand the rugged environment. The disadvantage of this approach is that the distributed control system would then consist of two versions of similar hardware: a basic, inexpensive version designed for the relatively mild control room and equipment room environments and a more expensive version designed for the rugged, remote environment. The resulting distributed system would have a high installation cost, since the volume of each type of module in the system would be reduced, the documentation required would increase, and the number of spare parts that the user would have to stock would double.

A better approach is to use the same standard electronic modules throughout the distributed system but surround them with a different packaging system when it is needed for protection against a more stringent environment. Some vendors provide a conformal polyurethane coating on the electronic modules to protect them from a corrosive atmosphere or dust-laden environment; however, this approach does not prevent corrosion of connectors. Also, it introduces installation and maintenance problems by preventing easy access to switches or socketed components on the circuit boards.

A simpler way to meet the specifications is to isolate the electronics from the harsh environment by means of sealed cabinets. If the elements to be housed in the cabinet are designed for 19 in. rack mounting, there is a variety of off-the-shelf sealed cabinets from which the user can select for the specific environment in question. For example, a NEMA 3 ("Outdoor—Dust Tight, Rain Tight, and Sleet-Resistant") or NEMA 4 ("Indoor—Water Tight and Dust Tight") cabinet can be used, depending on the location. The main problem in using a sealed cabinet is finding a way to dissipate the heat generated by the electronics and power supplies mounted in the cabinet. This can be done without an active cooling system if the system uses low-power CMOS electronics and if the power density (watts per cubic foot) of the package is low. Otherwise, active cooling of the cabinet by means of a heat exchanger or other mechanism (e.g., a thermoelectric heat pump—see Reference 8.9) must be used to keep the interior of the cabinet within the temperature limits of the electronics.

8.4. POWER SYSTEM ISSUES

As in the case of packaging, considering the power supply and distribution portion of a distributed control system often is regarded as a routine, unglamorous task that is neglected until the last moment when designing or evaluating such a system. However, selecting the proper structure of the power subsystem can have a major impact on the cost and reliability of the resulting distributed system. This section will summarize the key requirements on the power subsystem and review some of the common design approaches used by vendors to meet these requirements. References 8.12–8.20 provide additional information on the design of power systems for industrial applications.

8.4.1. Power System Requirements

As for *any* electronic industrial control system, the power subsystem in a distributed control application must convert available line power to the voltage and current levels required by the electronic modules (most of which use digital components), the cooling hardware, and (often) many of the sensors and transmitters in the field. Typical conditions under which this conversion must take place are as follows:

1. The power system must accommodate line power that varies considerably in voltage, frequency, and quality from one country to another around the world. In most cases this is some combination of 115/230 V, 50/60 Hz nominal, with a typical variation of up to ±10% in voltage and ±2 Hz in frequency. *Harmonic distortion* (variation from pure sine wave) can be up to 3% RMS or more.
2. The delivered power must be at the levels that the system components require. Most components used in the electronic modules require power at 5 V nominal, with less power required at other levels in the ±15 V range. Power to the cooling hardware can usually be at line voltage and frequency. Power to field-mounted transmitters usually is at 24 V DC, and power to relays and solid-state switching gear usually is at 48 V DC, 125 V DC, or at line voltage and frequency. Of course, each user often has special requirements that must be met on a custom basis.
3. The power must be delivered over the full range of conditions listed in Section 8.3 on packaging for the control room, equipment room, and distributed environments. Special attention must be paid to the temperature environment, since the capacity of most power systems decreases significantly as the temperature increases above the normal design range.
4. The power system must include sufficient fuses and current-limiting resistors to protect the power supplies from likely component failures and human errors (e.g., shorting outputs to ground).
5. The electronic modules must be isolated from power line transients, electromagnetic interference (EMI), and radio frequency interference (RFI).

In addition to these basic requirements, there are several other corollary requirements for industrial control applications:

1. The power system for all or a significant portion of the distributed control system must not be subject to a single-point failure of an active element; that is, the system should not have to be shut down if a single element (such as an individual power supply) fails.
2. If such a single-point failure occurs, it must be possible to remove and replace the failed element with a good one without shutting the power system down.
3. All power sources and output voltages must be monitored and alarms sent automatically to the operator if a failure occurs (that is, the power system must be included in the total system diagnostic hierarchy).
4. The power system must be designed to allow plant personnel to remove and replace failed electronic modules or cooling components without shutting the power system down.
5. If the power monitoring system detects an impending total loss of power, it must send a "power fail interrupt" signal to the electronic modules in time to allow them to shut down in an orderly manner.
6. The power system should be designed to permit operation despite the loss of the primary line power source for a specified period of time (usually, 15 minutes to one hour). This capability can be an option that the user selects at time of purchase to allow sufficient time to shut the plant down in an orderly and safe manner after line power is lost.

One critical issue related to the design of the power subsystem is grounding provisions and practices. In a distributed control system, the various consoles, cabinets, and other elements can be geographically distributed throughout the plant site. Since the ground potential can vary significantly from one location to another at the site, it is important that the distributed system be designed to eliminate or minimize ground loops, electrical noise, and other grounding-related problems. While a complete discussion on grounding practices is well beyond the scope of this chapter, a few comments in this area should be made regarding the design of the power and packaging system:

1. The power system must have a provision for a safety ground conductor to be connected at the power entry point. Generally, the cabinet structure is connected to this ground point through the power system within the cabinet.
2. If a power subsystem in one cabinet also provides power to com-

ponents in other cabinets, there must be a mechanism for connecting the structures of the latter cabinets to the safety ground point in the former cabinet.

3. Within each cabinet, a separate grounding system (*system common*) must be provided to allow the common terminals of the DC power supplies, the shields of the process I/O signal wiring, and the signal commons (signal grounding points) to be tied together at a single point or ground bus. It must be possible to connect this bus to site ground through a conductor that is separate from the safety ground connection. In the case of multiple cabinets powered by a single electrical supply, there must be a means to allow interconnection of the system common buses in each of the cabinets.

4. The shared communications facility that *integrates* the distributed control system elements from an informational point of view must provide *isolation* from a power and grounding point of view. That is, the system commons for the various cabinets or clusters of cabinets in a distributed system must *not* be electrically connected to each other through the plant communication system. Isolation is usually accomplished through the use of transformer coupling or fiber optics in the shared communications facility.

The user should consult the relevant electrical codes for specifics on the grounding requirements in a particular installation and how they affect the configuration of the power portion of the distributed control system.

8.4.2. Power System Design Issues

Unlike many aerospace and military applications, the industrial control application does not put a significant premium on minimizing the size and weight of the power system. Also, the production volumes of industrial power systems are relatively small compared to commercial applications. As a result, one usually cannot justify a specialized design of the basic power supply elements for industrial use. Instead, most distributed control system vendors use commercially available off-the-shelf power supplies to perform the basic function of converting AC line power to the needed voltage and current levels in the system. Specialized filtering, monitoring, load-sharing equipment, and other hardware, then surround these standard power supplies to form a total power system that meets the needs of the industrial control application.

One overall objective in power system design is to match the size and cost of the power subsystem to the portion of the control system being powered. This can be a difficult task, since there is a wide variation in the amount of power required in any one cabinet or cluster of cabinets. This amount can range from the relatively little power required for a few single-loop control modules to the greater amount necessary for a reasonably large data acquisition and control system. Special care must be taken at the low end of the size range, since the packaging and power components are likely to comprise a significant portion of the volume and cost of the total equipment in a small system. Most distributed control system vendors solve this problem by offering power subsystems in a range of sizes; as much as possible, each subsystem is designed to be modular to allow a range of power levels without changing the structure of the subsystem.

There are a variety of power system configurations that meet the requirements described previously in this chapter. The remainder of this section will discuss two typical configurations to illustrate some of the design possibilities and the pertinent issues. Each configuration is composed of similar basic elements; they differ in how the elements are arranged to form a total system. In the discussion, the configuration is assumed to supply the power needs of a single cabinet or cluster of cabinets; the precise power capacity of the configuration is not a significant issue in the discussion.

Figure 8.5 illustrates configuration 1. This architecture is designed to

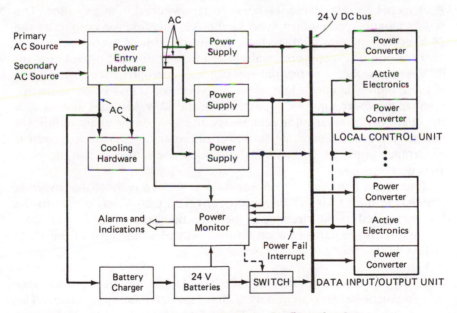

Figure 8.5. Power System—Configuration 1

convert the AC line power to a 24 V bus that in turn supplies the LCUs, DI/OUs, and other devices in the cabinet. The power entry hardware includes the circuit breakers, line filters, fuses, and other hardware used to separate the external line power source (or sources) from the other power system hardware within the cabinet. A standard application generally requires only a single source. Critical applications may require a separate independent source (say, from a diesel-generator). In configuration 1, one or more standard commercial power supplies convert the line power to the 24 V DC level supplied to the bus. The number of these supplies is selected to meet the power requirements for the cabinet (perhaps including an extra supply to accommodate a single supply failure). If multiple AC sources are available, the design of the power entry hardware connects these sources to the power supplies in one of two ways: either (1) the primary and secondary AC sources are each wired to separate power supplies for redundancy; or (2) the primary source is connected to *all* of the power supplies and the secondary source is switched in only if the primary source fails.

As mentioned previously, the cooling hardware (fans and heat exchangers) generally is powered from the AC source (or sources) through the power entry hardware. If the power system is required to operate despite a loss of both AC sources, a set of batteries supplies the 24 V bus with sufficient power to get the system through the expected time of outage. A charger keeps the batteries ready to be switched in at any time. The power monitor continuously checks the AC sources, the outputs of the 24 V power supplies, and the battery outputs. If it detects a loss of one of these outputs, it triggers an alarm to the operator and provides an indication of the failure so that the user can take appropriate repair measures. If the monitor detects a loss of both sources or a loss of an excessive number of power supplies, it switches in the 24 V batteries and notifies the operator. If the monitor detects that the 24 V bus is about to fail, for whatever reason, it generates a power-fail interrupt signal to the active electronics in the LCUs or DI/OUs to allow them time to shut down in an orderly fashion.

Note in configuration 1 that separate power conversion hardware is required in the LCUs or DI/OUs to convert the 24 V bus power to the levels required by the circuitry in the units themselves. This power conversion hardware can add a substantial amount to the cost of the LCU or DI/OU, for the following reasons:

1. The power supplies that feed the 24 V DC bus are usually relatively inexpensive, providing only a first level of power regulation. The power converters in the LCUs or DI/OUs perform the final regulation.

2. In many applications, each LCU or DI/OU must have redundant power converters since the control system cannot tolerate a single-point power failure that would cause the loss of a large number of control loops or data points.

The extra cost of this power conversion hardware is not significant if it can be prorated over a large number of loops or points per LCU or DI/OU. For this reason, configuration 1 is used most often in distributed control systems with relatively large LCUs or DI/OUs.

A different power system architecture, shown in Figure 8.6 as configuration 2, can be more effective for distributed control systems that have relatively small LCUs (e.g., single-loop controllers) or DI/OUs. This approach eliminates the need for power conversion circuitry in the LCUs and DI/OUs by producing the full range of required voltages in bulk supplies, then making these voltages available to the LCUs and DI/OUs over multiple power buses. As Figure 8.6 shows, power entry hardware performs the same set of functions as it does in configuration 1. Multiple power supplies (standard, off-the-shelf models) generate the ranges of voltages required by the LCUs and DI/OUs. Redundant supplies of each type are usually a standard offering, since otherwise the failure of a single supply would lead to the loss of all power to at least one of the buses.

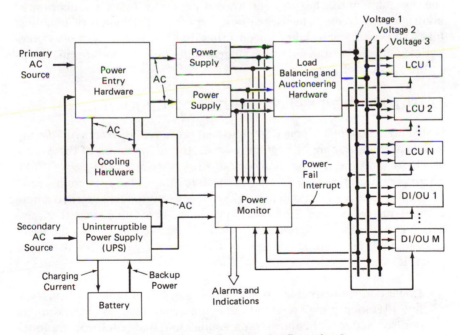

Figure 8.6. Power System—Configuration 2

Load balancing and auctioneering hardware manages the outputs of the redundant supplies and provides the final regulation of the power to the buses. This hardware also includes sufficient filtering capacity to absorb the voltage transients that occur when an LCU or DI/OU is connected to or disconnected from the power bus, thus satisfying one of the repair requirements listed previously in this section (i.e., plant personnel must be able to remove or replace system elements without shutting the power system down).

As in the case of configuration 1, the cooling hardware in configuration 2 is driven from the AC source power; also, a power monitor produces alarms and indicates any failures in the input AC sources or the DC power supplies. Note, however, that in configuration 2 the power monitor does not switch in any backup batteries, since the backup power capability is provided in a different manner than in configuration 1. In this case, since the system has no 24 V DC bus, the backup battery is an integral part of an uninterruptible power system (UPS) that is used as the secondary AC input to the power entry hardware. The UPS is a standard product, consisting of a battery charger, sufficient battery capacity to handle the expected time of AC power loss, and an inverter to generate the AC input to the power system.

As stated previously, these two configurations by no means exhaust the possible approaches to structuring a power system for a distributed control environment. The user or designer of the distributed system must take the final responsibility for ensuring that the power system is compatible with the overall control system architecture and the specific needs of the application.

8.5. FUTURE TRENDS IN DISTRIBUTED CONTROL

Distributed control as applied to industrial processes is a relatively young technical field, tracing its beginnings back to the invention of the microprocessor and the development of the first systems in the early 1970s. There is no question that the market introduction of the first commercial distributed control system in late 1975 was a milestone that marked a new era in industrial control. However, even in the short time since then, the field has undergone a significant amount of change that makes the early systems look primitive in the light of the technology of the 1980s. Some examples of this evolution are as follows:

- Local control units that once were no more than replacements for a few PID loops now are able to execute a combination of continuous control, sequential control, data acquisition, and batch control functions. Accomplishing each of these functions no longer requires the use of separate hardware.

- Configuring these control functions once meant an endless amount of button-pushing, with constant references to a stack of manuals. The development of CAD technology now allows the user to draw, edit, and duplicate control configurations directly on a CRT screen and then download them directly to the controllers.
- The bandwidth of the shared communications facilities in a distributed system has increased by a factor of 40 or more. The use of fiber optics as a transmission medium is common. The capability of direct peer-to-peer communication from any LCU to any other in the system now is taken for granted.
- CRT displays that once only mimicked simple panelboard instrumentation devices have been supplanted by color graphics displays that provide the operator with an easily understandable view of plant operations, from the highest level of supervisory control down to the individual loop level.
- The transition from using dedicated stations to using shared displays has taken place more swiftly than first anticipated. This has significantly reduced concerns about the ability of operators to adapt to the use of shared displays. At the same time, the introduction of video games and personal computers in the commercial marketplace is producing a new generation of future operators to whom video displays are second nature.

As dramatic as these developments have been, the pace of technological progress in the late 1980s and the 1990s will lead to equally dramatic innovations in the distributed control field in the future. Some of the likely trends of development in the areas of system architecture, control capabilities, operator interfaces, and applications are summarized in the following paragraphs. References 8.21–8.34 provide additional information on future trends in distributed control.

Trends in System Architecture. One major architectural trend that already is under way is the expansion in scope and the corresponding integration of functions of the distributed control system in the industrial plant. *Horizontal expansion* is occurring in the sense that many more of the plant instrumentation and control functions previously performed by separate, independent subsystems are now being integrated into a single plantwide system. Examples of these independent subsystems are programmable controllers used for safety and interlock functions, thermocouple data loggers, and sequence-of-events monitors. Of course, a degree of separation in function will remain when needed for redundancy or safety reasons. However, similar hardware will be used to implement the functions, thus reducing the amount of personnel training required and the number of different spare parts kept on hand. Another factor encouraging horizontal expansion is the continuing emphasis on optimizing plantwide production operations and minimizing overall energy usage. This can only be accomplished through the plantwide integration of monitoring and control functions. (See References 8.21–8.23 regarding trends in this area.)

These influences toward complete integration of plant operations also will encourage the *vertical expansion* in scope of the distributed control system. Currently, a different vendor often supplies the hardware at each level of information and control in the plant: from the sensors and analyzers that obtain the basic measurement information in the plant, through the first level of regulatory control, and up to the higher levels of plant production computer systems and corporate information systems. The task of providing interfaces to ensure a coherent flow of information between levels is not trivial, but it is simplified significantly if most of the layers are implemented with distributed control hardware that has been designed from the beginning to support an integrated database. The information in this database can then be used at the highest levels in the control hierarchy to provide on-line plant performance information and an analysis of alternative plant operating strategies.

Another architectural trend that is expected to continue is the standardization of communications interfaces, both within the distributed system and in the gateways between the distributed system and other users or generators of plant information. As Chapter 5 described, a start has been made in this area. However, so far no major user has insisted that the vendors of these systems adhere to any particular communication standard; nor has a de facto standard based on a single dominant vendor's system architecture emerged. As the proliferation of distributed control system products continues, it is likely that the major users of distributed control systems will become more interested in generating communication standards that will allow mixing and matching of vendor hardware. If and when such standards emerge, they will support the movement towards this horizontal and vertical integration of disparate systems. These standards would also contribute to the "technological transparency" of the instrumentation and control systems installed in a plant; that is, the user could update portions of these systems with hardware having additional capabilities while maintaining compatibility with the rest of the equipment in the plant. This compares favorably with the current situation, in which the introduction of new hardware often forces the user to tear out a major portion of an existing system.

The final architectural trend that will be noted here is the gradual disappearance of mainframe computers from the operating levels of plant control systems. As described earlier in Section 8.2, many of the functions previously performed by these computers are being taken over by dedicated microprocessor-based devices. Due to the increasing performance and decreasing costs of microprocessor technology, these dedicated devices are providing functionality that meets or exceeds the capability of much larger computers used a few years ago. Also, these devices are usually designed to be "configured" (not programmed) to perform their dedicated function. This eliminates the user's dependence on specialized computer programmers for startup and maintenance of the equipment performing the high-level functions in the plant. Mainframe computers, if used at all, will "migrate upwards" in the control hierarchy to the levels of corporate management information systems and company-wide operations control.

Trends in Controller Capabilities. The continuing increase in power and capacity of the microprocessors, memories, and associated support chips that make up a distributed control system is a trend that will have a significant impact on the capabilities of the LCUs in such a system (see Reference 8.24, for example). One impact is to increase the speed of execution of the algorithms in the LCUs. At present, some controllers are able to execute the algorithms only two or three times a second. This sampling and processing rate is too slow to handle fast control loops such as compressor surge controls and boiler windbox pressure controls. Hardware advances will make it possible for controllers to execute their control algorithms at a rate ten to 50 times per second. This will allow digital controllers to be used in the full range of applications implemented today with analog controllers.

In general, enhancing controller power will not lead to a significant increase in the *number* of control functions that an individual controller can implement. As pointed out in Chapter 2, this number depends more on the architectural philosophy of the user (e.g., a preference for single-loop versus multi-loop control) than on the capabilities of the controller supplied by the vendor. However, the increase in controller performance certainly will remove any limitations previously imposed by the hardware on the type of control architecture the user prefers for the particular application.

This performance trend also will accelerate the use of high-level programming languages to implement customized control functions at the LCU level. General-purpose languages such as extended BASIC are already available; batch control languages and specialized languages (such as LISP for artificial intelligence applications) will also become available as the increased speed and memory capabilities of the controllers make their implementation feasible and cost-effective.

Two other trends related to controllers will continue. First, any remaining custom wiring between controllers will disappear as the various controller types become absorbed within a single distributed control system. Once a signal enters the system, it will be made available to all controllers using the shared communications facility (again, with the possible exception of safety-related subsystems that require independent inputs). Second, the movement towards computer-aided design of control systems will accelerate, expanding into the areas of system documentation, equipment selection and configuration, and system integration and checkout. The automation of these functions will cut the costs of specifying and engineering a control system dramatically, especially in the area of documentation. These capabilities will allow automatic documentation of changes to the control system during checkout, startup, and field use, a function difficult to accomplish (and therefore rarely done) today.

Trends in Operator Interfaces. The current designs of operator interfaces in distributed control systems have been influenced greatly by the historical use of panelboard instrumentation as the primary operator interface in the control of industrial processes. To encourage plant operators to accept the new hardware, designers of CRT-based interfaces have used many of the characteristics of panelboards in the layout of displays and keyboards in the new equipment. Clearly, some immediate work is required to incorporate current knowledge of what constitutes a good interface design into standard display formats and keyboard and touch screen layouts. However, the general acceptance of VDUs as the primary operator interface mechanism in distributed systems has opened the door to developing new concepts in the interfaces between humans and machines.

This development is likely to be an evolutionary, trial-and-error process rather than a drastic change from the approaches used today. The process will require a significant amount of interaction between vendor and user to generate new interface concepts that are well-accepted by the operators while remaining technically feasible and cost-effective. The technical advances now being made in the operator interface area will make this evolutionary process an interesting one, since the available interface options in both hardware and software will increase exponentially. Some examples are as follows:

- High-resolution, bit-mapped color CRT technology will become cost-effective for industrial control applications. Flat-panel display technology will later replace CRT-based displays.

- Voice I/O hardware will develop to the point where the interface equipment will understand simple operator commands (say, for alarm acknowledgments or display paging). (See References 8.25–8.27, for example.)
- Many improvements will occur in the software area: Operating displays will include high-resolution *windows* that allow the operator to select information from two or more displays and superimpose it on the screen (e.g., to allow control stations to be configured temporarily at any location on a custom graphics display or to provide "HELP" information without requiring the operator to switch displays). The capability for showing "three-dimensional" displays (either in two-dimensional or true three-dimensional form) will be provided for specialized information and status applications. Color graphics will include simple animation of certain process operations. The operator will have more flexibility in customizing certain displays to match his or her particular method of operation.
- Improvements in optical storage and other memory technologies will allow the operator to store and recall essentially unlimited amounts of information. (See References 8.28 and 8.29.) This will be of substantial help in constructing operator guides and advisories in case of emergencies, thus replacing bulky operations manuals. These guides will not only aid in the diagnosis of problems in the plant, but also will offer some advice on the options available to solve the problems. The guides also can be used for operator training and for answering questions about the display equipment during operations. Integrating expert system technology with operator interface devices will make these operator aids feasible, cost-effective, and maintainable.

It also should be pointed out that advancements in flat-panel displays and optical storage devices will make it possible to use the operator interface equipment in a wider range of plant environments. CRTs and rotating memory devices (e.g., floppy disks and hard disks) used in current interfaces have a limited range of application because of their sensitivity to dust and vibration. Flat-panel displays and optical storage devices are much better in this regard.

One unmistakable trend in both the design and the application of operator interface devices is the tremendous increase in the amount of information becoming available to the operator. Early VDUs allowed the operator to control about 200 loops and monitor up to 500 data points. Current units are being designed to handle at least an order of magnitude more of information. This expansion in scope of monitoring and control will place a tremendous burden on the operator unless the VDU is designed to filter and organize the information to present it in a more meaningful way. Future distributed control systems will provide significant assistance to the operator in this area through improved signal validation techniques, alarm prioritization structures, operator advisories, and automated fault diagnostic capabilities (for both plant equipment and instrumentation and control hardware). References 8.30–8.34 discuss these trends.

Application Knowledge—the Key Trend. As distributed control systems become more standardized and the major vendors' systems become saturated with the most recent technology, a major factor in evaluating and designing these systems will be the amount of knowledge and experience that the vendor has in the user's intended area of application. This knowledge will be especially important as horizontal and vertical expansion in scope of the distributed control system continues. To provide a system that is effective in a particular application, the vendor designing that system must be aware of:

1. The requirements on and characteristics of the various subsystems that make up the total instrumentation and control system for the application;
2. The specialized sensors and analyzers that are used in that application;
3. Any specialized control hardware and control or computing requirements for that application;
4. The modes of plant operation in that application, including the methods used in plant startup, shutdown, and change in operating modes.

This knowledge will not replace the expertise of the user, who knows the plant better than anyone else. However, if the vendor does *not* have this application background and experience, it is likely that the distributed control system the vendor supplies will not have the hardware interfaces and the control and computational packages needed to help the user put together a system that works well in the application. This applications factor always has been present, but it occasionally has been obscured by the new technology inherent in distributed control systems. The glamour of a particular hardware or software product is no substitute for a solid base of experience in solving the real problems of the user.

REFERENCES

High-Level Functions

8.1 Kennedy, J.P., "Computer Control in the Design of a Grass Roots Plant," in *Chemical Engineering, Deskbook Issue,* pub. by *Chemical Engineering* magazine, vol. 86, no. 21, October 15, 1979, pp. 55–66.

8.2 Williams, T.J., "Computer Control—The Medium for Process Control in the Future," ASME International Computer Technology Conference, San Francisco, August 1980, pp. 121–132.
8.3 DiBiano, R., Hales, G., and Autenrieth, A., "Advantages of Third Generation Computer Control," *Hydrocarbon Processing,* vol. 61, no. 6, June 1982, pp. 117–121.
8.4 Hodson, W.R., "An Overview of Distributed Process Control and Motor Control with a Master Computer," Instrument Society of America International Conference, Philadelphia, October 1982.
8.5 "Q and A on Digital Control Systems," *Hydrocarbon Processing,* vol. 62, no. 6, June 1983, pp. 69–73.

Packaging

8.6 National Electrical Manufacturers Association, "Enclosures for Industrial Controls and Systems," Standard IS1.1–1977, 1977.
8.7 Ballantyne, A.D., "Redesign of a Commercial Microcomputer for Severe Environments," *Computer Design,* vol. 19, no. 5, May 1980, pp. 193–198.
8.8 Calder, W., "Electronic Instruments: Hostile Environments Seek Vendor/User Solutions," *InTech,* vol. 29, no. 3, March 1982, pp. 51–53.
8.9 Barber, R.W., "Consider Thermoelectric Heat Pumps for Your Instrument Cooling Needs," *InTech,* vol. 29, no. 5, May 1982, pp. 55–56.
8.10 Olson, D.H., and Scharringhausen, D., "Effectively Using Distributed Control Concepts," *Hydrocarbon Processing,* vol. 63, no. 10, October 1984, pp. 59–61.
8.11 Von Brecht, R.C., "Prefabricated Control Modules," *Chemical Engineering,* vol. 92, no. 10, May 13, 1985, pp. 85–90.

Power System

8.12 Morrison, R., "Answers to Grounding and Shielding Problems," *Instruments & Control Systems,* vol. 52, no. 6, June 1979, pp. 35–38.
8.13 Snigier, P., "Special Report: Power Supplies," *Digital Design,* vol. 10, no. 2, February 1980, pp. 50–62.
8.14 Heider, R.L., "Avoid Plant Computer Problems with Proper Power and Ground Wiring," *InTech,* vol. 27, no. 4, April 1980, pp. 34–38.
8.15 Morris, H.M., "Using an Uninterruptible Power Supply Can Save Your Data," *Control Engineering,* vol. 28, no. 12, December 1981, pp. 62–64.
8.16 Shafer, F.K., "Diverse UPS Technologies Provide Design Alternatives," *Digital Design,* vol. 13, no. 6, June 1983, pp. 81–96.
8.17 Laduzinsky, A.J., "Micros Generate New Power Supply Market," *Control Engineering,* vol. 30, no. 10, October 1983, pp. 72–74.
8.18 Eppich, K., "Selecting Uninterruptible Power Systems," *Instruments & Control Systems,* vol. 57, no. 6, June 1984, pp. 51–57.
8.19 Wilson, D., "Designer's Guide to Uninterruptible Power Supplies," *Digital Design,* vol. 14, no. 8, August 1984, pp. 60–66.
8.20 McAlister, J., "Control Disturbances? Check Grounding," *Chemical Engineering,* vol. 91, no. 26, December 24, 1984, pp. 77–78.

Future Trends

8.21 Keyes, M.A., "The Future of Process Control," *TAPPI Journal,* vol. 67, no. 2, February 1984, pp. 56–61.

8.22 Dallimonti, R., "From the Sensor to the Boardroom—Total Plant Information Management," *Proceedings of the Third Annual Control Engineering Conference,* Control Engineering, Barrington, Illinois, 1984, pp. 133–138.

8.23 Haggin, J., "Process Control on Way to Becoming Process Management," *Chemical & Engineering News,* vol. 62, no. 21, May 21, 1984, pp. 7–13.

8.24 Bond, J., "Architectural Advances Spur 32–Bit Micros," *Computer Design,* vol. 23, no. 6, June 1, 1984, pp. 125–136.

8.25 Groner, G.F., and Gilblom, D.L., "Speech: A Better Way for Machines to Communicate with Operators," *InTech,* vol. 31, no. 5, May 1984, pp. 63–66.

8.26 Cleaveland, P., "What's New in Voice I/O?" *Instruments & Control Systems,* vol. 57, no. 11, November 1984, pp. 32–39.

8.27 Meng, B., "Speech Recognition: Not a Typical Engineering Problem," *Digital Design,* vol. 15, no. 6, June 1985, pp. 49–57.

8.28 Pingry, J., "Optical Disk Technology Creates a New Class of Peripheral," *Digital Design,* vol. 14, no. 8, August 1984, pp. 68–77.

8.29 Jones, K., "What's in Store for the Optical Drive Market," *Electronic Business,* vol. 11, no. 1, January 1, 1985, pp. 200–206.

8.30 Damsker, D.J., "Alarm Monitoring and Reporting Systems in a Distributed Control Environment," *IEEE Transactions on Power Apparatus and Systems,* vol. PAS–102, no. 9, September 1983, pp. 3177–3183.

8.31 Powell, R.E., "Distributed Control Systems: The Missing Tools," *Process Industry Management Association Journal,* vol. 66, no. 1, January 1984, pp. 26–30.

8.32 Kaplan, G., "Nuclear Power Plant Malfunction Analysis," *IEEE Spectrum,* vol. 20, no. 6, June 1983, pp. 53–58.

8.33 Krigman, A., "System, Heal Thyself: Self-Test and the Cost of Instrument Ownership," *InTech,* vol. 29, no. 6, June 1982, pp. 9–20.

8.34 Eimers, G.W., "Network, Heal Thyself: A Diagnostic Primer," *Computer Design,* vol. 21, no. 10, September 1982, pp. 213–220.

APPENDIX
GLOSSARY OF ACRONYMS

A/D Converter—Analog-to-digital converter (hardware used to convert input measurements to digital form)

ADCCP—Advanced data communications control procedures (bit-oriented data communications protocol standard)

ADLC—Advanced data link control (type of data link protocol)

AFIPS—American Federation of Information Processing Societies (group of technical societies)

ANSI—American National Standards Institute

CAMAC—Computer-automated measurement and control (instrumentation interface and communication standard)

CCR—Control complexity ratio (a measure of the complexity of a particular control system's logic configuration)

CID—Computer interface device (hardware that allows a general-purpose computer to share data with the rest of the distributed control system)

CMOS—Complementary metal-oxide semiconductor (one type of computer semiconductor memory)

CPU—Central processing unit (the part of a digital computer that performs most of its computational functions)

CRC—Cyclic redundancy check (technique used in digital communication systems to detect or correct transmission errors)

CRT—Cathode ray tube (one type of video display unit)

CSMA/CD—Carrier sense/multiple access with collision detection (a type of protocol for access to the communication system network)

D/A converter—Digital-to-analog converter (hardware used to convert digital information into analog outputs to the process)

DDC—Direct digital control (control system that uses a computer or other stored program device in the control loop)

DDCMP—Digital data communications message protocol (character-oriented communications protocol standard)

DI/OU—Data input/output unit (device that interfaces to the process for the sole purpose of acquiring or sending data)

DMA—Direct memory access (type of communication channel used to transfer data between digital devices)

EAROM—Electrically alterable read-only memory (type of computer memory that is normally unchangeable; its contents can be changed only under special conditions)

EEPROM—Electrically erasable and programmable read-only memory (later version of EAROM that is simpler to use)

EIA—Electronic Industries Association

EMI—Electromagnetic interference (type of electrical noise that can affect electronic circuits adversely)

EWICS—European Workshop on Industrial Computer Systems (European industrial computer control standards group)

HDLC—High-level data link control (type of data link protocol)

HLCD—high-level computing device (microprocessor-based device used to perform computer-like functions)

HLHI—High-level human interface (device that allows a human to interact with the total distributed control system over the shared communications facility)

HLOI—High-level operator interface (type of HLHI designed for use by a process operator)

I&CS—Technical journal formerly known as *Instrumentation and Control Systems*

IEE—Institution of Electrical Engineers (engineering society in England)

IEEE—Institute of Electrical and Electronics Engineers (engineering society in the United States)

IFAC—International Federation of Automatic Control (international technical society specializing in control systems)

IFIP—International Federation for Information Processing (international group of technical societies)

InTech—Journal previously known as *Instrumentation Technology*

I/O hardware—Input/output hardware (computer hardware used to carry signals into and out of the processing hardware)

ISA—Instrument Society of America (control instrumentation society in the United States)

ISO—International Standards Organization

LAN—Local area network (one type of communication system)

LCD—Liquid crystal display (type of digital display device)

LCU—Local control unit (a control device that performs closed-loop control and interfaces directly with the process)

LED—Light-emitting diode (type of digital display device)

LLEI—Low-level engineering interface (type of LLHI designed for use by an instrumentation engineer)

LLHI—Low-level human interface (device that allows a human to interact with a local control unit)

LLOI—Low-level operator interface (type of LLHI designed for use by a process operator)

MAP—Manufacturing automation protocol (communication system standard advocated by General Motors)

μP—Abbreviation for *microprocessor*

MNOS—Metal-nitride-oxide semiconductor (one type of computer semiconductor memory used in EAROMs)

MUX—Multiplexer (hardware used to transmit several signals over a single conductor)

NEMA—National Electrical Manufacturers Association (Industrial association in the United States)

NOVRAM—Nonvolatile random-access memory (one type of nonvolatile semiconductor computer memory)

OSI—Open systems interconnection (a connection between one communication system and another using a standard protocol)

P&ID—Piping and instrumentation diagram (drawing that shows both process elements and related monitoring and control devices)

PI—Proportional-integral (simplified form of PID control)

PID—Proportional-integral-derivative (one form of control algorithm used in industrial applications)

PLC—Programmable logic controller (microcomputer-based control device used to replace relay logic)

POL—Problem-oriented language (one type of high-level computer language used in process applications)

PROWAY—PROcess data highWAY (a data highway network standard)

RAM—Random-access memory (type of computer memory used for temporary storage of data; allows the CPU to have fast access to read or change any of its memory locations)

RFI—Radio frequency interference (type of electrical noise that can affect electronic circuits adversely)

ROM—Read-only memory (type of computer memory used for permanent storage of programs or data)

RTD—Resistance temperature detector (industrial temperature measuring device)

SAMA—Scientific Apparatus Makers Association (industrial association in the United States)

SDLC—Synchronous data link control (type of data link protocol)

TAPPI—Technical Association of the Pulp and Paper Industry (technical society)

T/C—Thermocouple (temperature-measuring device)

TDMA—Time division multiplex access (type of protocol for access to communication system network)

TTL—Transistor–transistor logic (type of digital circuitry)

UPS—Uninterruptible power supply (type of power supply that can provide electrical power even when line power is lost)

UVROM—Ultraviolet-erasable read-only memory (type of computer memory that can be erased or changed only by exposure to ultraviolet light)

VDU—Video display unit (any one of several types of shared human interface devices that use digital video technology)

INDEX